Focus on Addictions

A Reference Handbook

TEENAGE PERSPECTIVES

Focus on
Addictions

A Reference Handbook

Kay Marie Porterfield

ABC-CLIO
Santa Barbara, California
Denver, Colorado
Oxford, England

Library of Congress Cataloging-in-Publication Data

Porterfield, Kay Marie.
    Focus on addictions : a reference handbook / by Kay Marie
Porterfield.
        (Teenage perspectives)
    Includes bibliographical references and index.
    1. Drug abuse—Handbooks, manuals, etc.   2. Alcoholism—Handbooks,
manuals, etc.   3. Tobacco habit—Handbooks, manuals, etc.   4. Eating
disorders—Handbooks, manuals, etc.   5. Compulsive behavior—
Handbooks, manuals, etc.   I. Title.   II. Series.
    RC564.3.P67   1992   616.86—dc20   92-26623

ISBN 0-87436-674-7

99 98 97 96 95 94 93   10 9 8 7 6 5 4 3 2

ABC-CLIO, Inc.
130 Cremona Drive, P.O. Box 1911
Santa Barbara, California 93116-1911

This book is printed on acid-free paper ⊖ .
Manufactured in the United States of America

Contents

Chapter 5: Eating Disorders: The Battle with Body Image, 149

Chapter 6: Obsessive-Compulsive Disorder and Impulse Control Disorders: Hooked on Self-Defeating Behaviors, 177

Chapter 7: Codependents: Addiction's Other Victims, 191

Foreword

An old Chinese curse goes, "May you live in exciting times." Today's young people have grown up under such a curse—or blessing. They live in a world that is undergoing dramatic changes on every level—social, political, scientific, environmental, technological. At the same time, while still in school, they are dealing with serious issues, making choices, and confronting dilemmas that previous generations never dreamed of.

Technology, especially telecommunications and computers, has made it possible for young people to know a great deal about their world and what goes on in it, at least on a surface level. They have access to incredible amounts of information, yet much of that information seems irrelevant to their daily lives. When it comes to grappling with the issues that actually touch them, they may have a tough time finding out what they need to know.

The Teenage Perspectives series is designed to give young people access to information on the topics that are closest to their lives or that deeply concern them—topics like families, school, health, sexuality, and drug abuse. Having knowledge about these issues can make it easier to understand and cope with them, and to make appropriate and beneficial choices. The books can be used as tools for researching school assignments, or for finding out about topics of personal concern. Adults who are working with young people, such as teachers, counselors, librarians, and parents, will also find these books useful. Many of the references cited can be used for planning information or discussion sessions with adults as well as young people.

Ruth K. J. Cline
Series Editor

Preface

Most teenagers in today's society are affected to some degree by the problem of addiction. Whether an adolescent struggles with peer pressure to drink, watches friends affected by drug use, or lives with an alcoholic parent, the impact can be deep and lasting. Related dysfunctions such as eating disorders and compulsions also take a heavy toll on teenage lives.

Adolescents need straight answers to their questions about substance abuse. *Focus on Addictions* is intended to provide some of these answers. The chapters in this book focus on the information today's teens need to know about alcoholism, drug addiction, tobacco, eating disorders, and compulsions such as gambling and other self-defeating behaviors.

These chapter divisions provide structure and organization for the material, but it is important to understand that although people can be addicted to different things or have different compulsive behaviors, they share some similar patterns—no matter what their substance or behavior of choice. It is also important to keep in mind that people who struggle with the dependencies on behaviors or substances discussed in this book rarely struggle with only one of them.

Each chapter includes basic information and an extensive, annotated resource list. These resources include a wealth of fiction and nonfiction books, pamphlets, and videos. All were selected for their usefulness and interest to teenagers. The majority of the print materials listed are written on a junior high or senior high school reading level. Some books written for adults were also selected because of their informational content, readability, and value to teens.

For the most part resources are listed at the end of the chapter that deals with the subject matter they primarily cover. Some books, pamphlets, and videos, however, deal with topics from more than one chapter in this book. Resources that address dual disorders, poly-addiction, and recovery, with a few exceptions, are listed at the end of chapter 1.

Bibliographical references immediately follow the text of the chapters. These listings are intended to provide documentation for the text and are not annotated. In some instances these sources are highly technical and would be difficult for the average teenage reader.

Answers about addictions cannot come from books and videos alone. For this reason, the resource section at the end of each chapter ends with an annotated listing of organizations and hotlines focusing on the problems covered in that chapter. Some of these groups offer information about addictions and chemical dependency. Many provide referrals to self-help and support groups that serve teenagers and their families. All of the organizations are eager to communicate with adolescents who have further questions.

CHAPTER 1

Addiction: The Trap of Dependency

Lan considered carefully before he spoke. "The one thing I know for sure," he said, "is that I'm dead set against drugs, any kind of drugs, and whatever will help to get rid of them, I'm in favor of."

As he was talking, Lan noticed Kurt leaning forward intently. "I'd just like to say," Kurt began, "that whether we decide to run an anti-drug campaign or stick with being the hotline and only the hotline, there's something I believe we should do as a group. That is," he spoke slowly as though he was searching for exactly the right words, "I think all of us on the hotline should sign a pledge to be drug-free. Not only promise that we're not going to smoke dope or crack or shoot heroin or whatever—that's obvious. But also pledge not to drink anything alcoholic. We're all underage for drinking in this state anyway, but I know that at least some of us manage to get beer and stuff when we want it." Including me, Kurt thought wryly.

"What about cigarettes?" Rob asked.

Kurt nodded. "No cigarettes, either. Smoking's not illegal, but it's an addiction that could ruin our bodies. I think if we're going to be on the hotline and trying to help kids with problems, then we need to be a hundred-percent clean ourselves. . . ."

The Two Faces of Adam by Carolyn Meyer
(New York: Bantam, 1991), 56–57.

When Lan and his friends, characters in a novel by Carolyn Meyer, started a hotline for teenagers, they quickly learned to broaden their definition of addiction. Saying no to illegal drugs and alcohol was

1

not enough; they needed to rule out cigarettes as well. Within the last decade, some researchers and addiction counselors have broadened their definition of addiction even further to include dependency on behaviors such as eating and gambling, in addition to dependency on chemical substances. Others disagree with this classification.

Addiction is a hot topic right now. Newspapers and magazines are full of stories about drinking, drugs, and the negative effects of smoking. Bookstores are crammed with volumes about how to break addictions to work, to spending money, to food, to exercise, and even to love. The latest "addiction" to be written about is codependency— depending on others for our own sense of self-worth. Whether people collect baseball cards or ceramic frogs or earrings, they often say they are addicted to the thing they collect. It all can make you wonder whether there is anything that is *not* an addiction these days.

On the surface, someone who is hooked on heroin and someone who goes through "withdrawal" when he or she cannot get a football "fix" on the weekends do seem quite a bit alike. After all, both of them have habits and they focus their lives around something external to them. Both of them depend on the substance or the behavior they use to make themselves feel good, and they get upset when they are deprived of it. Sometimes they get so upset that they make the lives of those around them miserable.

Even though society casually lumps many behaviors together under the generic label of addictions and uses drug abuse terms to describe all kinds of dependencies, the real situation is not quite this simple. On a deeper level, some major differences exist between the physical addictions that drug users, alcoholics, and smokers experience and habits such as watching football games every Sunday afternoon or giving in to a chocolate craving every day after school. When we use the term *addiction* without clearly understanding what it means, we oversimplify a wide range of behaviors that are very complex.

What Is Addiction?

The spectrum of behaviors connected with addiction is broken into five types by some addiction specialists: patterns, habits, compulsions, impulse control disorders, and addictions.

Patterns are the ways we have for organizing our lives. Most of us tend to sleep at night, and we eat breakfast in the morning, rather than at 4:00 in the afternoon. We go to school or work on weekdays and at least try to do homework on school nights. We may arrange our lives so that we clean our rooms about once a week and reward ourselves by going out to a movie afterward. Many of our social interactions are based on patterns as well. When someone gives us a compliment, many of us smile and say, "Thank you." When we meet someone new, we shake his or her hand and introduce ourselves. Patterns keep our world in order. Without them life would be confusing at best.

Habits are a little different. More individual and ingrained, they are the things we often or usually do. Some of these "rituals" are harmless, such as usually making sure the stereo is turned off before we go to sleep or always taking a shower at night. Others are not quite so harmless. For example, we may usually wait until the last minute to study for a test or always leave the television on when we leave the living room.

Most of the time breaking or changing a habit is relatively simple. When someone points out to us that we are wasting electricity, we focus our attention on turning off the TV. For a while, we may forget or we may feel sort of uncomfortable about changing our habit, especially if we had a reason for leaving the TV on. Maybe we liked our immediate environment to contain a little background noise. But we can see the sense in changing our ways, and in time we learn to do just that on our own or with just a little help from parents and friends.

Compulsions, the third type, have a basis different from the routines called habits. They are the things people do to relieve anxiety. Compulsive individuals who fear leaving the house may check all the doors and windows and the stove many times before they can actually tear themselves away. A student who feels very nervous about passing tests in school may compulsively read the same material over and over again, unable to stop. When people have compulsions, they feel extremely anxious if they cannot do what they feel they need to do exactly when they feel the need to do it. Their lives are organized around meeting their compulsions, and to change these behaviors, which are based on deep underlying fears and anxiety, they usually have to seek professional help from a counselor or therapist to work on the hidden causes of the anxiety.

Impulse control disorders, the fourth type, are like compulsions in many ways with one major difference. When a person has an impulse control disorder, he or she relieves anxiety by doing something that provides immediate gratification or pleasure but that in the long run tends to be self-destructive. Someone who bakes and eats a pan of brownies every time he or she feels insecure about his or her looks eventually puts on weight and as a result feels even more anxious than before. This leads to even more impulsive eating and weight gain. A vicious cycle of psychological dependency is begun, and the person trapped in the middle of it eventually comes to believe he or she could not survive without the particular behavior.

The people society currently refers to as compulsive eaters or compulsive gamblers or love, food, shopping, or work addicts suffer from an impulse control disorder. They are not actually considered compulsives, because their routines bring them pleasure above and beyond feelings of anxiety relief. Neither are they physically addicted to their rituals, so they are not addicts in the precise sense of the word. Even so, ultimately their entire lives may be focused on engaging in their "quick fix" of choice, leaving destroyed relationships in their wake.

Impulse control disorders can be very difficult to correct because the immediate pleasure they bring is a powerful motivation to continue the self-destructive behavior. Treatment for these disorders usually includes a combination of psychotherapy and behavior modification.

Addiction, the last type, is a process in which a person becomes physically dependent on a substance or substances such as alcohol, drugs, or tobacco. It may begin as an impulse control disorder, with a person trying to relieve anxiety or reward herself or himself by taking a drink or popping a pill. In time, though, prolonged chemical use can change the body's tolerance and metabolism. When a person who is physically addicted tries to stop drinking, taking drugs, or smoking, he or she goes through physical withdrawal as the body adapts to life without the chemical substance.

The Process of Addiction

Addiction to a chemical substance usually does not happen overnight. Sometimes the process takes years. In other instances, when a powerful chemical such as heroin or crack cocaine is involved, the process of physical dependency can occur in only days or weeks.

Initially, chemical use may take the form of abuse, using a substance that is harmful to the body, the mind, or both. Soon such use can become a habit. This is followed by psychological dependency as a substance user comes to rely on her or his drug of choice to alter mood. Next, physical dependency occurs. The user's body adapts to the drug and tolerance increases. At this stage it takes more and more of the substance to get the desired mood-altering effect.

When a person who is physically addicted to a chemical stops taking it, his or her body puts up a fuss. Because the body has learned to adapt to the presence of that substance, it must suddenly readjust to life without drugs, alcohol, or nicotine. Withdrawal from chemicals can be mild to severe, depending on the chemicals involved.

Although some addicts can stop using the substance they are addicted to and begin their recovery with weekly visits to a counselor, others must go through detoxification (detox). During this time their withdrawal symptoms are physically monitored by medical professionals. Afterward, recovering addicts may require inpatient treatment in a hospital setting for days or weeks. Inpatient chemical abuse treatment involves intensive individual and group counseling sessions in a controlled living environment where alcohol and illegal drugs are not available.

The Brain and Addiction

Although some people who know little about chemical dependency believe that addicts are people who lack willpower and that it should be easy for addicts to stop their chemical use, brain researchers know differently. Certain chemicals in drugs, alcohol, and tobacco interact with the body, especially the brain, causing users to be physically dependent.

Our moods and emotional states are determined by the release of the brain's neurotransmitters, chemical messengers that send information from one brain cell to another. These neurotransmitters are released from the brain's nerve endings, or neurons, and are sent to receptors, fitting into these receptors like keys in locks. Opiates, cocaine, alcohol, tranquilizers, stimulants, and hallucinogens all either imitate the brain's own chemical messengers or block them from being received by the neuron receptors, thus changing mood. Addictive drugs also affect the pleasure center of the brain and provide immediate gratification to the user.

Despite the harmful consequences of chemical abuse, addicts are powerless to stop by just making the choice to do so. In addition to having cravings, addicts' bodies eventually adapt to these substances because of the effects of chemicals on the brain. An addict no longer drinks or takes drugs to get "high"—he or she does it just to feel normal, just as smokers do not feel "right" without a cigarette.

Focused entirely on satisfying their addictions, addicts find that other areas of their lives become unmanageable. As the body's tolerance for drugs or alcohol increases, addicts must drink more and more or use more and more drugs just to feel okay. Because of this fact, addicts face the risk of overdose. If they are deprived of the substance, they suffer withdrawal.

Patterns of Dependency

Although psychologists and medical researchers have yet to uncover what could be called an addictive personality, they do recognize that individual problems that involve repeated behaviors or chemical indulgence tend to overlap neat boundaries, sometimes defying labels.

    Much of the confusion about whether a particular dependency should be called a compulsion, an impulse disorder, or an addiction comes from the fact that once the vicious cycle of dependency has begun, people who suffer from these different problems tend to act in very similar ways. Some of the behavioral characteristics people share when they have compulsions, impulse control disorders, or addictions are

- Denying to others and sometimes to themselves that they have a problem
- Trying to stop using the substance or stop doing the behavior but failing
- Protecting their access to the substance or behavior by being secretive about it
- Using the substance or behavior to relieve anxieties or to block uncomfortable feelings and to forget problems
- Regretting the substance use or behavior and feeling ashamed about it afterward
- Experiencing uncontrollable mood swings including fear, anxiety, anger, and helplessness
- Distorting reality and making rationalizations that they can quit tomorrow or that the behavior is not that big of a problem
- Blaming others for making them engage in the behavior
- Neglecting other parts of their lives in order to engage in the behavior or use the substance
- Planning life around the substance or behavior, being preoccupied about it very often, and being willing to do almost anything to get the substance or do the behavior

Poly-Addictions and Dual Diagnosis

Many addicts are poly-drug dependent. They take two or more chemical substances, such as cocaine and alcohol or amphetamines and barbiturates, to self-medicate themselves or to regulate their moods.

By the same token, many people who are physically addicted to chemicals either experience or have experienced impulse control disorders or compulsions in their lives. It is quite possible for a person to have addiction, compulsion, and impulse control problems all at once. A bulimic can also be an alcoholic. An anorexic may get physically addicted to amphetamines in order to lose weight. Someone who has a compulsive need to wash his or her hands may discover that taking drugs lowers the anxiety and the need to engage in the compulsive act, so he or she gets hooked on drugs. A compulsive gambler may develop alcoholism. A compulsive shopper might have an eating disorder as well. Such people are referred to as having a dual diagnosis.

Unless the underlying issues that caused repeated problem behavior patterns in the first place are treated, often a recovering compulsive eater or alcoholic or drug addict may simply "switch addictions," giving up one problem only to develop another. In this instance, the compulsive eater might substitute drinking or shopping for food, or the alcoholic might substitute love affairs or candy bars for drinking.

Problems caused by repeated behavior patterns—whether those patterns are spending money, drinking beer, or binging on food and then vomiting—have a profoundly negative impact on those who suffer from them as well as on friends and family members. Despite the fact that these problem behavior patterns are very serious, they can be overcome through treatment.

Recovery

Many counselors believe that no one-shot cure exists for the disorders discussed above but that recovery is a lifelong process. That certainly is true for physical addictions such as alcoholism and other forms of chemical dependency. Once a person's brain chemistry is altered and the body develops a tolerance for a substance, that person has little if any hope of being able to have a drink without falling back into alcoholic drinking patterns or to smoke a cigarette without becoming a smoker all over again. For that reason, abstinence, which means stopping all use of the addictive substance, is the first step in dealing with addiction.

People with pattern problems such as eating disorders or compulsive spending face a different set of issues in recovery. They must learn to understand and control their impulses. After all, it is impossible to live without eating or to survive in our society without spending money.

No matter what sort of pattern has caused problems in a person's life, help is available through counseling, inpatient treatment programs, and self-help support groups such as Alcoholics Anonymous (AA) or other Twelve-Step programs based on AA's successful approach. Counseling and support groups are also available for friends and family members. Once the person who suffers from addiction, compulsion, or impulse control disorders admits to the problem and is willing to face it honestly, help is usually only a phone call away.

REFERENCES

Bristler, Phyllis, and David Bristler. *The Vicious Circle Phenomenon: Our Battle for Self-Control—How To Win the War.* Birmingham, AL: Diadem Publishing, 1987.

Diagnostic Statistical Manual III (DSM III), revised. Washington, DC: American Psychiatric Association, 1987.

Kaplan, Harold I., and Benjamin J. Sadock, eds. *Comprehensive Textbook of Psychiatry,* 5th edition. Baltimore, MD: Williams & Wilkins, 1989.

Milkman, Harvey, and Stanley Sunderwirth. *Craving for Ecstasy: The Consciousness of Chemistry and Escape.* Lexington, MA: Lexington Books, 1987.

Nicholi, Armand M., Jr. *The New Harvard Guide to Psychiatry.* Cambridge, MA: Harvard University Press, 1988.

Snyder, Solomon H. *Drugs and the Brain.* New York: Scientific American Library, 1986.

Stimmel, Barry. *The Facts about Drug Use: Coping with Drugs and Alcohol in Your Family, at Work, in Your Community.* Yonkers, NY: Consumer Reports Books, 1991.

Resources
for Finding Out about Addictions

Fiction

Young adult novels about addictions are listed at the beginning of the resource section of the chapter that deals with that specific addiction or disorder.

Nonfiction

BOOKS

Carnes, Patrick. **A Gentle Path through the Twelve Steps: A Guidebook for All People in the Process of Recovery.** Minneapolis, MN: CompCare, 1989. 250p.

This workbook is based on the Twelve Step recovery program originally developed and practiced by Alcoholics Anonymous. Over 40 exercises help readers examine their own addiction issues and begin to work the steps no matter what their addiction.

Donlan, Joan. **I Never Saw the Sun Rise: The Private Diary of a Fifteen-Year-Old Recovering from Drugs and Alcohol.** Minneapolis, MN: CompCare, 1977. 200p.

Partially written when Donlan was heavily into drug and alcohol abuse and partially written as she was recovering, this gripping true story tells about the reality of addiction from someone who's been there. This book offers hope to other teens with similar problems.

Glick, Stephen. **Little by Little the Pieces Add Up.** Minneapolis, MN: Deaconness Press, 1990. 392p.

A daily meditation book, *Little by Little* offers hope, inspiration, and information to teenagers who are breaking free from chemical addiction. According to the author, "Recovery is like putting together a puzzle without knowing what it looks like. But with persistence, information is collected and, little by little, the pieces add up, and the puzzle of our lives takes shape."

Hall, Lindsey, and Leigh Cohn. **Recoveries: True Stories by People Who Conquered Addictions and Compulsions.** Carlsbad, CA: Gurze Books, 1987. 224p.

This collection of seven personal accounts covers alcoholism, anorexia, bulimia, smoking, cocaine, and narcotics. Its supportive and gripping pages highlight the common threads shared by those who have been addicted and are now in the recovery process.

————. **Self-Esteem Tools for Recovery.** Carlsbad, CA: Gurze Books, 1990. 126p.

This book focuses on raising and maintaining self-esteem so it is no longer necessary to look outside of ourselves for acceptance and feelings of worth. The book is filled with specific tools, exercises, and examples that teenagers can easily relate to. It deals with recovery from chemical dependency, eating disorders, codependency behaviors, and compulsions.

Johnson, Vernon, ed. **Everything You Need To Know about Chemical Dependence.** Minneapolis, MN: Johnson Institute, 1991. 496p.

Written in lay language by the founder of the Johnson Institute, a nationally respected treatment center, this book tells families what they need to know about chemical dependency. Johnson looks at what to do as a family before, during, and after addiction. The information in this book is easy to access and to understand.

Larsen, Earnie. **Stage II Recovery: Life beyond Addiction.** New York: Harper & Row, 1985. 102p.

When people first recover from alcoholism or drug addiction, their main priority is to stay away from the substance they are addicted to. When they hit the second stage of recovery, they must begin to work on fixing their broken lives and relationships. This book talks about that second stage.

Levinson, Nancy, and Joanne Rocklin. **Getting High in Natural Ways: An Infobook for Young People of All Ages.** Los Angeles: Hunter House, 1986. 112p.

The mind/body conection is an important one for anyone wanting to explore alternatives to drugs. Levinson not only provides suggestions and exercises for accentuating the positive but also includes pointers about how to cope with problems. Chapters on exercising, dance, laughter, and relaxation make this a valuable resource.

McFarland, Rhonda. **Coping with Substance Abuse.** New York: Rosen Publishing Group, 1990. 162p.

McFarland, a certified drug and alcohol counselor, writes about both alcohol and drug dependency from a family systems approach. In addition to covering the basics of the problem, she talks about codependency between chemically addicted teens and their parents, how to cope with a drug-abusing brother or sister, and coping with friends who drink and use drugs. In her final chapter McFarland forecasts drug and alcohol issues of the coming decade.

Mann, Peggy. **Arrive Alive: How To Keep Drunk and Pot-High Drivers Off the Highways.** New York: McGraw-Hill, 1985. 512p.

This book gives statistics for injuries and deaths related to drunk driving. It also looks at successful prevention solutions that can be used in any community.

Marshall, Shelly. **Young, Sober and Free.** Center City, MN: Hazelden Educational Materials, 1983. 137p.

The stories of 14 teens recovering from drug or alcohol addiction are recounted in this book written especially for teenagers. The book not only covers the trap of addiction but also leaves readers with a solid understanding of recovery techniques.

The Minnesota Vikings Change the Play: Team Up against Alcohol and Other Dangerous Drugs. Minneapolis, MN: Deaconness Press, 1989. 96p.

This book is a collection of interviews with Minnesota Viking football team members Wade Wilson, Scott Studwell, and Tim Irwin. They talk honestly about the pressures of being a professional athlete and advise readers about how to cope with their own peer pressure as well as how to find drug-free alternatives when dealing with pain, stress, and disappointment.

Nakken, Craig. **The Addictive Personality: Roots, Rituals, Recovery.** Center City, MN: Hazelden Educational Materials, 1988. 125p.

How addictions begin, the pressures that push people into addiction, and a look inside the minds of addicts are all covered in this book. Of special interest is the exploration of why some people recover from one addiction only to take up another one.

Orlandi, Mario, Donald Prue, and Annette Spence. **Substance Abuse.** New York: Facts on File, 1989. 128p.

This book is full of facts about all types of chemical dependency. In addition to up-to-the-minute information, it contains advice. Why people use drugs, alcohol, and tobacco; how those substances affect their bodies; prevention; and treatment are all dealt with as well.

Pursch, Joseph, M.D. **Dear Doc . . . A Noted Authority Answers Your Questions on Drinking and Drugs.** Minneapolis, MN: CompCare, 1985. 350p.

If you have questions about where normal use ends and addiction starts, this book is the place to find answers. Dr. Pursch, who has served as the head of the Betty Ford Center, writes in a straight-forward and informative style for both the people who think they might be chemically dependent and the people who care about them.

Ryan, Elizabeth. **Straight Talk about Drugs and Alcohol.** New York: Facts on File, 1988. 160p.

In addition to facts and statistics based on research, Ryan offers interviews with young substance abusers. This book contains an overview of drug and alcohol use, information about how it affects our society, details about both long- and short-term effects on users, and advice about how to make wise decisions in situations involving drugs and alcohol. No matter what addiction or compulsion an adolescent is recovering from, this workbook can help. Based on the first four steps of Twelve Step programs, it guides readers to look at the losses and consequences caused by addiction and at making life changes that last.

Seymour, Richard, and David Smith. **Drugfree: A Unique, Positive Approach to Staying Off Alcohol and Other Drugs.** New York: Facts on File, 1987. 256p.

The authors, two drug treatment experts, write about addiction and recovery myths in this book, as well as about common substances and their effects. They also discuss how to overcome blocks to finding help and how to take some of the stress out of recovery.

Twerski, Abraham. **Addictive Thinking: Why Do We Lie to Ourselves? Why Do Others Believe Us?** Center City, MN: Hazelden Educational Materials, 1990. 105p.

This book explores the distorted thought processes that allow addicts and their families to become frozen in denial of the problem and of its painful consequences. By using case studies and personal stories, the author also covers the topic of relapse and presents some strategies for learning to break free from addictive thought patterns.

U.S. Journal. **The Treatment Directory.** Deerfield Beach, FL: Health Communications, 1991. 130p.

This comprehensive directory helps people dealing with alcoholism, drug addictions, eating disorders, or codependency to find the best treatment programs for them.

W., Dana. **Getting a Life: The Young Person's Guide to Drug-Free Living.** Center City, MN: Hazelden Educational Materials, 1991. 240p.

Humorous and hard-hitting, this book is a guide for teenagers about what life is like during recovery. A compilation of teens' experiences with recovering from chemical dependency, *Getting a Life* tackles important subjects including sexuality, peer pressure, and dealing with authority figures.

Yoder, Barbara. **The Resource Recovery Guide: The Best Available Information on Addictions and Codependency.** New York: Fireside Books, 1990. 314p.

In addition to extensive resource lists, this book contains facts and personal accounts of addiction and recovery. Recovery hints include everything from how to choose a family therapist to how to tell whether you are a compulsive shopper. Chapters on drugs, alcohol, and compulsive behaviors are included along with chapters on sugar, caffeine, incest, abuse, and AIDS.

PAMPHLETS

About Teens and Drugs. South Deerfield, MA: Channing L. Bete Co., 1987. 15p.

This cartoon booklet takes a broad look at the dangers of drug use and provides alternatives. Of special interest are sections on how to tell whether a friend is using drugs and what to do to help that person.

Alcohol, Tobacco and Other Drugs May Harm the Unborn.
Rockville, MD: National Clearinghouse for Alcohol and Drug
Information, 1990. 80p.

The most recent research findings on the effects of alcohol are
presented in this booklet, along with the effects of tobacco and both
illegal and prescription drugs on the growing fetus, the mother, and
the baby after it is born.

**The Fact Is . . . Alcohol and Other Drug Abuse Affects the Lives of
Millions of Americans.** Rockville, MD: National Clearinghouse on
Alcohol and Drug Information, 1988. 5p.

This leaflet gives answers to the most often asked questions about
alcohol and drug use. Statistics are included on how many people
use drugs, what drugs they use, death rates from drug use, and how
much addiction costs society.

**The Fact Is . . . Alcohol and Other Drugs Can Harm an Unborn
Baby.** Rockville, MD: National Clearinghouse on Alcohol and Drug
Information, 1989. 13p.

This pamphlet provides background information about the impact of
alcohol and illegal drugs on a growing fetus. A list of informational
resources is included.

Hull-Mast, Nancy. **How We Got Better: Teens Answer the
Most-Asked Questions about Recovery.** Park Ridge, IL: Parkside
Publishing Corporation, 1989. 15p.

Teenagers in recovery answer in their own words questions such as
"Am I too young to be addicted?" "What is addiction?" and "How
can I face the people I've hurt?" They also tell readers how they came
to be addicted, what addiction was like, and how they got
themselves into treatment.

Leite, Evelyn. **How It Feels To Be Chemically Dependent.**
Minneapolis, MN: Johnson Institute, 1987. 14p.

This pamphlet, which focuses on denial, can help chemically
dependent people break through their own denial. It also aids
friends and family members in understanding what their loved one
is experiencing.

Mann, George A. **The Dynamics of Addiction.** Minneapolis, MN:
Johnson Institute, 1987. 12p.

Detailing both the physical and the psychological aspects of addiction, this booklet also includes information on how stress and family history can affect the addictive process.

Montagne, Mary. **Staying Straight: Adolescent Recovery.** Minneapolis, MN: Community Intervention, 1987. 36p.

This pamphlet discusses the process involved in healing from addictions with special emphasis on the issues that face adolescents as they begin recovery.

The Recovery Dictionary. Park Ridge, IL: Parkside Publishing Corporation, 1989. 8p.

This basic booklet was compiled by clinical advisors for teens and adults who are bewildered by the specialized vocabulary of recovery. It is a good guide for anyone first learning about addictions.

Sassatelli, Jean. **Breaking Away: Saying Good-Bye to Alcohol/Drugs.** Minneapolis, MN: Johnson Institute, 1989. 24p.

Breaking free from alcohol, drugs, or both, is not an easy process. For many teenage addicts the relationship with their chemical of choice is the most important relationship in their lives. This booklet focuses on helping readers see how chemical dependency affects addicts' relationships with family, friends, and, most important, themselves.

Scherling, Donald. **Better All the Time: A Young Person's Recovery Workbook.** Minneapolis, MN: Parkside Publishing Corporation, 1989. 30p.

Filled with exercises, this book covers the first four steps of the Twelve Step recovery program. Readers are helped to look at the consequences of their addiction.

Zarek, David, and James Sipe. **Can I Handle Alcohol/Drugs? A Self-Assessment Guide for Youth.** Minneapolis, MN: Johnson Institute, 1987. 32p.

Filled with quizzes, questionnaires, and exercises, this booklet aids teenagers in taking a look at how drinking and drug use might affect or already is affecting their lives. Some areas covered are the severity of the problem, some of the roadblocks to recovery, and options for treatment.

PERIODICAL

LISTEN Magazine
6830 Laurel Street, NW
Washington, DC 20012-9979

This monthly magazine provides information about smoking and alcohol and drug use through articles, puzzles, and poems. It is packed with alternatives to getting high on chemicals. Subscriptions cost $12.95 per year.

Nonprint Materials

Addiction: The Problems, the Solutions
Type: VHS video
Length: 24 min.
Cost: Purchase $169
Distributor: Sunburst Communications
               39 Washington Avenue
               Box 40
               Pleasantville, NY 10570-9971
Date: 1991

This video defines addiction as any kind of repeated behavior that leads to continued use, compulsive use, lack of control, and finally chaos. In addition to chemical dependency and eating disorders, compulsive behaviors such as gambling and exercise are covered in a series of interviews with teens, a medical expert, and a psychologist. Self-esteem is discussed as an important part of both prevention and recovery. A teaching guide is included.

Athletes and Addiction: It's Not a Game
Type: VHS video
Length: 32 min. (edited), 55 min. (unedited)
Cost: Rental $85, purchase $250
Distributor: Coronet/MTI Film and Video
               108 Wilmot Road
               Deerfield, IL 60015-5196
Date: 1991

Narrated by Jim McKay and Lynn Swann, this specially edited ABC Sports production gives viewers an intimate look at why some athletes have fallen prey to chemical dependency and how they have struggled to recover. The video includes interviews with Edmonton Oiler hockey player Dave Hunter, and ice skater Tai Babilonia.

Chemical Dependency: A Disease of Denial

Type: VHS video
Length: 20 min.
Cost: Purchase $195
Distributor: Hazelden Educational Materials
                 P.O. Box 176
                 Center City, MN 55012-0176
Date: 1991

The psychological, biological, and social aspects of chemical dependency are explored in this film. It includes commentary from the director of the Mayo Clinic's Addictive Disorders Department and from recovering individuals. There is a special emphasis on denial.

Choices and Consequences

Type: 16mm film, VHS video
Length: 33 min.
Cost: Purchase $525 (film); $495 (video)
Distributor: Johnson Institute
                 7151 Metro Boulevard
                 Minneapolis, MN 55439-2122
Date: 1987

Izzie, Stuart, and Eric are three teenagers involved to different degrees with drugs and alcohol. When the police find illegal substances in the teens' car, Izzie is court-ordered to attend a drug awareness group at school. She is successful in her recovery. Stuart and Eric are not quite so lucky. They relapse. This video is helpful to teenagers with chemical dependency problems and those teens who want to help their substance-dependent friends without becoming enablers.

Corralling Your Cravings

Type: VHS video
Length: 30 min.
Cost: Rental $75, purchase $80
Distributor: Coronet/MTI Film and Video
                 108 Wilmot Road
                 Deerfield, IL 60015-5196
Date: 1986

Produced by WGBH-TV in Boston in conjunction with *American Health* magazine, this video demonstrates the biology of addiction as mood-altering chemicals interact with the brain's pleasure centers. The video provides a good introduction to understanding why people become addicted to drugs and alcohol and offers suggestions about how to break bad habits.

D.A.R.E. To Say "No"
Type:	16mm film, VHS video
Length:	16 min.
Cost:	Rental $75, purchase $400 (film); rental $75, purchase $280 (video)
Distributor:	Coronet/MTI Film and Video
	108 Wilmot Road
	Deerfield, IL 60015
Date:	1988

D.A.R.E. (Drug Abuse Resistance Education) teaches teenagers how to say no to drugs. This video features dramatized scenes that reinforce the need to refuse to use chemicals and that show firm and tactful ways to say no. It was produced by Disney Educational Productions.

15 and Getting Straight
Type:	VHS video
Length:	48 min.
Cost:	Purchase $225
Distributor:	Intermedia
	1300 Dexter North
	Seattle, WA 98109
Date:	1989

This video, which stars Drew Barrymore, Tatum O'Neal, and David Birney, dramatizes the struggles of adolescents recovering in a chemical dependency unit. The stories of six teenagers are woven together. Their addictions include marijuana, cocaine, alcohol, and crack cocaine, and their fight to put their lives back together is a powerful one.

From behind the Mask
Type:	VHS video
Length:	15–20 min. each
Cost:	Purchase $129 (individual videos); purchase $483 (complete seven-video set)
Distributor:	Intermedia
	1300 Dexter North
	Seattle, WA 98109
Date:	1989

This seven-video set of programs was taped in an adult chemical dependency treatment program. The videos cover disease, denial, feelings, codependency, family of origin, detachment, and responsibility. Because everyone involved in putting these videos together was recovering from drug or alcohol dependency, they bring a unique understanding to this series.

Go for It! Natural Highs
Type: VHS video
Length: 30 min.
Cost: Purchase $189
Distributor: Sunburst Communications
               39 Washington Avenue
               Box 40
               Pleasantville, NY 10570-9971
Date: 1989

Matt, the teenage host of this tape, is recovering from alcoholism. He shares with viewers other ways of getting high besides using alcohol and drugs. These natural highs include surfing, music, and basketball. Other teens also talk about their strategies: running, student activism, meditation, and just having fun. In addition to offering concrete strategies for getting high naturally, this upbeat video discusses the biology of feeling good naturally.

Hard Facts about Drugs: Alcohol, Marijuana, Cocaine and Crack
Type: VHS video
Length: 22 min.
Cost: Purchase $59
Distributor: Guidance Associates
               P.O. Box 1000
               Mount Kisco, NY 10549-0010
Date: 1988

Dramatic scenes show how these drugs devastate the students who make up a typical high school class during the four years leading to their high school graduation.

Introduction to Street Drug Pharmacology
Type: VHS video
Length: 50 min.
Cost: Purchase $99.95
Distributor: Parkside Publishing Corporation
               205 West Touhy Avenue
               Park Ridge, IL 60068
Date: 1988

This tape of a lecture by Randall Webber provides an easy-to-understand scientific overview of street drugs—what they are, how they are used, and what they do to users. The neuro-chemical part of addiction, loss of control, and physical tolerance are all covered. Special emphasis is placed on currently popular drugs including cocaine.

The Invisible Line

Type: 16mm film, VHS video
Length: 31 min.
Cost: Rental $100, purchase $525 (film); rental $100, purchase $475 (video)
Distributor: Gerald T. Rogers Productions
               5215 Old Orchard Road
               Suite 900
               Skokie, IL 60071
Date: 1987

Jason is a teenager who begins drinking beer and wine at parties. Next he moves to pot, pills, and then cocaine. This dramatic portrayal shows an adolescent who begins drinking and using drugs "recreationally" and then moves on to addiction and finally overdose. This production has been evaluated and approved by the National Federation of Parents for Drug-Free Youth.

The Rehearsal

Type: VHS video
Length: 22 min.
Cost: Rental $100, purchase $350
Distributor: Gerald T. Rogers Productions
               5215 Old Orchard Road
               Suite 900
               Skokie, IL 60071
Date: 1989

Six high school students rehearsing a play about a family learn the basics about alcohol and drug addiction. The facts about what addiction is, who it happens to, and why it happens are presented in an entertaining way in this video, which was given a first place award by the National Council on Family Relations.

Relapse Prevention

Type: VHS video
Length: 20 min.
Cost: Purchase $249
Distributor: Altschul Group Corporation
               930 Pitner Avenue
               Evanston, IL 60202
Date: 1991

A relapse, which is going back to using drugs or alcohol, does not happen all of a sudden. There usually are warning signs well ahead of time. This video examines the blame, denial, and self-pity that signal a possible retreat from recovery. It tells how to recognize these warning signs and what to do about them.

Saying No to Drugs and Alcohol

Type:	16mm film, VHS video
Length:	16 min.
Cost:	Purchase $345 (film), $295 (video)
Distributor:	Perennial Education
	930 Pitner Avenue
	Evanston, IL 60202
Date:	1991

Peer pressure to drink and use drugs begins early for teenagers. This video explores what it is like to be a 13-year-old faced with the choice between trying to fit in and saying no to substance abuse. Both the choices and the consequences of each are presented.

Secret Addictions: Women, Drugs and Alcohol

Type:	VHS video
Length:	32 min.
Cost:	Rental $85, purchase $495
Distributor:	Coronet/MTI Film and Video
	108 Wilmot Road
	Deerfield, IL 60015
Date:	1991

Women at all income levels and of all races can become addicted. In this video a number of women talk about their problems with chemical dependency and how they were motivated to go into treatment. There is an exploration of how society's expectations of women make their addiction and recovery issues different from those of men.

Secret Addictions: Women in Treatment

Type:	VHS video
Length:	32 min.
Cost:	Rental $85, purchase $495
Distributor:	Coronet/MTI Film and Video
	108 Wilmot Road
	Deerfield, IL 60015
Date:	1991

Single and married women and mothers and their children talk about addiction and the recovery process. This video includes a look at group therapy, parenting training classes, and residency rehabilitation centers along with interviews with professionals. Of special interest is the information that many women addicts were abused as children.

Slipping into Darkness

Type:	VHS video
Length:	17 min.
Cost:	Purchase $249
Distributor:	Altschul Group Corporation
	930 Pitner Avenue
	Evanston, IL 60202
Date:	1991

The stories of alcoholics and drug users who went through recovery and then retreated back into chemical dependency are covered in this video. Counselors are interviewed about how addicts can cope with a relapse and get back into recovery.

Stand Up for Yourself

Type:	16mm film, VHS video
Length:	15 min.
Cost:	Rental $60, purchase $345 (film); rental $60, purchase $260 (video)
Distributor:	Churchill Films
	12210 Nebraska Avenue
	Los Angeles, CA 90025
Date:	1987

This film shows teenagers ways they can better say no to drugs, alcohol, and cigarettes without losing their friends. It models refusal skills and offers encouragement to stand up to peer pressure.

Steps One, Two and Three for Young People

Type:	VHS video
Length:	30 min.
Cost:	Purchase $225
Distributor:	Hazelden Educational Materials
	P.O. Box 176
	Center City, MN 55012-0176
Date:	1991

This collage of music, images, and voices of recovering teenagers focuses on struggles with denial, powerlessness, and spirituality.

Built-in pauses in the video make it very effective as a classroom discussion tool.

Student Assistance Program

Type: VHS video
Length: 20 min.
Cost: Purchase $149
Distributor: Altschul Group Corporation
930 Pitner Avenue
Evanston, IL 60202
Date: 1991

Aimed at teenagers, this video talks about how to avoid chemical dependency and what to do about a drug abuse habit if they already have one. The main focus is on student assistance programs. Practical suggestions are given for setting up school support groups, finding counselors who are willing to listen, and finding drug treatment outside the school.

Twelve Steps: The Video

Type: 16mm film, VHS or Beta video
Length: 40 min.
Cost: Purchase $300 (film), $39.95 (video)
Distributor: Gerald T. Rogers Productions
5215 Old Orchard Road
Suite 900
Skokie, IL 60071
Date: 1989

A dramatic and sensitive introduction to Twelve-Step programs as a means of addiction recovery, this production is a good relapse prevention tool. In addition to alcoholism and drug addiction, it covers other life stress problems and is approved by Alcoholics Anonymous World Services.

Organization

The National Clearinghouse for Alcohol and Drug Information
P.O. Box 2345
Rockville, MD 20852
(301) 468-2600

This national clearinghouse distributes a number of informational pamphlets and resource directories that cover all types of substance abuse. It also has posters and videos. In addition the clearinghouse can provide referrals over the phone.

CHAPTER 2

Alcoholism: Dying for a Drink

While she cut up stuff for a salad I peeled some carrots. She told me about her years of drinking and how she'd stopped and what her life had been like since she had. She drank for seven years before she hit what she called her "bottom." She explained that alcohol seemed to move much more rapidly in teenagers than in adults. She also said that everyone was different. Two adult alcoholics could drink exactly the same amount and one might go on for twenty or twenty-five years, while the other might hit bottom in five or ten. Then she said it was possible I hadn't hit bottom yet and that maybe I had years of drinking ahead of me. After all, I'd never been jailed or institutionalized. The only sure things she knew about alcoholic drinking were that there were only two ways it could end—insanity or death—and that the only way to arrest the disease was to stop drinking.

"Do you think I should go to an A.A. meeting?" I asked.

"Should?"

"Well, you know what I mean."

"Should isn't part of my vocabulary anymore . . . at least I try to live without it. You do what you'd like to do."

"What if what I'd like to do is drink?" I asked, testing her.

"If you really want to drink, you will. If you want to try not to, I can help."

I felt mad again. "Don't you even care if I drink?"

"Of course I care. But there's nothing I can do unless you're willing. Try to remember one thing: chances are you wouldn't have just one drink or even two. Chances are you'd have lots of drinks and end up drunk doing God knows what. Is that what you want?"

I didn't know. But did drink always mean drunk? And did drunk always mean trouble? So far it hadn't always meant that, but it did happen often enough. And the thing was I couldn't predict it. Drink almost always meant drunk and I never, never knew if drunk would mean trouble. If only I could control it. But I couldn't— that was the problem. I just seemed to be going around in circles. I didn't know what to do.

The Late Great Me by Sandra Scoppettone
(New York: Bantam Starfire, 1976), 205–206.

Geri Peters was a high school junior when her boyfriend, Dave, gave her her first bottle of wine. It seemed like a magic potion. As she became more and more caught up in drinking, she reached a point where she forgot to eat, and later she became involved in an incident at school. One of her teachers, Kate Laine, confronted Geri about her alcoholism. But Geri's dad forbade his daughter to associate with a known alcoholic, even if she was a teacher and was recovering. His daughter could not be one of them, he insisted. Against his wishes, Geri accepted an invitation to dinner at Kate's house and took Kate's suggestion to go to an A.A. meeting. All the while Geri kept struggling to avoid facing the truth about herself—that she was addicted to alcohol and that if she continued, she would wind up as Kate warned, insane or dead.

Alcoholism has been called the disease of denial, and for good reason. People who are alcohol dependent are not the only ones who play the dangerous game of pretending they do not have a problem. Family members—like Geri's father—friends, and society as a whole often conspire to keep alcoholism a secret.

Despite the fact that one out of every ten drinkers in this country will develop alcoholism, we are bombarded from all sides by liquor ads that promise this beer or that wine cooler will make us popular, well liked, and the life of the party. The most abused drug in the United States today, alcohol is tightly woven into the fabric of U.S. life. Although it is legal, at least for those age 21 or over, alcohol can cause big problems. The consequences of alcohol abuse and addiction in the United States are truly staggering.

Facts about Alcohol

According to the National Council on Alcoholism

- In 1986 the U.S. liquor industry spent $1.17 billion to advertise their products.
- Sixty-six percent of adults in the United States drink.
- About 10 percent of adults in this country have alcohol problems. In 1985 there were 10.6 million alcoholics in the United States and 7.3 million alcohol abusers.
- This 10 percent is responsible for half of the alcohol consumed in this country.
- In 1986 the amount of pure alcohol sold in the United States was enough for slightly over 2.5 gallons for every man, woman, and child in the United States. This is the same as 3 gallons of wine per person or 29.8 gallons of beer.
- Almost 5 percent of all the deaths in the United States in 1980 were either directly or indirectly attributable to alcohol.
- In 1986, 23,990 people died in traffic accidents related to alcohol. This figure was an increase over previous years. Alcohol-related accidents account for just over half of all traffic deaths.
- About 4.6 million teenagers between the ages of 14 and 17 say they have experienced negative consequences as a result of alcohol use. These consequences include arrest, injury, and accidents.
- According to the National Institute on Alcohol Abuse and Alcoholism, in 1984 more than half a million Americans were in treatment for alcoholism or alcohol abuse.

Alcoholic Beverages

Beer, wine, and distilled spirits, or liquor, are the three main categories of drinks classified as alcoholic beverages. All contain varying amounts of ethanol, which is sometimes called grain alcohol, a chemical that is rapidly metabolized by the body, producing intoxication. (Another kind of alcohol, rubbing alcohol or isopropyl, is a poison and if it is drunk is often fatal.)

The alcohol content of alcoholic drinks is usually stated in percentage by volume or proof. The percentage by volume of drinks is equal to half of the proof. If an alcoholic beverage says 100 proof on the label, then it contains 50 percent ethanol. Most beer is about 4 percent alcohol, or 8 proof, and wines are usually 10 to 12 percent alcohol, or 20 to 24 proof. Whiskey and other distilled spirits are usually 80 to 100 proof, or 40 to 50 percent alcohol.

Alcohol has been around for a long time, probably for nearly as long as people have lived on Earth. Drinking has been an acceptable part of life in the United States since the country was founded. In fact drinking became such a problem that in 1919 Congress ratified the Eighteenth Amendment prohibiting the manufacture, sale, and consumption of alcoholic beverages. During Prohibition organized crime began to flourish, making and selling bootleg booze to Americans who were more than willing to drink it. Prohibition ended in 1933 and was generally believed to be an experiment that failed. Today alcohol is a legal drug except for minors.

The Physical Effects of Drinking

When a person takes a drink of an alcoholic beverage, about 20 percent of the ethanol, in the form of small water- and fat-soluble molecules, passes through the lining of the stomach and enters the bloodstream. Eighty percent passes through the wall of the small intestine. Because alcohol is a liquid and does not need to dissolve, this process happens very rapidly. Not every drinker absorbs alcohol at the same rate. A drinker who has an empty stomach absorbs ethanol through the stomach lining much more quickly than does someone who has just eaten. In both cases, however, all of the alcohol is absorbed. Only the rate of absorption is changed. The more diluted the alcohol is, the more slowly it is absorbed, so drinking shots of undiluted 100 proof whiskey makes a drinker intoxicated much more quickly than does sipping beer or wine.

Once it is in the bloodstream, alcohol is distributed throughout the body, including the brain. Because the brain has a large blood supply, the alcohol concentration there is higher than in other parts of the body, almost as high as it is in the bloodstream. Alcohol affects the brain by changing both how the drinker views the world and his or her behavior.

On a short-term basis, drinking alcohol increases the drinker's heart rate and dilates blood vessels in the extremities such as the fingers and toes and in the skin. Blood pressure is slightly reduced. In small amounts alcohol increases appetite. Urine output increases as well.

Just as the rate of absorption is different for different people, the way in which alcohol is distributed throughout the body varies from drinker to drinker. As a general rule, a person who is thin can drink the same amount as a heavier person, but the smaller person will have higher levels of alcohol in the bloodstream and will feel ethanol's effects faster. On the other hand, the thin drinker's body will process, or metabolize, the ethanol faster, so alcohol's effects will decrease more rapidly than they will for the heavier person.

The metabolizing of alcohol, during which the molecule is broken down to its smaller parts, begins in the stomach. Most of the alcohol, however, is metabolized by the liver. Here an enzyme called alcohol dehydrogenase goes to work to turn the ethanol into acetaldehyde and hydrogen. Acetaldehyde is then transformed into acetate, which is further broken down into carbon dioxide and water that are eliminated by the body.

The liver's metabolic process is constant; it does not speed up simply because a person has had more to drink. The average rate at which alcohol is metabolized by the human body is one-third of an ounce per hour, which works out to about an ounce of whiskey or a can of beer. If a drinker consumes more than this, blood alcohol content rises, increasing the effects of ethanol both on the brain and on the body.

Alcohol: The Mood-Altering Drug

Alcohol's impact on the brain is that of a depressant. Initially a drinker's inhibitions are lowered by drinking, and he or she may seem giddy or excited. Mood swings occur as well as loss of control over behavior. As more alcohol is consumed, however, and the blood alcohol concentration measures over .10 percent, the depressing action of ethanol on the brain cells becomes obvious. Slurred speech, slowed reaction time, and lack of coordination are all symptoms of intoxication. Given enough alcohol, drinkers become anesthetized or numb, eventually falling asleep or passing out. Overdoses of alcohol cause comas and even death.

Exactly how fast an individual will become intoxicated can depend on several factors in addition to the ones discussed above. The first is the rate at which alcohol is metabolized by and excreted from the system. Women, because they tend to have lower levels of the enzyme alcohol dehydrogenase, show the effects of drinking more quickly than do men of the same weight. Many women also report that during certain times of the menstrual cycle alcohol has more of an impact on them than at other times. People of both Asian and Native American heritage tend to metabolize alcohol much more slowly than do other ethnic groups.

Whether a person reacts to alcohol by being relaxed, happy, angry, or even violent depends a great deal on the drinker's personality, his or her state of mind, and the situation in which he or she is drinking. As a general rule, though, the more a person has to drink, the less these situational factors come into play.

How quickly a drinker will sober up again depends on his or her individual metabolism. Some heavy drinkers produce more alcohol dehydrogenase, and so they might sober up more quickly than other people who have not developed an alcohol tolerance. Black coffee and cold showers do not remove alcohol from a drinker's bloodstream and tissues; only their metabolism can do that.

Because alcohol is toxic (a poison), the morning after a drinker has overindulged, he or she may be faced with nausea, a headache, and sensitivity to sounds and light—a hangover.

Problem Drinking or Alcoholism?

According to the American Psychiatric Association's *Diagnostic Statistical Manual III,* most Americans are light drinkers and more than one-third do not drink any alcohol at all. A number of people do drink heavily, though, and enjoy it less, tossing down beers or wine coolers or shots of bourbon until they numb out. However, not everybody who drinks heavily is an alcoholic.

Some people are called problem drinkers, alcohol abusers, or irresponsible drinkers because they have not crossed the invisible line into the territory of physical addiction. Theirs is a psychological dependency on alcohol. According to the Office for Substance Abuse Prevention of the National Clearinghouse for Alcohol and Drug Information, alcohol abusers are people who experience negative social or personal consequences for their drinking such as arrests, loss of jobs, health problems, or problems with personal relationships. They are people who unwisely let their drinking habits interfere with the rest of their lives. Although alcohol may be at the center of their lives for limited periods of time, they are able to control the amount they drink and the times they drink.

Drinkers who are alcoholics show many of the same symptoms with a big difference. Because alcoholics are physically dependent on the ethanol in their drinks, they cannot control how much or when they will drink. At the deepest personal level, they do not believe they could survive physically or emotionally without alcohol. They have a higher tolerance for alcohol than do nonalcoholics, either because they metabolize ethanol faster or because their central nervous systems are less profoundly affected by the drug. Over time, it takes more and more alcohol for them to feel high. Many alcoholics do not even drink for the euphoria ethanol produces but instead drink to avoid feeling sick when withdrawal sets in.

People who are alcoholics often have memory losses called blackouts. Once they start drinking, they cannot quit until they are intoxicated or perhaps even have passed out. No matter how hard they try to cut down on their drinking, they cannot. When they are forced to go without a drink, alcoholics who have reached the advanced stage of the disease display withdrawal symptoms such as the shakes or D.T.s (delirium tremors), during which they see things or hear voices that do not really exist. Their heart rate speeds up and they may be short of breath or experience chills and fever. Some alcoholics who are in withdrawal have seizures. For this reason it is important for an alcoholic to seek medical help, usually at a detox, or detoxification, center rather than trying to stop drinking alone.

Alcoholism is a disease that progresses over time and is often fatal if it is not treated. Alcoholics die from overdoses of alcohol and from the effects of chronic heavy drinking on the brain, heart, liver, and other organs. In addition alcoholics as a group tend to have higher death rates from suicide, murder, and accidents than do other people.

The Course of the Disease

Although researchers still are not certain why some people become alcoholics and others do not, they have found that dependence on alcohol tends to run in families. Studies of adopted twins have shown that the passing of alcoholism from parents to children happens at a statistically significant rate, even when children are not raised by their alcoholic biological parents. In addition to an inherited predisposition, a person's environment and personality undoubtedly play a role in the development of alcoholism.

Male alcoholics, who have been studied much more than female alcoholics, tend to begin becoming ethanol dependent as teenagers or in their 20s. Because the addiction progresses slowly, they may not even be aware that they have a problem until their late 30s or 40s. It is rare for a man to cross the line of alcohol dependence after he turns 45. Women, on the other hand, tend to begin problem drinking and to develop symptoms of alcoholism later in life. Some researchers believe the disease progresses much faster in women than it does in men. A woman, after 3 or 4 years of heavy drinking, may develop a degree of dependency it takes a man 15 to 20 years to reach.

As the disease of alcoholism progresses, along with the alcoholic's physical tolerance for the drug, his or her behaviors change. The person makes more and more excuses for his or her actions as denial sets in. Whereas others drink to feel high, the alcoholic drinks to feel normal. An alcoholic's thinking gets confused as he or she sinks deeper into denial. He or she often begins to hide the drinking and may start avoiding friends and family members.

Long-Term Effects of Alcohol on the Body

Chronic abuse of alcohol over long periods of time usually does a great deal of damage to the drinker's body. An alcoholic's life expectancy is reduced by 10 to 12 years compared to someone who is not an alcoholic. Some of the physical consequences of long-term alcoholism or alcohol abuse are

1. Brain damage: Acute alcohol intake (drinking large amounts at one time) can cause irreversible damage to brain cells and even destroy them altogether. Memory loss, a decrease in learning ability, and loss of judgment are some results. Alcoholics may also suffer from Korsakoff's syndrome, a type of psychosis caused by lack of nutrition.
2. Liver damage: The alcoholic's or long-term heavy drinker's liver swells and becomes tender. It also stores fat. Eventually cells may die and the organ develops scars called cirrhosis. This damaged tissue cannot replace itself with healthy cells, and as the disease progresses the alcoholic's liver may eventually shut down completely. High blood sugar and alcoholic hepatitis are other problems that can occur.
3. Stomach problems: Peptic ulcers are not uncommon among advanced alcoholics. Stomach inflammations often occur as well, because alcohol irritates the stomach's lining.
4. Circulatory disease: People who abuse alcohol over a period of time may develop heart pains, irregular heartbeats, coronary artery disease, and high blood pressure. Even ingesting large quantities of alcohol over a relatively short period of time can cause direct damage to the heart's cells and make a person develop an irregular heartbeat, which can cause death. Some alcoholics develop anemia because ethanol disrupts the bone marrow. Bleeding disorders are not uncommon because a long-term heavy drinker's blood does not clot well.

5. Malnutrition: Because alcoholic beverages contain sugar, alcohol, and little else, they provide few vitamins and many empty calories. As the disease progresses, an alcoholic will usually stop eating a balanced diet as his or her caloric intake becomes composed of more and more alcohol and less and less food. Vitamin deficiencies become a major problem and cause flabby muscles, the shakes, decreased stamina, and a lowering of resistance to infections.

6. Cancer: Research shows that long-term heavy drinking can cause mouth, throat, tongue, voicebox (larynx), stomach, and liver cancer. Those who drink and smoke raise their chances of cancer 44 times over people who abstain from both alcohol and tobacco. In addition, cancer survival rates for drinkers are lower than those for nondrinkers.

Kinds of Alcoholics

It is important to understand that there is no such thing as a typical or average alcoholic. The image of an old wino staggering around skid row is only a tiny part of the picture. In fact, skid row bums only account for 1 out of 20 alcoholics. People who are addicted to alcohol come from all income levels and all races and nationalities; they can be male or female. Alcohol causes problems for people in nearly every age group, including the elderly and children. The average age at which U.S. teenagers begin to drink is 12.

When people are dependent on alcohol, their drinking patterns may vary, too. Some alcoholics drink slowly and steadily, nursing drinks all day long and never appearing extremely drunk. Others get drunk once or twice a week, but only at parties on weekends. Still others may not drink for months and then they "binge," drinking to excess for several days at a time and finally sobering up for a few more months until the next binge. Some alcoholics limit their consumption to situations when others are present. Still others drink alone and may drink only moderately or not at all in the presence of others.

Alcoholism and Teenagers

More than any other drug, alcohol profoundly affects teenagers' lives. Recent surveys show that adolescents are beginning drinking younger—usually at age 12. Another survey conducted by *Weekly*

Reader in 1987 showed that over one-third of all kids in the fourth grade had been pressured by friends to drink alcoholic beverages. Alcohol counselors report that it is not rare for 10- to 12-year-olds to have serious drinking problems. As a rule, the younger people are when they begin drinking, the more problems they tend to develop, such as truancy, teen pregnancy, and vandalism.

Because many teen drinkers tend to be physically smaller than their adult counterparts, the alcohol they drink affects them more quickly and profoundly. After all, they have less blood and a smaller body mass to dilute the ethanol they consume. Even though most teens are too young to incur any long-term physical effects for their abusive drinking yet, they may be victims of fatal automobile accidents and even alcohol poisoning from drinking too much at one sitting. According to the National Clearinghouse for Alcohol and Drug Information, alcohol use is present in over half of all teen suicides.

Teenagers begin drinking for a number of reasons. Some of them see heavy drinking as an accepted part of their families. The tendency toward alcohol use and abuse is higher among people with an alcoholic parent than it is among those with parents who were moderate drinkers or nondrinkers. Children of alcoholics have a four times greater risk of developing alcoholism than do children of parents who are not alcoholics.

Peer pressure can be an important factor in a teenager's decision to drink, in addition to cultural influences. Personal problems are a factor as well. Some teenagers report drinking to try to handle anger, sadness, and frustration. Some teens also drink in an attempt to feel better about themselves.

FACTS ABOUT TEENAGE DRINKING

According to the National Council on Alcoholism and Drug Dependence

- Alcohol is the number one drug of choice among American teenagers.
- In 1989 two-thirds of all high school seniors drank.
- More than one-third of high school seniors are occasional heavy drinkers, which means they had more than five drinks in a row within the previous week.
- One-third of all high school seniors have friends who get drunk at least once a week. The same number of students do not believe there is a risk in having four or five drinks every day.

- Alcohol is the top killer of teens. About 10,000 people from the ages of 16 to 24 die alcohol-related deaths every year.

The San Francisco–based Advocacy Institute, which monitors alcohol issues, conducted a study that shows almost 2 out of 5 teenagers drink on a weekly basis, consuming a total of 1.1 billion cans of beer each year. Over one-third of all wine coolers made in the United States are consumed by teens who are not old enough to legally drink.

Alcoholism and Women

An estimated half of all alcoholics are women, but in the past women addicted to alcohol escaped detection and avoided treatment because society forced them to hide their alcoholism. A man who was a heavy drinker was looked up to as somebody who knew how to have a good time, whereas a woman who showed the same behavior was thought to be a "fallen" woman.

Women's drinking patterns are changing today, especially those of teenage girls. Even though teenage boys drink more often and drink larger quantities of alcohol than do teenage girls, that gap has been closing over the past 15 years. By age 17, only 14 percent of boys abstain from drinking alcohol as compared to 15 percent of girls.

Women often abuse other drugs in combination with alcohol. In 1983 Alcoholics Anonymous noted that 40 percent of its female membership reported poly-addictions. Of women alcoholics age 30 or younger, 64 percent had multiple addictions.

Material provided by the National Council on Alcoholism and Drug Dependence indicates that women will spend as much as $30 billion on alcohol in 1994. That figure is up from $20 billion spent 10 years earlier.

Fetal Alcohol Syndrome

Fetal alcohol syndrome (FAS) is the term used for a group of birth defects that may occur in babies of mothers who drink heavily during pregnancy. Among these defects are mental retardation, central nervous system problems, growth deficiencies, deformed facial features, and deformed organs. Even moderate drinking by pregnant women can cause problems in newborns. These milder problems, which can include low birth weight, behavioral problems, and mild deformities, are called fetal alcohol effects, or FAE.

There is no known time during a woman's pregnancy that it is safe for her to drink, so the best course of action for pregnant women is to not drink at all. The more alcohol a woman consumes during pregnancy, the more she increases the risk that her baby will develop FAS or FAE. Conversely, stopping drinking at any time during pregnancy lowers that risk.

According to the National Council on Alcoholism and Drug Dependence

- Fetal alcohol syndrome is one of the three major causes of birth defects. It is the only one that is easily preventable.
- Approximately 5,000 babies are born with FAS every year in the United States. That is 1 baby in every 750 born.
- The economic cost of treating FAS babies born in 1980 was an estimated $14.8 million. Caring for FAS children under 18 years old cost $670 million, and it cost $760 million to treat adults who were suffering from fetal alcohol syndrome.
- Fetal alcohol effects can be seen in as many as 36,000 newborns every year.
- As few as 1 or 2 drinks a day consumed by a pregnant woman can lower her baby's birth weight and cause behavior problems as well as deformities.
- Drinking as little as 1 or 2 drinks a week increases a pregnant woman's risk of spontaneous abortion (miscarriage).
- As many as 1 out of 3 women mistakenly believes that drinking more than 3 drinks a day during pregnancy is safe.

Drinking and Driving

Traffic accidents are another major consequence of alcohol use and abuse in the United States today.

- A little over half of all highway deaths in the United States are from alcohol-related accidents.
- Drivers under 21 years old have the highest rates of fatal, alcohol-related automobile accidents according to the National Council on Alcoholism and Drug Dependence.
- In 1986, 9,000 young people between the ages of 15 and 24 were killed in alcohol-related car fatalities according to the National Highway Traffic Safety Administration.

- Two out of every 5 Americans will be involved in an alcohol-related car crash at some time during their lives according to the National Council on Alcoholism and Drug Dependence.

Alcohol's Other Social Costs

Alcohol causes other safety problems besides traffic accidents. According to the National Council on Alcoholism and Drug Dependence, 83 percent of all fire fatalities are alcohol related and 53 percent of the victims are alcoholics. Often fires are started by alcoholics who smoke and then pass out with their cigarettes still lit.

The economic costs of alcoholism are staggering. In 1988 alone alcohol abuse cost the United States $85.8 billion in health care and in reduced work productivity. In 1985 about 95,000 people died from either alcoholism or alcohol-related deaths.

Alcohol, Crime, and Violence

Alcoholism does not only damage alcoholics, the fetuses of pregnant women who drink, and the innocent victims of alcohol-related traffic accidents. Although no one has been able to prove that drinking causes violence, the two are linked statistically. According to the National Institute on Alcohol Abuse and Alcoholism

- As many as 77 percent of child abusers reported drinking right before the abuse took place
- Two out of 5 parents who abuse their children have a history of heavy drinking
- Seventy-two percent of attackers in reported assaults had been drinking
- Half of all murders are alcohol related
- Half of all rapists had been drinking before the attack

Treatment

When alcoholics seek treatment, they must first go through the process of detoxification (detox), so that alcohol no longer alters their thinking. Then they either go into an inpatient treatment center or live at home and attend A.A. meetings or counseling sessions. Most treatment for alcoholism combines a variety of methods.

Many experts agree that an individual's recovery from alcoholism is a lifelong process. For that reason, most alcohol-dependent people who no longer drink say they are recovering rather than saying they have recovered. Although some alcoholics can stop drinking and stay sober as soon as they enter treatment for the first time, others relapse, or go back to drinking, many times before they can attain a long period of sobriety. Even though no cure exists for alcoholism, after treatment it is possible for alcoholics to live happy, productive, and alcohol-free lives.

ALCOHOLICS ANONYMOUS

Probably the most popular method of alcoholism treatment today is the group called Alcoholics Anonymous (A.A.), which was founded in 1935. Since that time it has grown so that there are A.A. meetings nearly every place in the United States. To become a part of A.A. or to work the program, as the Twelve Steps are called, the alcoholic must admit that alcoholism is a disease that is progressive and that the only solution is to stop drinking entirely. Even though A.A. is a spiritual group, it does not follow a particular religion.

The Twelve Steps of Alcoholics Anonymous have been modified and used by a number of organizations dealing with other problems besides alcohol use. The steps are

1. We admitted we were powerless over alcohol—that our lives had become unmanageable.
2. We came to believe that a Power greater than ourselves could restore us to sanity.
3. We made a decision to turn our will and our lives over to the care of God as we understood God.
4. We made a searching and fearless moral inventory of ourselves.
5. We admitted to God, to ourselves, and to another human being the exact nature of our wrongs.
6. We were entirely ready to have God remove all these defects of character.
7. We humbly asked Him to remove our shortcomings.
8. We made a list of all persons we had harmed and became willing to make amends to them all.
9. We made direct amends to such people wherever possible, except when to do so would injure them or others.

10. We continued to take personal inventory and when we were wrong, promptly admitted it.
11. We sought through prayer and meditation to improve our conscious contact with God as we understood God, praying only for knowledge of God's will for us and the power to carry that out.
12. Having had a spiritual awakening as a result of these steps, we tried to carry this message to others and to practice these principles in all our affairs.

COUNSELING

Both individual and group counseling can be effective for people who are trying to come to terms with their alcohol addiction. Such therapy is a way to tackle the underlying psychological factors that cause stress and therefore may trigger a drinking episode. Counseling also helps recovering alcoholics to learn a new set of coping skills in order to live an effective alcohol-free life. Because many alcoholics have forgotten how to feel and how to handle their emotions without the numbing effects of drinking, counseling can provide a safe place for them to sort through those feelings and learn to communicate them.

Although alcoholics numb their feelings by drinking, they also cut themselves off from healthy relationships. Because an alcoholic's primary relationship is to alcohol, friends and family members often suffer. Within the past few years, alcohol counselors have discovered that family counseling can help both alcoholics and their families to put the pieces back together and to learn to relate to one another in growth-promoting ways.

ANTABUSE

Antabuse, also called disulfiram, is a drug that slows down the way alcohol is metabolized. When an alcoholic takes Antabuse and then drinks he or she experiences a negative reaction within a few minutes. This reaction includes nausea and vomiting, flushing, restlessness, headaches, a rapid heart rate, and chest pains. Because the effects of drinking are so unpleasant for people who are taking Antabuse, this drug provides strong motivation to stay sober. However, because Antibuse can have side effects, often it is not prescribed until an alcoholic has tried and failed repeatedly to stay away from drinking.

REFERENCES

Diagnostic Statistical Manual III (DSM III), revised. Washington, DC: American Psychiatric Association, 1987.

Duncan, David, and Robert Gold. *Drugs and the Whole Person.* New York: John Wiley & Sons, 1982.

"Fact Sheet on Alcohol Related Birth Defects." New York: National Council on Alcoholism and Drug Abuse, 1990.

"Fact Sheet on Alcoholism and Alcohol Related Problems." New York: National Council on Alcoholism and Drug Abuse, 1990.

"Fact Sheet on Teenagers and Alcohol." New York: National Council on Alcoholism and Drug Abuse, 1990.

Jones-Witters, Patricia, and Weldon L. Witters. *Drugs and Society: A Biological Perspective.* Monterey, CA: Wadsworth Health Sciences, 1983.

Julien, Robert M. *A Primer of Drug Addiction.* San Francisco: W. H. Freeman and Company, 1981.

Stimmel, Barry. *The Facts about Drug Use: Coping with Drugs and Alcohol in Your Family, at Work, in Your Community.* Yonkers, NY: Consumer Reports Books, 1991.

U.S. Department of Health and Human Services. *The Economic Costs of Alcohol and Drug Abuse and Mental Illness: 1985.* San Francisco: Public Health Service, 1990.

Resources
for Finding Out about Alcoholism

Fiction

Bell, W. **Crabbe's Journey.** New York: Little, Brown, 1986. 169p.

Franklin Crabbe, a gifted student, is unappreciated by his parents. He is also an alcoholic with a wealthy father who drinks too much and a mother who takes tranquilizers. He escapes to the woods to live on the land. There he meets another runaway and begins to face himself and his problem head-on. Filled with suspense, this story documents Franklin Crabbe's journey to maturity.

Due, Linnea A. **High and Outside.** New York: Bantam Books, 1982. 195p.

Seventeen-year-old Nikki's parents do not question her social drinking because she is a modern teenager. Besides, she is one of the top players on the girls' softball team at her school. Before long, however, Nikki's drinking is no longer social—she is downing fifths of gin and having blackouts. Nikki's road to seek help is not an easy one.

Ellis, Hugh. **Legacies of an Alcoholic Family.** Deerfield Beach, FL: Health Communications, 1988. 140p.

This novel about the trials and tribulations of alcoholism and the triumph of recovery follows a family through three generations of drinking and codependency.

Franklin, Lance. **Takedown.** New York: Bantam Books (Varsity Coach), 1987. 138p.

The star wrestler of his high school, Kevin hurts his shoulder during a scrape with a dirt bike. The lingering injury bothers him during the season, and he learns to "cope" with the pain by taking a few drinks before matches. When Kevin's coach discovers the wrestler's secret, he takes steps to help Kevin.

Howe, Fanny. **Taking Care.** New York: Avon Books, 1985. 160p.

Pam at 16 is transferred to a new school because she is wild and tough. Both of her parents have a drinking problem, so she does everything she can to make her family life appear normal and at the same time deal with her own craving for alcohol. Her life changes when she goes against the wishes of her atheistic parents to explore her own spirituality and begins to do volunteer work at a hospital.

The Invisible Enemy: Alcoholism and the Modern Short Story. St. Paul, MN: Graywolf Press, 1989. 256p.

These 15 short stories by best-selling authors including Susan Minot, Alice Adams, John Cheever, and Raymond Carver detail the powerful impact of alcoholism on all levels of society.

Knoedler, Michael. **Callie's Way Home.** Center City, MN: Hazelden Educational Materials, 1990. 160p.

Sixteen-year-old Callie thought coming face to face with her alcoholism and being in a treatment center was tough, but then she has to deal with even more when she gets out of the treatment center. Before she knows what is happening she is forced to adapt to a new town and a new stepdad who has a drug problem. The stress is enough to make her want to drink again. This book about reentry after treatment is especially relevant for teens who have been through treatment themselves as well as for those who want to gain an understanding of what their friends just out of treatment may be going through.

Major, Kevin. **Far from Shore.** New York: Laurel-Leaf Library, 1983. 192p.

Chris Slade at 15 has failed tenth grade, cannot find a summer job, and has a horrible home life. A heavy drinker, he starts hanging out with tough kids and having blackouts. Finally he is accused of committing a crime he cannot remember.

Ogren, Thomas. **Happy Hour.** Syracuse, NY: New Readers Press, 1990. 112p.

Eddie Moreno, a young alcoholic, will do anything to stay high, including risking losing his wife, his family, and his job. When he can hide his addiction no longer, he finds help through Alcoholics Anonymous. This hard-hitting, high-interest book is written for adult readers with low-level reading skills.

Scoppettone, Sandra. **The Late Great Me.** New York: Bantam (Starfire), 1976. 249p.

A teenage girl's struggle with alcoholism is told with gripping realism and humor. This book has become a classic.

Snyder, Anne. **My Name Is Davey—I'm an Alcoholic.** New York: Signet (Vista Books), 1978. 133p.

Drinking makes Davey's life more interesting, especially because he shares his wild times with Maxine, who drinks heavily as well. Maxine begins Alcoholics Anonymous meetings and enters into recovery, but Davey insists his drinking is not a problem. When he convinces Maxine to drink again, the results are tragic.

Strong, Bryan. **Serena's Secret.** Santa Cruz, CA: Network Publications, 1987. 84p.

When 15-year-old Serena is pressured to experiment with alcohol, she has to make some tough choices. This interactive book lets the reader make those choices and then find out how the choices affect Serena, her friendships, and her family.

Voigt, Cynthia. **Izzy, Willy-Nilly.** New York: Fawcett Juniper, 1986. 272p.

Isobel is 15 when her date drinks too much and smashes his car, in which she is riding. Her right leg, crushed beyond repair, has to be amputated. As the survivor of an alcohol-related crash, Izzy finds that her whole life is changed. This novel tells of her struggle to move beyond bitterness and to become all that she can be.

Wagner, Robin S. **Sarah T.: Portrait of a Teenage Alcoholic.** New York: Ballantine, 1986. 120p.

Sarah's struggle with alcoholism is one many teens can empathize with.

Nonfiction

BOOKS

Alcoholics Anonymous, 3d edition. New York: Alcoholics Anonymous World Services, 1976. 605p.

Termed the Big Book in A.A. circles, this is the text of the original Twelve Step program. In addition to personal stories of drinking and recovery, the book goes into depth about the A.A. recovery program and how it works.

Alibrandi, Tom. **Young Alcoholics.** Minneapolis, MN: CompCare, 1978. 239p.

This book is based on a survey of 2,500 teenagers. Although the book is written primarily for parents as a prevention and intervention tool, much of the information contained in these pages is of interest to teenagers who want to learn more about alcohol and the adolescent experience.

Claypool, Jane. **Alcohol and You.** New York: Franklin Watts, 1988. 96p.

This up-to-date book covers all aspects of alcohol dependency for teens. It talks about when and why teens drink, how alcohol affects them, and where they can find help for themselves or for friends who need it.

Coffey, Wayne. **Straight Talk about Drinking: Teenagers Speak Out about Alcohol.** New York: NAL Plume, 1988. 256p.

Wayne Coffey, a recovering alcoholic himself, interviews 50 teenagers to get their opinions about alcohol. He combines that information with his own experience.

Cohen, Susan, and Daniel Cohen. **A Six Pack and a Fake I.D.** New York: M. Evans, 1986. 150p.

Every teenager must decide whether to drink or not to drink. The authors provide information so teenagers can make an informed choice. They present both sides of the drinking question and avoid using scare tactics. Legal issues of drinking also are discussed.

Evans, Glen, Robert O'Brien, and Morris Chafetz. **The Encyclopedia of Alcoholism.** New York: Facts on File, 1991. 400p.

This reference book contains current research and information about alcohol dependency. It is indexed and cross-referenced so it is easy to use. This is one of the most comprehensive books available about alcoholism.

Grosshandler, Janet. **Coping with Alcohol Abuse.** New York: Rosen Publishing Group, 1985. 139p.

This overview of teens and alcoholism includes sections on the effects of alcohol, teenagers' drinking habits, the various types of alcoholism, the stages of the disease, and dual addictions. Also covered are treatment strategies including student assistance programs, rehabilitation treatment centers, and Alcoholics Anonymous.

————. **Coping with Drinking and Driving.** New York: Rosen Publishing Group, 1985. 134p.

Although this book covers such broad topics as why adolescents drink and what alcohol does to their bodies, most of the material focuses specifically on how drinking impairs driving skills. It also covers the legal aspects of drinking and driving, the aftermath of losing a loved one in an alcohol-related auto accident, and what teens can do to help prevent this national problem.

Mann, Marty. **Marty Mann Answers Your Questions about Drinking and Alcoholism.** New York: Henry Holt, 1981. 132p.

This brief book, written in question-and-answer format, gives quick and informative answers to the most common questions about alcoholism. The book addresses symptoms of alcoholism, the causes of the disease, and options for treatment.

Martin, Father Joseph. **Chalk Talks on Alcohol.** New York: Harper & Row, 1982. 184p.

Using a sense of humor and his in-depth understanding of alcoholism, Father Martin discusses the dynamics of alcoholism, how it affects the family, and how to get an alcoholic into treatment. Father Martin has lectured on alcohol and alcoholics for three decades.

Milam, James, and Katherine Ketcham. **Under the Influence: A Guide to the Myths and Realities of Alcoholism.** New York: Bantam, 1981. 253p.

Under the Influence focuses on the physical processes of alcohol addiction and explores the drug's impact on the body as the disease progresses. This book is written for adults but uses relatively simple language.

Milgram, Gail. **Coping with Alcohol.** New York: Rosen Publishing Group, 1987. 138p.

This book centers on the ambivalence most Americans feel about alcohol. Although alcohol is a legal drug and is in many instances socially acceptable, it causes major problems for active alcoholics. Given the confusion, myths abound. Taking a values clarification approach, Milgram leads the reader through information on what alcohol is, how alcohol affects drinkers, alcoholism, problems alcohol causes other than alcoholism, and the impact alcoholism has on families. The purpose of the book is to provide teens with the facts so they can consciously develop their own attitudes about alcohol and discuss those attitudes with parents, teachers, and peers.

Silverstein, Herma. **Alcoholism.** New York: Franklin Watts, 1990. 112p.

This book surveys the different forms that alcoholism takes, the warning signs of the disease, and how alcoholism affects the drinker. It also covers treatment options and lists organizations that can help people who live with an alcoholic.

Taylor, Barbara. **Everything You Need To Know about Alcohol.** New York: Rosen Publishing Group, 1988. 64p.

The focus of this easy-to-read book (fourth- to sixth-grade reading level) is on helping teens decide whether or not they are irresponsible drinkers or are addicted to alcohol. Some of the chapters in this book are "What Is Alcohol," "Attitudes toward Alcohol," "The Effects of Alcohol on the Body," and "The Treatment of Alcoholism."

Wholey, Dennis. **The Courage To Change.** New York: Warner Books, 1986. 298p.

This book is a collection of personal stories about alcoholism and recovery told by famous people such as Doc Severinsen and Grace Slick. The commentary in this book draws together the common themes in the stories and discusses what it is that gives alcoholics the courage to change.

PAMPHLETS

About Alcohol. Santa Cruz, CA: Network Publications, 1990. 5p.

Written in easy-to-read language, this booklet explains exactly what alcohol is, as well as what effects it has on the body and on the emotions. Alcohol addiction is covered, as are the dangers of drinking during pregnancy.

Alcohol! Marta and Sean Talk to Teens. Santa Cruz, CA: Network Publications, 1990. 7p.

Marta and Sean have decided to quit drinking. In this pamphlet, they share with readers their own health and legal problems caused by alcohol. Tips on how to avoid drinking in the first place and how to stop the habit once you have started are covered here as well.

Alcohol Alert #10: Alcohol and Women. Rockville, MD: National Clearinghouse for Alcohol and Drug Information, 1990. 4p.

This leaflet examines the consequences of alcohol abuse on women and the different issues women alcoholics face in treatment.

Alcohol and Youth Fact Sheet. Rockville, MD: National Clearinghouse for Alcohol and Drug Information, 1987. 5p.

This pamphlet answers some of the most-asked questions about teenagers and alcohol consumption. It also discusses the effectiveness of alcohol-abuse prevention efforts.

Alcoholism: A Treatable Disease. Minneapolis, MN: Johnson Institute, 1987. 17p.

This booklet examines denial, which probably is one of the biggest stumbling blocks to recovery, and also addresses intervention and treatment.

Fact Sheet on Alcohol-Impaired Driving. Rockville, MD: National Clearinghouse for Alcohol and Drug Information, 1989. 1p.

A fact sheet about alcohol-related accidents, this was prepared from information provided by the National Highway Traffic Safety Administration.

Special Focus: Preventing Alcohol-Related Birth Defects. Rockville, MD: National Clearinghouse for Alcohol and Drug Information, 1985. 75p.

This reprint from *Alcohol Health and Research World* is filled with articles on current research into the effects of alcohol on unborn babies. It also details prevention programs that try to lower the incidence of alcohol-related birth defects.

Stamper, Laura. **Getting Help, Gaining Hope: The Second and Third Steps for Teens.** Minneapolis, MN: Deaconess Press, 1990. 20p.

A.A.'s Second and Third Steps are all about asking for help and choosing to change. Stamper, a chemical dependency counselor, uses personal stories to help adolescent readers go beyond the excuses substance abusers often use to avoid fully participating in their own recovery. This easy-to-read and easy-to-understand booklet covers A.A.'s emphasis on relying on a Higher Power for recovery.

————. **Taking the First Step: Being Honest with Yourself.** Minneapolis, MN: Deaconess Press, 1989. 14p.

This pamphlet tells the stories of five adolescents as they go through chemical dependency treatment in order to add meaning to A.A.'s First Step. Nonjudgmental and nonthreatening, the pamphlet helps readers take a long, hard look at their own drug use and helps them get started on the road to recovery.

Young People and AA. New York: Alcoholics Anonymous, 1979. 40p.

Ten stories by young people who are recovering alcoholics serve as an introduction to the Alcoholics Anonymous program for adolescents. There is a description of how A.A. works as well as a quiz and basic information about alcoholism.

Nonprint Materials

Advertising Alcohol: Calling the Shots, 2d edition
Type: VHS video
Length: 30 min.
Cost: Rental $43, purchase $350
Distributor: Cambridge Documentary Films
                P.O. Box 385
                Cambridge, MA 02139
Date: 1991

Recommended by the National PTA and the National Council on Alcoholism, this video shows how liquor advertisers use images that are far from the truth to advertise their wares. A major goal of these advertisers is to turn young people into alcohol consumers. Entertaining and thought-provoking, this video provides teenagers with the knowledge they need to be wise consumers.

Alcohol: All the Kids Do It
Type: 16mm film, VHS video
Length: 30 min.
Cost: Purchase $525 (film), $395 (video)
Distributor: The Health Connection
                12501 Old Columbia Pike
                Silver Spring, MD 20904-6600
Date: 1985

A high school athlete who has a good chance of earning a place on the Olympic diving team finds out the life-changing consequences of drinking and driving in this program, which stars Scott Baio.

Alcohol: Choices for Handling It

Type: 16mm film, VHS video
Length: 13 min.
Cost: Rental $75, purchase $325 (film); rental $75, purchase $235 (video)
Distributor: Coronet/MTI Film and Video
108 Wilmot Road
Deerfield, IL 60015
Date: 1976

Providing teens the facts in a humorous and nonjudgmental way, this video coaches viewers so they are better prepared to say no to alcohol.

Alcohol: Pink Elephant

Type: 16mm film, VHS video
Length: 15 min.
Cost: Purchase $420 (film), $240 (video)
Distributor: Britannica Educational Corporation
310 South Michigan Avenue
Chicago, IL 60604
Date: 1976

An alcoholic sees a pink elephant who convinces him that he has a problem. This program presents the basic facts about what causes alcoholism and how it is treated in a humorous and lively way.

Alcohol and Cocaine: The Secret Addiction

Type: 16mm film, VHS video
Length: 36 min.
Cost: Purchase $545 (film), $395 (video)
Distributor: The Health Connection
12501 Old Columbia Pike
Silver Spring, MD 20904-6600
Date: 1988

An ABC documentary, this program uses both graphics and interviews to show how alcohol and cocaine have a great deal in common. It includes brain cell research and information on how the predisposition to addiction may be inherited.

Alcohol and Human Physiology

Type: 16mm film, VHS video
Length: 21 min.
Cost: Purchase $475 (film), $375 (video)

Distributor: The Health Connection
                 12501 Old Columbia Pike
                 Silver Spring, MD 20904-6600
Date: 1984

This program discusses the damaging effects of alcohol on the digestive, circulatory, muscular, skeletal, urogenital, and nervous systems. It includes interviews with six recovering alcoholics who tell about how drinking damaged them physically.

Alcohol Facts: For Teenagers Only

Type: VHS video, filmstrips and audiocassettes
Length: 31 min.
Cost: Purchase $145 (video), $129 (filmstrips)
Distributor: Sunburst Communications
                 39 Washington Avenue
                 Box 40
                 Pleasantville, NY 10570-9971
Date: 1984

This filmstrip or filmstrip on videocassette presents facts about alcohol that are especially relevant to teenagers. The emphasis of the program is that by knowing the facts, teenagers can better protect themselves against the problems drinking can cause. The presentation is split into two parts: facts about drinking and facts about coping.

Comeback: The Bob Welch Story

Type: 16mm film, VHS video
Length: 26 min.
Cost: Rental $60, purchase $440 (film); rental $60,
                 purchase $330 (video)
Distributor: Churchill Films
                 12210 Nebraska Avenue
                 Los Angeles, CA 90025
Date: 1981

Bob Welch, a former pitcher for the Los Angeles Dodgers baseball team, started drinking when he was a teenager. By the time he was 21, he was an alcoholic. Friends took him to treatment and later he was able to make a comeback. This video tells his story.

Cruel Spirits: Alcohol and Violence

Type: 16mm film, VHS video
Length: 32 min.
Cost: Rental $75, purchase $595 (film); rental $75,
                 purchase $495 (video)

Distributor: Coronet/MTI Film and Video
                  108 Wilmot Road
                  Deerfield, IL 60015
Date: 1989

Alcohol use consistently has been tied to rape, child abuse, and battering. Researchers talk about why this is so and explain that not only does alcohol seem to unleash aggression, but that it increases chances of becoming a victim of violence as well.

Death in the Fast Lane
Type: 16mm film, VHS video
Length: 15 min.
Cost: Rental $50, purchase $290 (film); rental $50,
                  purchase $265 (video)
Distributor: Coronet/MTI Film and Video
                  108 Wilmot Road
                  Deerfield, IL 60015
Date: 1982

This presentation, which won an Emmy Award, looks at the enormous problem of teenage drinking and at the community action groups that have begun in response to the problem. The film was produced by the ABC news program *20/20*.

Drinking Driver: What Could You Do?
Type: 16mm film, VHS video
Length: 14 min.
Cost: Rental $75, purchase $400 (film); rental $75,
                  purchase $250 (video)
Distributor: Coronet/MTI Film and Video
                  108 Wilmot Road
                  Deerfield, IL 60015
Date: 1988

This program focuses on helping teenagers involved in dangerous situations regarding drinking and driving—for their own safety and that of others.

Drinking in America
Type: VHS video
Length: 38 min.
Cost: Purchase $350
Distributor: New Dimension Media
                  85803 Lorane Highway
                  Eugene, OR 97405
Date: 1987

From the Whiskey Rebellion to Prohibition, Americans have held many different attitudes about drinking. This video traces those attitudes throughout U.S. history using dramatized scenes to show just how historically complex the issues of alcohol and alcoholism are in the United States.

Driving under the Influence

Type:	16mm film, VHS video
Length:	22 min.
Cost:	Rental $60, purchase $485 (film); rental $60, purchase $395 (video)
Distributor:	Alfred Higgins Productions, Inc. 6350 Laurel Canyon Boulevard North Hollywood, CA 91606
Date:	1984

This award-winning film tells the true stories of drivers who caused fatal accidents when they were drunk. Also interviewed are people injured in such accidents as well as friends and relatives of people killed in accidents caused by drunk drivers. The program points out that legal drunkenness is not necessary for the worst to happen and that teens are the worst offenders when it comes to drunk driving.

Drugs and Drinks Don't Mix

Type:	16mm film, VHS video
Length:	19 min.
Cost:	Purchase $395 (film), $345 (video)
Distributor:	Perennial Education 930 Pitner Avenue Evanston, IL 60202
Date:	1985

Anyone who takes medication, whether it is over-the-counter cold medicine or a prescription, can find the combination of medication and alcohol to be deadly. This film warns about the physiological and psychological side effects of stimulants and depressants when they are taken in combination with alcohol.

Epidemic: Deadliest Weapon in America

Type:	16mm film, VHS video
Length:	30 min.
Cost:	Rental $75, purchase $595 (film); rental $75, purchase $495 (video)
Distributor:	Coronet/MTI Film and Video 108 Wilmot Road Deerfield, IL 60015
Date:	1985

This film, produced by the Gannett Broadcast Group, pulls no punches as it concentrates on the horrible deaths and injuries caused by drunk driving. It includes interviews with surviving family members of people killed in drunk driving accidents, who beg viewers to form tougher attitudes against driving under the influence of alcohol.

Facing It—My Friend's an Alcoholic

Type:	16mm film, VHS video
Length:	25 min.
Cost:	Rental $60, purchase $475 (film); rental $60, purchase $355 (video)
Distributor:	Churchill Films
	12210 Nebraska Avenue
	Los Angeles, CA 90025
Date:	1985

A. J. finds himself ensnared in his friend Terry's drinking problem. At first A. J. tries to cover it up and then he enlists Terry's girlfriend to help make Terry quit. In the end A. J. and Terry's girlfriend discover they need professional help for Terry.

A Family Talks about Alcohol

Type:	16mm film, VHS video
Length:	25 min.
Cost:	Rental $60, purchase $475 (film); rental $60, purchase $355 (video)
Distributor:	Churchill Films
	12210 Nebraska Avenue
	Los Angeles, CA 90025
Date:	1983

A family gets upset when the mother, who is a recovering alcoholic, is late for a birthday party. The importance of communication is stressed in this film, which also talks about the harmful physical and mental effects of alcohol.

The Final Score

Type:	16mm film, VHS video
Length:	23 min.
Cost:	Rental $60, purchase $455 (film); rental $60, purchase $340 (video)
Distributor:	Churchill Films
	12210 Nebraska Avenue
	Los Angeles, CA 90025
Date:	1989

Alex, who is an athlete, has a girlfriend and gets good grades. His life is turned upside-down when he has too much to drink and drives away from a party only to hit a little girl. He is not even aware of what he has done until the next day at school, when he is arrested.

Inheriting Alcoholism

Type:	VHS video
Length:	29 min.
Cost:	Rental $75, purchase $80
Distributor:	Coronet/MTI Film and Video
	108 Wilmot Road
	Deerfield, IL 60015
Date:	1989

People with alcoholic parents run a high risk of becoming alcoholics themselves. This film talks about the research being done on finding a gene responsible for an inherited predisposition to alcohol. It also covers the psychological problems caused by being parented by alcoholics and how alcoholic parents may be at least partially responsible for kids turning out to be alcoholics.

It Won't Happen to Me

Type:	16mm film, VHS video
Length:	31 min.
Cost:	Rental $85, purchase $595 (film); rental $85, purchase $495 (video)
Distributor:	Coronet/MTI Film and Video
	108 Wilmot Road
	Deerfield, IL 60015
Date:	1988

Martin's life has to start falling apart, including a suspension from school and a threat of jail, before he will get help for his drinking problem. He finally finds help in a support group. This award-winning drama weaves the stories of other kids in the group together with Martin's memories.

Just Beer

Type:	16mm film, VHS video
Length:	17 min.
Cost:	Purchase $345 (film), $295 (video)
Distributor:	Perennial Education
	930 Pitner Avenue
	Evanston, IL 60202
Date:	1984

Using a series of dramatic stories, this video shows teens that, contrary to the popular myth, beer causes problems. In addition to the dramatizations, there are interviews with teens who have stopped drinking beer.

Medical Effects of Alcohol

Type:	16mm film, VHS video
Length:	13 min.
Cost:	Rental $20, purchase $395 (film); rental $20, purchase $230 (video)
Distributor:	Britannica Educational Corporation
	310 South Michigan Avenue
	Chicago, IL 60604
Date:	1985

Alcohol is not only a drug but also a toxin. This program examines the physical effects of alcohol on drinkers.

My Friends, My Friends: Alcohol and Automobiles

Type:	VHS video
Length:	21 min.
Cost:	Rental $60, purchase $295
Distributor:	Churchill Films
	12210 Nebraska Avenue
	Los Angeles, CA 90025
Date:	1990

This powerful video tells the stories of three teenagers who killed people in automobile accidents when they were driving under the influence of alcohol. It covers both the personal and the legal consequences of drinking and driving and is a good video to spark discussion.

No Accident

Type:	16mm film, VHS video
Length:	13 min.
Cost:	Purchase $255 (film), $195 (video)
Distributor:	Perennial Education
	930 Pitner Avenue
	Evanston, IL 60202
Date:	1986

Produced by the National Film Board of Canada, this film is about the death of a young child caused by a drunk driver and how that death inspires the child's father to tell teenagers about the after-effects of such an "accident."

No Second Chance

Type: 16mm film, VHS video
Length: 14 min.
Cost: Rental $50, purchase $325 (film); rental $50,
                 purchase $260 (video)
Distributor: Coronet/MTI Film and Video
                 108 Wilmot Road
                 Deerfield, IL 60015
Date: 1987

Teenagers who drink and drive cause over 8,000 traffic fatalities each year. This drama tells the story of a popular 17-year-old who faces life as a paraplegic because he drove home from a party after drinking.

No Victory: Teens Driving Drunk

Type: VHS video
Length: 28 min.
Cost: Purchase $295
Distributor: Perennial Education
                 930 Pitner Avenue
                 Evanston, IL 60202
Date: 1991

"Whenever you drink, you're such a jerk," Lisa said before she slid into the car beside Steve, her boyfriend. Those were the last words that Steve, a top high school student and athlete, would hear. This excellent video is about how to stop friends from driving drunk.

One Too Many

Type: 16mm film, VHS video
Length: 30 min.
Cost: Rental $75, purchase $550 (film); rental $75,
                 purchase $250 (video)
Distributor: Coronet/MTI Film and Video
                 108 Wilmot Road
                 Deerfield, IL 60015
Date: 1985

Michelle Pfeiffer and Val Kilmer are the stars in this condensed version of an ABC prime time special. Two high school couples find their lives tragically changed forever by drunk driving. Dramatic and powerful, this program will cause viewers to rethink their attitudes about drinking and driving.

Personal Touch: Jason Robards on Alcoholism

Type: 16mm film, VHS video
Length: 15 min.

Cost:	Rental $75, purchase $335 (film); rental $75, purchase $260 (video)
Distributor:	Coronet/MTI Film and Video
	108 Wilmot Road
	Deerfield, IL 60015
Date:	1985

Actor Jason Robards shares his own battle with alcohol in this video produced by the ABC news program *20/20*.

Preventing Fetal Alcohol Syndrome

Type:	VHS video
Length:	24 min.
Cost:	Purchase $345
Distributor:	Perennial Education
	930 Pitner Avenue
	Evanston, IL 60202
Date:	1991

This video takes a look at the causes, treatment, and prevention of fetal alcohol syndrome (FAS), a condition believed to affect almost 6,000 babies each year. In addition to interviews with medical experts, there are interviews with mothers and families of FAS children.

Saying No to Drinking Drivers

Type:	16mm film, VHS video
Length:	23 min.
Cost:	Rental $60, purchase $455 (film); rental $60, purchase $340 (video)
Distributor:	Churchill Films
	12210 Nebraska Avenue
	Los Angeles, CA 90025
Date:	1986

It can be very difficult under peer pressure for a teenager to refuse to ride with a driver who has been drinking. This film covers several situations when adolescents may be faced with such a choice and provides strategies for saying no.

Sentenced for Life: Straight Talk about Drunk Driving

Type:	VHS video
Length:	40 min.
Cost:	Purchase $209
Distributor:	Guidance Associates
	P.O. Box 1000
	Mount Kisco, NY 10549-0010
Date:	1990

Through interviews with drunk drivers and victims who have survived alcohol-related accidents, this video examines the feelings the survivors share—loss, remorse, guilt, anger, and frustration at not being able to change the past. *Sentenced for Life* won an award at the National Educational Film and Video Festival.

Smashed, Loaded, Blasted, Bombed: What You Should Know about Alcohol

Type: VHS video
Length: 50 min.
Cost: Purchase $209
Distributor: Guidance Associates
              P.O. Box 1000
              Mount Kisco, NY 10549-0010
Date: 1989

Teenagers share why they drink in this video and offer strategies about how to say no to drinking. The focus is on building self-esteem and a strong value system. In addition to providing suggestions for handling peer pressure, the video offers tips about where to go for help for alcohol problems.

Staying Alive: Decisions about Drinking and Driving

Type: VHS video
Length: 42 min.
Cost: Purchase $209
Distributor: Guidance Associates
              P.O. Box 1000
              Mount Kisco, NY 10549-0010
Date: 1985

As a result of drinking and driving, three teenagers die in a car wreck. This dramatization uses flashbacks to intensify the pace, and it talks about successful national efforts to keep drunk drivers off the road.

Straight Talk about Drinking

Type: 16mm film, VHS video
Length: 30 min.
Cost: Rental $75, purchase $595 (film); rental $75,
              purchase $495 (video)
Distributor: Coronet/MTI Film and Video
              108 Wilmot Road
              Deerfield, IL 60015
Date: 1989

Based on the book *Straight Talk about Drinking: Teenagers Speak Out,* by Wayne Coffey, this program is filled with interviews with teenagers who tell why they drink and talk about the consequences that have affected them personally. Interviews with a medical expert and a counselor about treatment programs are included as well as warning signs of a potential drinking problem.

Teenage Drinking: A National Crisis

Type:	16mm film, VHS video
Length:	32 min.
Cost:	Rental $75, purchase $575 (film); rental $75, purchase $250 (video)
Distributor:	Coronet/MTI Film and Video 108 Wilmot Road Deerfield, IL 60015
Date:	1982

Four teenagers who were or currently are heavy drinkers talk about their past and present drinking patterns. Their honest comments provide an analysis of peer pressure, irresponsible parents, and trying to grow up too fast.

Teenage Substance Abuse: An Open Forum with John Callahan

Type:	16mm film, VHS video
Length:	22 min.
Cost:	Rental $75, purchase $495 (film); rental $75, purchase $325 (video)
Distributor:	Coronet/MTI Film and Video 108 Wilmot Road Deerfield, IL 60015
Date:	1989

John Callahan is a cartoonist and recovering alcoholic. His story about how he tried to cope with a difficult childhood by drinking, the denial of his alcoholism, and a drunk driving accident that left him in a wheelchair is powerful and touching. Teenagers, too, describe their struggles with alcohol and reveal their coping strategies in this Disney Educational Productions film.

Teens and Alcohol: The Hidden Problem

Type:	VHS video
Length:	37 min.
Cost:	Purchase $199

Distributor: Sunburst Communications
                 39 Washington Avenue
                 Box 40
                 Pleasantville, NY 10570-9971
Date: 1989

Focusing on the consequences of irresponsible drinking, this video argues that even when teens do not become addicted to alcohol, their behavior can have a high cost. When Jennifer holds a drinking party the kids start to fight, sexual rumors begin, and kids drive home drunk. This thought-provoking story may cause teens to think twice about drinking.

Thanks for the One Time

Type: 16mm film, VHS video
Length: 45 min.
Cost: Rental $75, purchase $650 (film); rental $75,
                 purchase $250 (video)
Distributor: Coronet/MTI Film and Video
                 108 Wilmot Road
                 Deerfield, IL 60015
Date: 1981

In this drama, a physician denies his alcoholism even though his work and family life are falling apart around him. An intervention finally brings him to treatment. All of the actors in this film have been personally touched by alcohol abuse.

There Is Hope

Type: VHS video
Length: 28 min.
Cost: Purchase $295
Distributor: Perennial Education
                 930 Pitner Avenue
                 Evanston, IL 60202
Date: 1986

The symptoms and characteristics of alcoholism are discussed in this video, but the main emphasis is on the fact that alcoholism is treatable. Exploring the different options for rehabilitation, the program offers hope to friends and family members of alcoholics as well as to alcoholics themselves.

Thinking about Drinking

Type: 16mm film, VHS video
Length: 18 min.

Cost: Rental $60, purchase $415 (film); rental $60,
                 purchase $375 (video)
Distributor: Alfred Higgins Productions, Inc.
                 6350 Laurel Canyon Boulevard
                 North Hollywood, CA 91606
Date: 1991

Covering the basic facts about many common drinks and the effects of alcohol on both the body and the mind, this film places a great deal of emphasis on the dangers of drinking and driving and of drinking during pregnancy.

Understanding Alcohol Use and Abuse
Type: 16mm film, VHS video
Length: 12 min.
Cost: Rental $75, purchase $320 (film); rental $75,
                 purchase $240 (video)
Distributor: Coronet/MTI Film and Video
                 108 Wilmot Road
                 Deerfield, IL 60015
Date: 1980

This video teaches the dangers of drinking in a lively and entertaining manner. Both the emotional and the physical consequences of drinking are covered in this program made by Disney Educational Productions.

Women, Drugs and Alcohol
Type: 16mm film, VHS video
Length: 21 min.
Cost: Rental $75, purchase $450 (film); rental $75,
                 purchase $400 (video)
Distributor: Coronet/MTI Film and Video
                 108 Wilmot Road
                 Deerfield, IL 60015
Date: 1980

Many women alcoholics are chemically dependent on prescription drugs as well. This film takes a look at doctors who overprescribe drugs, the signs of dual alcohol/drug addiction, and how to kick these habits.

The Young Alcoholic: A Family Dilemma
Type: 16mm film, VHS video
Length: 30 min.

Cost: Rental $70, purchase $500 (film); rental $70,
                 purchase $450 (video)
Distributor: Coronet/MTI Film and Video
                 108 Wilmot Road
                 Deerfield, IL 60015
Date: 1982

Intervention is a strategy that works to get alcoholics past denial
and into treatment. Filmed at a workshop conducted at the Maxwell
Institute in New York, this program illustrates how intervention
works.

Organizations

Alcoholics Anonymous (A.A.)

Box 659
Grand Central Station
New York, NY 10163
(212) 686-1100

The oldest of all support/recovery groups for alcoholics, A.A. has
about 75,000 meetings scattered throughout the United States and
the world. Members share their experiences with alcoholism and
work together in the recovery process using the Twelve Steps.
A.A. publishes a newsletter, *The Grapevine,* and offers literature
about recovery.

Calix Society

7601 Wayzata Boulevard
Minneapolis, MN 55426
(612) 546-0544

Calix Society is a national organization of Catholics recovering from
alcoholism. People who belong to this group use the Twelve Steps of
A.A. to maintain their sobriety. Special emphasis is placed on
spirituality in the Catholic tradition. A priest serves as spiritual
director for each group.

J.A.C.S. (Jewish Alcoholics, Chemically Dependent Persons, and Significant Others)

197 East Broadway
Room 208
New York, NY 10002
(212) 473-4747

Contrary to the myth believed both outside and within the Jewish community, people with Jewish heritage can and do become alcoholic. This group holds meetings, does networking, publishes literature, and organizes retreats. Although this national organization is small, it helps interested people start groups throughout the country.

Mothers Against Drunk Driving (MADD)
669 Airport Freeway, Suite 310
Hurst, TX 76053
(817) 268-6233

MADD, begun in 1980, is the biggest organization in the United States fighting against drunk driving. MADD offers publications, videos, workshops, and a student resource publication.

National Association of Lesbian and Gay Alcoholism
204 West 20th Street
New York, NY 10011
(212) 713-5074

This referral and support organization can provide callers with information about alcohol treatment programs and individual therapists who can help deal with the issues of being gay and alcoholic. The association publishes a newsletter and holds a national conference as well as having a library. There is a membership fee.

National Black Alcoholism Council, Inc. (NBAC)
53 West Jackson Boulevard, Suite 828
Chicago, IL 60604
(312) 663-5980

NBAC focuses on alcohol issues in the black community. The organization offers publications, has a speakers' bureau, and manages Blacks Against Drunk Driving (BADD) groups on the campuses of black colleges.

National Council on Alcoholism and Drug Abuse
12 West 21st Street
New York, NY 10010
(800) 622-2255

The National Council on Alcoholism provides information about alcoholism and other forms of chemical dependency. It compiles annual statistical reports about the impact alcohol has on society.

Women for Sobriety
Box 618
Quakertown, PA 18951
(215) 536-8026

Women for Sobriety, a national organization dealing with the issues women face in recovery, uses a "New Life" program based on 13 statements of acceptance rather than the Twelve Steps. This program centers on how to overcome depression and guilt. There is a small membership fee, and members receive a newsletter. Currently there are about 300 groups in the United States. Groups are limited to 6 to 10 women.

Hotlines

Alcoholism and Drug Addiction Treatment Center
(800) 382-4357

Twenty-four hours a day, this hotline provides referrals to alcohol and drug treatment centers for both adults and teenagers.

National Council on Alcoholism and Drug Abuse
(800) 622-2255

This hotline refers callers to local councils on alcoholism and sends out printed material on alcoholism. The hotline operates 24 hours a day.

CHAPTER 3

Drug Addiction: America's Tragedy

July 22

    I could tell Mom had been crying when she came to see me today, so I tried to be very strong and put on a really happy face. It's a good thing I did because they are sending me to an insane asylum, a looney bin, a crazy house, freak wharf, where I can wander around with the other idiots and lunatics. I am so scared I cannot even take a full breath. Daddy tried to explain it all very professionally but it was obvious that he had been completely unhinged by the whole thing. But not as much as I am. No one could be.

    He said that when my case was taken before the juvenile judge, Jan and Marcie both testified that I had been trying for weeks to sell them LSD and marijuana and that around school I was a known user and pusher.

    Circumstances really were quite against me. I have a drug record and Daddy said that when Mrs. Larsen's neighbor heard me screaming, she and the gardener came over to see what was happening and thinking I had gone insane they locked me in a small closet, ran to check the baby who had apparently also been awakened by my screams, and called the police. By the time they got there I had injured myself severely and was trying to scratch the rough plaster off the walls to get out and had beaten my head against the door until I had a brain concussion and a fractured skull.

    Now they are going to send me to the Boobie Hatch which is probably where I belong.

Go Ask Alice by Anonymous (New York:
Avon Flare, 1967), 152–153.

The author of the journal upon which the book *Go Ask Alice* is based was a real teenager caught up in the dark world of drug abuse. She smoked pot, popped pills, and dropped acid until finally her addictions caught up with her. This entry comes toward the end of her diary, which tells the story of a life that ended in overdose. Unfortunately the wild ups and downs, the struggle to stop using drugs, and ultimate tragedy are the far too common results of the problems of drug abuse and addiction in this country today.

Facts about Drugs

- In 1988, 80 percent of all Americans aged 18 to 25 had used an illegal drug, and 64 percent of the people aged 26 to 34 admitted experimenting with illegal drugs (*National Household Survey on Drug Abuse*, 13–14).
- Even though illegal drug use among American high school seniors, college students, and young adults has declined from the 1970s, the United States still has the highest rate of drug use in the industrialized world (*Drug Prevention Curricula*, 2).
- By the time they graduate from high school, one-quarter of all American teenagers regularly use illegal drugs (*Drug Prevention Curricula*, 2).
- The illegal drugs most frequently reported to cause drug abuse–related deaths in teenagers are narcotics, antidepressants, alcohol in combination with other drugs, and cocaine (*NIDA Capsules*, 2).
- The illegal drug economy is an estimated $57 billion industry. Heroin addicts often have a $100 a day habit, one that must be fed day in and day out (Dobrin, 1).
- Cleaning up the fallout from illegal drugs cost the United States $44.1 billion in 1985. Most of that figure was required as a result of decreased productivity in the workplace; other costs included law enforcement and health care (*The Economic Costs of Alcohol, Drug Abuse and Mental Illness*, 167).

Psycho-Active Drugs

Researchers have divided the types of psycho-active, or mood-altering, drugs into several categories based on the physical and mental effects these drugs have on users. These categories are hallucinogens, stimulants, depressants/sedatives, narcotics/opiates, and inhalants. Although in the past marijuana was considered to be a hallucinogen, today many experts put it in a class by itself.

Marijuana

Marijuana is also known as pot, grass, Mary Jane, reefer, weed, dope, Maui wowie, smoke, and THC. Composed of the dried leaves of the *Cannabis sativa* plant, marijuana is smoked either in the form of hand-rolled cigarettes called joints or in pipes. Sometimes it is mixed with food and eaten. According to a 1988 household survey on drug abuse conducted by the National Institute on Drug Abuse, 11.6 million Americans had used marijuana during the past month and over 20 million had used it during the last year. By 1988, a total of 65.7 million Americans, one-quarter of the people who live in this country, had tried the drug (*National Household Survey on Drug Abuse,* 17). It is the most widely used illegal drug in the United States. Although drug enforcement efforts have cut back the imports of grass coming into the country, the amount produced by marijuana farmers in the United States has doubled over the past few years.

Grown for thousands of years, cannabis, sometimes called hemp, was used to make rope and cloth because of its tough fibers. Before marijuana was made illegal, doctors prescribed the substance for headaches and menstrual cramps. Today marijuana's medical use is limited to suppressing nausea in cancer patients who are undergoing chemotherapy.

Even though it was known to change peoples' moods when it was smoked or eaten, marijuana did not become popular for recreational use in this country until the 1920s, during Prohibition, as a substitute for alcohol. As a reaction to the spread of marijuana use, most states made the drug illegal by 1937. The legal punishments for marijuana possession and use were as stiff as those for heroin because law enforcement authorities believed smoking dope would make people go into a frenzy, which they referred to as reefer madness. Because in the past most of the drug education about marijuana was exaggerated, young people tended to discount all warnings about it. In the 1960s and 1970s many believed the drug was harmless. Recent, more potent kinds of marijuana and the ability to do more accurate studies on the drug are causing many researchers to take a harder look at the consequences of dope smoking.

The chemical responsible for marijuana's mood-altering changes is delta-9-tetrydrocannabiol or, as it is called more often,

THC. The more THC marijuana contains, the more potent is its impact on a user's mental state. Hashish or hash, a more concentrated form of the drug that is high in THC, is made from the resin of cannabis flowers. Since the 1970s marijuana growers have been breeding more potent strains of cannabis, and they can control growing conditions to increase the amount of THC in their plants by as much as ten times. As the strength of the drug has gone up, so has the price.

Marijuana or hash smokers begin to feel the effects of THC in about one to five minutes. Those changes peak in about an hour and wear off after three or four hours. When people smoke dope, the THC enters their bloodstreams through their lungs and travels to their brains. Grass causes users to feel euphoric. It relaxes inhibitions, makes people hungry, and causes disorientation, especially in a user's sense of time. Studies show that marijuana reduces short-term memory and concentration and impairs coordination. Biological changes that occur when someone uses pot include an increased heart rate by as much as 50 percent, reddening of the eyes, dryness of the mouth and throat, and a lowering of body temperature. Although users often believe that marijuana sharpens their senses, there is no physical evidence that the drug heightens eyesight, skin sensitivity, taste, or hearing. Negative reactions to pot can include panic and fatigue.

Over a period of time, grass can cause smokers to become less motivated or to "burn out." They lose ambition, withdrawing from activities that interested them in the past. Confusion, apathy, and uncertainty become a way of life. Research shows that smoking two joints a week for three months is enough to cause some of these long-term changes to take place. About half of the chemicals in marijuana leave the body within a day after it is smoked, but because THC is stored in the fatty tissues of the brain and other organs, people who use marijuana more than twice a month are always affected by the chemical.

In addition to problems with motivation, chronic dope smoking can cause respiratory problems. Lung cancer is one of the most frightening possibilities. One joint contains twice as much tar as a cigarette. Other cancer-causing agents are 5 to 10 times higher in marijuana smoke than in tobacco smoke. Research shows that smoking 4 or more joints a week causes the same amount of damage to a smoker's lungs as smoking 16 cigarettes a week. Smoking dope can also cause emphysema, bronchitis, and other lung and throat problems.

There is evidence, too, that people who smoke marijuana regularly experience other negative physical effects. Chronic marijuana smokers have a more difficult time than other people fighting off infections. Some have abnormal white blood cells. It also affects the reproductive system. Heavy use of marijuana suppresses production of testosterone, the male sex hormone. Because THC is stored in the tissues of the female reproductive system, heavy marijuana use can cause a woman to stop menstruating and can affect ovulation.

No evidence exists that users can become physically addicted to smoking grass, but long-term users can become psychologically dependent on the drug. Over time, they may need to smoke more joints to feel the same effects, and some users eventually believe they cannot cope unless they are high. Grass can become the focus of their lives, negatively affecting school, work, and relationships. People who only smoke marijuana occasionally do not go through withdrawal when they stop, but some people who smoke it regularly do experience insomnia, hyperactivity, and loss of appetite when they attempt to kick their habit.

Hallucinogens

Hallucinogens are substances that cause users to hallucinate, or to see things that are not there. The most popular forms of hallucinogens in the United States today are LSD, PCP, and Ecstasy. Psilocybin mushrooms and mescaline or peyote, part of a type of cactus, are weaker forms of hallucinogens and are rarely sold on the street.

LSD

LSD (also called acid, paper acid, blotter, windowpane, or green star) is made from lysergic acid. In nature lysergic acid is found in ergot, a fungus that grows on grains. Probably the most potent hallucinogen, LSD is similar in chemical structure to a chemical that occurs naturally in the brain. In many ways the effects of dropping acid are much like those of psychosis, or a break from reality. In fact, soon after LSD began to be manufactured in 1943, researchers used the drug to artificially create mental illness in human research subjects.

Originally scientists believed LSD was a wonder drug with many medical uses. Among these were the treatment of alcoholism and use as a substitute for heroin. It was also thought that LSD would ease the agony of terminal cancer patients. The military studied the drug as a possible way to brainwash prisoners of war and as a chemical weapon to disorient the enemy. By the 1960s LSD spread from the laboratory and the campus to the streets as a recreational drug.

According to the *National Household Survey on Drug Abuse*, in 1988, 7 percent of Americans had used LSD at some time in their lives and about 2 percent had used the drug within the past year.

LSD is colorless and tasteless, and its effects are unpredictable. It is 1,000 times more powerful than mescaline and 100 times more powerful than psilocybin. The drug's effects begin to be felt about half an hour to an hour and a half after it is taken into the body. When LSD is absorbed into the system, it causes the pupils of the user's eyes to dilate and increases heart rate and blood pressure. Other physical symptoms include sweating, loss of appetite, a dry mouth, and shakiness.

Emotionally, LSD causes mood swings, and some people who use it report feeling several very intense emotions all at once. The user's sense of time changes, and he or she may see things and experience sensory distortions so that colors seem to have sounds or sounds may take physical form. Depending on the amount of the drug taken and the circumstances under which it is taken, LSD's effects can cause the user to panic or, in street slang, to have a "bad trip." With relatively high doses, the mind-altering effects of LSD may last from 10 to 12 hours.

Although LSD users do not become physically addicted to the drug, they do develop tolerance for its effects and may begin to take larger and larger doses. People who take high doses of LSD or who use it frequently sometimes experience long-term changes in thinking. The heaviest users develop symptoms that are a lot like those of organic brain damage. Memory suffers and so does abstract thinking. In some cases people who have taken LSD in the past have flashbacks or recurring altered states of consciousness, much like the ones they had when they were on the drug, even after LSD has left their systems. These flashbacks are unpredictable and in some cases may continue for years after drug use has stopped. Researchers still are not sure whether mental impairments and flashbacks eventually go away or whether these effects of LSD may be permanent.

PCP

In the 1950s, PCP (phencyclidine)—also called angel dust, white powder, peace pills, super joint, busy bee, hog, or elephant tranquilizer—was invented as an anesthetic to alleviate pain in human beings. It was also used as a tranquilizer to immobilize monkeys and other primates. As soon as researchers discovered that it had dangerous side effects on people, it was removed from the market for human use. Although PCP was largely ignored among drug users when it first began hitting the streets in the mid 1960s, by the late 1980s its use had soared in large urban areas such as Washington, D.C.

PCP is sold in many forms: white powder, clear liquid, tablets, capsules, and rock crystal. Users may swallow it, sniff it, or inject it. When PCP is smoked, it is usually sprinkled on marijuana. In street slang, this combination is called green tea leaves or super joint.

One of the reasons PCP is so popular on the drug scene today is because it is easy and cheap to manufacture. For about $100 worth of equipment and supplies, an amateur chemist can make 1 pound of PCP, which sells for about $25,000 on the street. Because it looks so much like other drugs, PCP is sometimes sold as LSD or even cocaine. Because the drug is manufactured illegally, people who buy it never know what they are getting. PCP poisoning, which causes high fever, kidney failure, and extremely high blood pressure, is hard to treat and may require weeks of hospitalization.

PCP works as a stimulant and also by blocking the user's pain receptors, and it starts to work in 15 minutes to half an hour from the time the user first ingests it. A PCP high lasts from 4 to 6 hours. In small amounts PCP causes an altered state that may feel similar to being drunk. Users experience disorientation, numbness, slurred speech, and slowed reflexes. They may even hear buzzing noises. Dizziness and floating sensations are also common. Rapid heartbeat and increased blood pressure are experienced as well. Flushed skin; drooling; heavy, labored breathing; and increased perspiration are other physical effects that can occur soon after PCP is used.

Some people become very withdrawn and apathetic when they take PCP, but others become angrily aggressive and even violent. The drug makes some users very paranoid. It also gives them hallucinations. This can lead to violent acts including self-inflicted injuries. Because researchers have not been able to find a direct link between the amount of PCP in a user's blood stream and the commission of violent acts, they suspect that the user's personality before he or she took the drug may be responsible for angry acts committed under the influence of PCP. This PCP madness or psychosis can last for days or weeks.

In fact, the symptoms of PCP use can so closely resemble those of schizophrenia, a mental disorder in which patients experience a total break with reality, that sometimes mental health workers make the wrong diagnosis when they encounter a PCP user. When a user is mistakenly treated with anti-psychotic drugs, heart and respiration rate are depressed further and the psychosis may last even longer.

In addition to causing jumbled speech and coordination problems, the use of PCP over periods of time also results in mood swings and hallucinations. Chronic users may hear or see things that do not really exist. They may also become depressed and develop memory and thinking problems so profound that the after-effects of PCP use have been called the Alzheimer's disease of adolescence. In laboratory experiments PCP has been found to kill the brain cells of animals. There is reason to believe that this drug may have the same effect on human beings.

Because users of PCP become tolerant to the drug's effects, they require larger and larger doses to feel the high they desire. Overdoses of PCP result in ruptured blood vessels in the brain, respiratory failure, kidney failure, coma, convulsions, and ultimately death.

Stimulants

Stimulants, or uppers as they are sometimes called, are drugs that increase physical activity and alertness by stimulating the body's central nervous system. Amphetamines are considered to be stimulants, as are cocaine, crack (a cocaine derivative), and, to a mild extent, caffeine.

AMPHETAMINES

First discovered and manufactured in 1887, amphetamines (including speed, white crosses, uppers, dexies, bennies, crystal, ice, L.A. ice, crank, and Ecstasy) were ignored by the medical profession until 40 years later, when they began to be used as a treatment for obesity and depression. Later amphetamines were prescribed for asthma. Eventually, these drugs became popular among people who needed to stay awake for long periods of time, such as truck drivers. By the early 1960s half of the amphetamines made by drug companies were being sold illegally. Ten years later they were recognized as being both dangerous and addictive, and the government set limits on how much of the drug could be produced.

Today amphetamines are still fairly easy for users to buy because they continue to be made by drug companies and prescribed by doctors. Some of the amphetamines sold on the street, though, are produced in makeshift street labs. These amphetamines sometimes are contaminated and so are doubly dangerous to users. Street drug manufacturers and drug dealers also have been known to cut, or dilute, amphetamines with drain cleaner.

Even though amphetamines are easy to obtain, the dangers of their use are well known, and few Americans take them today.

According to the 1988 *National Household Survey on Drug Abuse*, in the 18–25 age group of Americans, only 11 percent have ever tried amphetamines and only 2 percent currently take them.

In their pure form, amphetamines are yellowish crystals. These crystals usually are crushed and made into pills. Some users, however, sniff the crystals or dissolve them in water and inject them. When speed is taken orally in the form of pills or tablets, its mood-altering effects usually begin after about an hour. When it is injected or snorted, effects occur immediately or within minutes.

The most recent variation of amphetamines is smokeable crystals called ice or crank. These affect the brain and body almost immediately. Ice first began to be used in Hawaii and on the West Coast but is quickly moving across the country. In some cities today it is used more frequently by teenagers than crack, a popular cocaine derivative. When ice or crank is smoked, its effects last longer than those of crack cocaine. Hallucinations, paranoia, and speech disorders may persist up to two days after a person smokes ice. Because ice is cheap to make ($700 a pound) and can be sold for as much as $225,000 a pound, its distribution is likely to escalate in the future.

After an amphetamine user has smoked crank or swallowed speed, the heart rate increases and both blood pressure and breathing rates go up. Sometimes amphetamine users get a dry mouth, sweat, become anxious, or have blurred vision. As soon as the central nervous system is stimulated, users report a sudden ecstatic feeling called a rush. Because the drug speeds up messages to the brain, users experience a false sense of self-confidence and power. Some actually think they are superhuman. They may talk more rapidly and get excited. They also can get restless, moody, and anxious.

After a few hours, the rush ends and the user either falls asleep or is depressed, because the overstimulated central nervous system needs to rest. This emotional low can be so severe that suicide may be attempted. As a rule of thumb, the higher the speed high, the lower the depression the user will fall into afterward.

Long-term damage from speed can be life threatening. Amphetamines kill brain cells and may even trigger small strokes and bleeding in the brain, which lead to disturbed thinking and speech difficulties. The heart-rate speedup, which is strongest when the drug is injected, can leave permanent heart damage. The strain that amphetamines place on the cardiovascular system may even lead to heart attack or stroke. If the drug has been cut or diluted with substances that do not dissolve in water and it is injected, arteries can be blocked. Kidney damage, lung problems, and stroke are other possible consequences from shooting impure speed.

Because amphetamines lower the appetite, chronic users often feel no need to eat for long periods at a time. When they stop eating, they suffer from vitamin deficiencies and malnutrition as well as from many other of the same problems to which anorexics fall victim. In addition to weight loss, signs of long-term amphetamine use that are associated with poor nutrition include acne, gum disease, and poor nail growth.

The psychological problems of amphetamine use over an extended period of time are just as frightening. Users may experience psychosis—a split from reality where they hear, see, and feel things that do not exist. They become irrational and may feel paranoid, convinced that people are out to get them. Fueled by their delusions and an abnormally high amount of energy, sometimes speed users become violent either to others or to themselves. They are like time bombs waiting to explode.

Amphetamines are addictive drugs. In the first place, physical tolerance to speed builds up very quickly. It only takes a matter of days for users to begin craving the drug at higher and higher doses in order to feel a rush. In laboratory experiments, when animals are given a choice between amphetamines and food and water, they will choose the drug, eating it until they have seizures and die.

Psychological dependency is a factor as well. Once a user experiences the superhuman and confident feelings the drug induces, he or she may be reluctant to go back to functioning with a normal amount of physical energy and self-esteem. When heavy users stop their amphetamine habit, they often experience withdrawal symptoms that include tiredness, problems with sleeping, irritability, hunger, and deep depression.

A number of look-alike drugs that are sold as amphetamines currently flood the market. These contain caffeine and other drugs usually found in over-the-counter diet pills and decongestants. Although these drugs are weak, when they are taken in large amounts they can have some of the same effects as speed: anxiety, restlessness, increased heart rate, and extremely high blood pressure.

COCAINE/CRACK

Cocaine (also called coke, snow, lady, toot, blow, stardust, nose candy, or flake), another central nervous system stimulant, is made from the leaf of the coca plant, which is grown in South and Central America. People have chewed these leaves in order to feel an energy boost for at least 5,000 years. It was not until the mid-1800s, though, that the pure drug was extracted from the leaves.

Fifty years later, doctors, including Sigmund Freud, the father of psychiatry, were certain they had found the cure for stomach disorders, respiratory illnesses, and sexual problems, as well as for opium and alcohol addictions. By the early 1900s cocaine was an ingredient in over 60 soft drinks or tonics that drugstores sold over the counter to people who wanted a "lift." In fact, Coca-Cola® got its name from the cocaine that was once used to make it.

Today soft drinks such as Coca-Cola do not contain cocaine, because, after it was realized that the drug had negative effects on people, the government outlawed all nonmedical uses of it in 1914. After cocaine was removed from the over-the-counter market until about 20 years ago, very few people outside of the arts community, such as musicians, artists, and writers, used it. Although the drug had been classified by the government as illegal by then, many people believed it was not addictive and did not cause users medical problems beyond irritation of the nasal passages or nasal ulcers.

Today, we know differently, but the number of Americans who use cocaine has risen dramatically within the past 50 years. According to the 1988 *National Household Survey on Drug Abuse*, more than 1 out of every 10 people in this country has used cocaine. Among young adults age 18 to 25, 1 out of every 4 has tried the drug during their lifetime and one-eighth have used it during the past month. Even though cocaine use in this country today has decreased slightly from the early and mid-1980s, it still is a major drug problem.

A white, crystal-like powder, cocaine is diluted with other substances such as aspirin, cornstarch lactose, talc, or even heroin. In this form it is most often sniffed or snorted. Once cocaine is snorted, it goes through the nasal tissue and into the bloodstream and then the brain, where it affects the user within 2 to 3 minutes. Sometimes the drug is mixed with water and injected. When it is injected into a vein, or "mainlined," the drug user feels cocaine's effects in only about 15 seconds.

As cocaine begins to affect the user's central nervous system, the eyes become dilated and the heart rate and blood pressure increase. Users breathe faster and their body temperature rises. Appetite decreases as they begin to feel a sense of well-being and experience more energy and alertness. These effects peak in about 20 to 40 minutes and disappear after about an hour.

People who use cocaine initially get hooked psychologically because they enjoy the feelings they get from snorting coke. Like an amphetamine high, a coke high is replaced by depression. When the high ends, users turn to the drug once again to lift themselves from "the blues." Because cocaine makes users feel confident and on top of the world, they may begin to take it to cope with daily stresses. Soon they are using cocaine to just feel normal.

The drug is physically addicting as well. Because it affects the part of the brain that scientists call the reward center, sometimes cocaine addicts go on runs or binges of nearly constant sniffing, smoking, or injecting. At the end of such a binge, the crash or depression is incredibly intense. It is not unusual, then, for coke addicts to turn to alcohol or heroin to sedate the central nervous system and allow them to sleep. In the process they may develop a dual addiction. This drug-induced up-and-down cycle causes incredible wear and tear not only on the body, but on the mind as well.

By the late 1970s cocaine use in the United States began to be epidemic. By then coke users had discovered a new way to make their rushes come even faster and to make them even more intense. Using ether, they made a heat-resistant variety of cocaine that could be smoked. When it was smoked it made a crackling noise, and so it came to be called crack. Also called rock, ready rock, and crystal, crack is almost pure cocaine.

Sold in chunks, crack can be smoked in a pipe or crushed and mixed with the tobacco in a cigarette. Because less dangerous chemicals than ether have been found to make crack, the drug has gone down in price, costing only about one-fifth to one-eighth of what a gram of cocaine costs. Users feel a rush within six to eight seconds after smoking crack, but the high is a short one, lasting only a few minutes. Because the highs are so intense and so short, users quickly develop a constant craving that often leads to habits that cost them as much as $500 a day.

Whether a person snorts, shoots, or smokes cocaine, the drug has a negative effect both on behavior and on the body. An acute reaction to cocaine brings on irritability and sometimes paranoia and violent aggressiveness. Sometimes users have hallucinations, and, depending on how much of the drug they use, they may experience a complete break with reality.

Frequent cocaine use can cause heart problems, too, because it shrinks the blood vessels and makes the heart work harder. Even though people who already have heart trouble may be more prone to cocaine-induced heart attacks, there have been reported cases of young people with healthy hearts suffering from cocaine coronaries. Seizures, comas, and strokes are all results of using cocaine.

When people withdraw from the drug, they have muscle pains, muscle spasms, and shakes. Their mental functioning decreases and their energy level is low. These withdrawal symptoms may start to appear from half a day to a week after the crash and may last several weeks. Because craving for the drug is so intense during the withdrawal phase, most users find it very difficult to quit without professional help.

Depressants

The group of drugs labeled as depressants retards the central nervous system's functions, reducing breathing, slowing heart rate, and lowering blood pressure. These drugs also calm anxiety and relax muscles. These last two effects are the reasons for their medical use. Sometimes these drugs are called sedatives or hypnotics. In fact, the first depressants discovered were used as anesthetics, to make patients unconscious during surgery and painful medical procedures.

Because their effects on the brain and body systems are similar to those of alcohol, depressants are extremely dangerous when mixed with alcohol. Some of these drugs are super-additive, which means that when they are mixed with each other their potency does not just double but is multiplied dramatically. An overdose of depressants slows the body systems so much that necessary functions eventually stop entirely and death results.

BARBITURATES

Barbiturates (also called phenobarbital, barbs, downers, yellowjackets, or reds) are drugs that are closely related to barbituric acid, which was first discovered right after the Civil War. Barbiturates were not used in medicine, however, until the twentieth century, when phenobarbital became popular as a painkiller.

Since that time about 50 different kinds of barbiturates have been made and sold by drug companies. Barbiturates are usually manufactured as pills that are taken orally. So many barbiturates are consumed in the United States today that if everyone took his or her allotted annual dose at once, we would all die of overdoses.

Depending on how much of the drug is taken, barbiturates can cause reactions from mild sedation, giddiness, and loss of inhibitions all the way to coma and death. In large doses these drugs cause slurred speech, staggering, lack of coordination, sleepiness, double-vision, confusion, and distorted thinking. Although most people who take barbiturates report feeling calm, a few people grow very depressed, and some even become violent under the influence of the drug.

When barbiturates are used over a period of weeks or months, tolerance for these drugs develops and the user must take more and more of them to feel their effects. One reason for the tolerance increase is that barbiturates trigger the production of enzymes in the liver that metabolize the drug. The more barbiturates a person takes, the faster the drugs are metabolized, so the user needs to take even more to produce the mood-altering results he or she desires.

The brain's chemical receptors can adapt to the presence of barbiturates, too, so that bigger doses are needed to feel the effects; both physical and psychological dependence are the result. This need for higher dosages is extremely dangerous because the tolerance the body develops toward the drug is selective. The breathing center of the central nervous system does not develop a tolerance, so the same dose required to make a long-term user feel giddy can also cause that person to stop breathing. As many as 5,000 people die from accidental or suicidal barbiturate overdoses each year.

Although barbiturates help put users to sleep and may be prescribed for patients by doctors for this reason, the sleep they induce is different from normal rest. When a person sleeps because he or she has taken barbiturates, dreaming is suppressed. Dreamless sleep over a period of time can cause emotional disturbances and even hallucinations during waking hours. Other mental side effects of high doses include amnesia and even permanent brain damage.

Users of barbiturates who take high dosages become physically dependent on the drug. When they stop taking it they experience withdrawal symptoms including restlessness and anxiety. They also experience a rebound effect of rapid eye movement (REM) sleep, causing many more dreams than usual, which can lead to insomnia. Severe withdrawal symptoms can include hallucinations and life-threatening convulsions. Medical experts believe withdrawal from barbiturates may be even more dangerous than withdrawal from heroin. Therefore, when a user stops taking depressants, he or she should be supervised by a doctor.

QUAALUDES

Quaaludes, the trademark name for methaqualone—also called sopers, ludes, quay, or quad—are one of the most popular antidepressant drugs used illegally. The drug was first designed to treat malaria. Later it was prescribed to relieve anxiety and to help people sleep at night. By 1973, though, the Food and Drug Administration (FDA) had classified methaqualone as a dangerous drug because it was discovered to cause users to be both physically and emotionally dependent.

Convulsions, coma, and death are the results of overdoses. Quaaludes also have been associated with automobile accidents because users become drowsy and have poor judgment when they are under the influence of the drug. Withdrawal symptoms from Qualuudes include anxiety, headaches, sleeplessness, stomach cramps, and nightmares. Convulsions may also occur.

MINOR TRANQUILIZERS OR BENZODIAZEPHINES

First manufactured in the early 1950s, minor tranquilizers (including Librium, Valium, Serax, Dalmane, Clonopin, Tranxene, and Vestran) are called minor to set them apart from major tranquilizers, which are prescribed for psychotic reactions. They are different chemically from barbiturates, but the effects they produce on the mind and the body are much the same. The one major difference is that benzodiazephines do not affect breathing as profoundly as do barbiturates. For this reason physicians believed benzodiazephines were a miracle drug for relieving anxiety and helping patients sleep, so doctors began widely prescribing them. In fact, minor tranquilizers quickly became the most prescribed drugs in the United States, earning billions of dollars for pharmaceutical companies. Minor tranquilizers have also become some of the most widely abused drugs in this country.

Used in pill form, these drugs are slowly absorbed by the body. It may take from eight hours up to an entire day for them to reach maximum levels in the user's bloodstream. Once in the body, however, they remain for several days.

When taken in high doses, minor tranquilizers can cause "drunken" behavior and confusion. Some people report experiencing a rage response during which violent behavior is exhibited. There is evidence that people who take these drugs can develop increased tolerance. Other side effects of minor tranquilizers include skin rashes, nausea, and a decreased sex drive. In very high doses, tranquilizers can cause death. This is especially true if they are taken with alcohol or other sedatives.

In time users can become physically addicted to minor tranquilizers. The withdrawal symptoms they experience when they stop taking the drug are much the same as those experienced by barbiturate users. Because these drugs remain in the body for so long before being excreted, withdrawal symptoms may not appear until a week after the drugs are stopped.

Narcotics

Narcotics, or opiates, are made from the resin contained in the seeds of the Asian poppy. These drugs have been used medically to relieve pain and stop diarrhea since the time of the ancient Greeks. All narcotics affect the eyes as well as the gastrointestinal system, dramatically shrinking the size of the pupils. Unpleasant effects of opiates include itching, drowsiness, nausea, vomiting, and watery eyes.

Opiates affect the central nervous system, too, producing feelings of euphoria, well-being, and contentment in most, but not all, users. Occasionally people become anxious when they use heroin. Sometimes users go back and forth between being super-relaxed and being alert. In street language, this is called being "on the nod."

Because tolerance for narcotics increases so quickly, addiction rates for narcotics users are extremely high. Soon an addict's life centers solely on finding and using the drug. In time the dosage must be increased for the user to feel the desired high. Narcotics overdoses produce shallow breathing, clammy skin, convulsions, comas, and sometimes death.

Physical withdrawal symptoms from opiate addiction resemble the flu, including chills and fevers, sweating, anxiety, and violent vomiting. These symptoms usually last from four days to a week. Sometimes people who are withdrawing from heroin have convulsions that can lead to death.

OPIUM

This drug comes in dark brown chunks or powder and it is usually smoked or eaten. In the 1800s, opium smoking became a big drug problem in the United States, and by the turn of the century about 1 in every 400 Americans was drug-dependent on opium or one of its variations—about the same number who are opium-dependent today. In 1914, once it was recognized as a dangerous and addictive drug, all nonmedical uses for opium were banned by the Harrison Narcotic Act.

MORPHINE

When morphine (also called morph, tab, white stuff, and monkey), a chemical compound in opium, was first isolated, it was thought to be a cure for opium dependency. Instead, it turned out to be an addictive drug in its own right. During the Civil War soldiers were given morphine as a painkiller, and later morphine addiction became known as the soldiers' disease.

CODEINE, DEMEROL, PAREGORIC, AND PERCODAN

These opiates are the ones most used for medical purposes today. Codeine (also called school boy) is used as a painkiller and is included in some prescription cough syrups as a cough suppressant. Paregoric is prescribed by doctors to prevent diarrhea. Demerol and Percodan are synthetically manufactured opiates that are used in pain medications. Because opiates are highly addictive, even in these forms, doctors are very careful about prescribing them.

HEROIN

Heroin (also called H, horse, smack, junk, stuff, brown sugar, and skag), a white or brownish-colored powder, is a version of morphine and is as much as five times more potent than morphine. It therefore is extremely addictive. In fact, heroin users can become addicted within a matter of days after they start to use the drug. Heroin makes up about 90 percent of the opiates used illegally in the United States today. In 1990 between 400,000 and 700,000 Americans were believed to be heroin-dependent.

Most heroin sold on the streets of this country is not pure. Instead it is cut, or diluted, with other substances such as sugar, baking soda, or quinine. Sometimes it is cut with substances such as fuel oils or strychnine, a rodent poison. Users face a high risk of not only addiction and overdose but poisoning as well. When a user dies as a result of heroin, it may happen so fast that he or she dies with a needle stuck in his or her arm. Often these acute fatal reactions are caused by contaminants that have been used to cut the heroin.

When it is taken orally, heroin is absorbed very slowly by the body. For this reason it usually is used by injecting it into a vein ("mainlining") or under the skin ("skin popping"). It can also be smoked or sniffed. Once in the body, it travels to the brain within half an hour to an hour. The user becomes flushed and sleepy. Afterward a heroin user feels a high that can last for a few hours. This high is followed by feelings of relaxation.

Within about 4 to 5 hours after a person uses heroin, the drug is metabolized and excreted. By about 8 to 12 hours after shooting up, a heroin user starts physically craving more of the drug. His or her eyes may begin to water, and yawning begins. These symptoms, along with a runny nose, sweating, and intense cravings, signal to the user that it is time for another injection. Severe withdrawal symptoms include stomach cramps, vomiting, diarrhea, and muscle spasms.

Because of unsterile needles and contaminated heroin, many users risk catching infectious diseases, including the human immunodeficiency virus (HIV), the virus that causes the acquired immunodeficiency syndrome (AIDS), and hepatitis, a liver disease that can cause cirrhosis of the liver. Users' immunity to these diseases is lowered because heroin affects the lymph nodes, a part of the body's infection-fighting system.

Heroin use depresses the central nervous system and can depress it so far that users become comatose or paralyzed from the destruction of the lining around the spinal cord. Nerve and muscle damage can follow an injection of contaminated heroin. Swelling of the blood vessels and irregular heart rhythms are other side effects of using heroin. Kidney damage and ultimate kidney failure can also occur. Finally, the endocrine gland system can be affected, causing everything from low blood sugar to an inability to function sexually.

METHADONE

Ironically, when methadone (also called dolls or dollies) was first made in Germany in the 1940s, physicians believed it would be an ideal cure for heroin addiction. But methadone, too, causes tolerance and dependence—as quickly as heroin if it is injected. It often is still administered orally to treat heroin addiction because it suppresses the craving heroin addicts feel as they are going through withdrawal.

When methadone is taken orally and under medical supervision it is not deadly. Because its effects only last for a day or two, addicts typically must take methadone every day. The drug is administered by clinics.

Because it is an opiate and it can produce a high when taken in large doses, methadone also is used illegally. Often methadone pills are crushed, dissolved in water, and injected. Because the binders— substances used to shape powder into pills—in these tablets do not dissolve in water, injecting methadone is very dangerous. In fact, some authorities believe that more addicts die from methadone injections than from heroin injections.

Inhalants

Most inhalants are not really thought of as drugs because they are not made for that purpose. But common household items such as gasoline, spray paint, paint thinner, hairspray, deodorants, Liquid Paper, Rubber Cement, nail polish remover, and airplane glue contain chemicals that when inhaled can alter the user's mood. These chemicals are also known as solvents.

When a person breathes solvents, she or he experiences coughing, giddiness, headaches, nosebleeds, nausea, and rapid heartbeat. Lack of coordination and poor judgment also result, and users can eventually fall into a stupor and faint. Some sniffers exhibit violent behavior. Kids between the ages of 12 and 17 are the biggest abusers of inhalants because these products are easy for them to obtain and are inexpensive.

When abused, solvents can be deadly. In general their effect on the body is similar to that of an anesthetic. They slow down the body's physical functions including heart and breathing rates. Heart failure and sudden death are the effects of an overdose. That is why items containing solvents carry a warning label urging people to use them out-of-doors or in a well-ventilated room.

Two other products used as inhalants have the opposite effect on bodily functions. They are amyl nitrite and butyl nitrite. Amyl nitrite, sometimes called poppers or snappers, is a bubble-enclosed liquid broken open and sniffed by heart patients to dilate the blood vessels and speed heart and breathing rates. Butyl nitrite, also called rush or locker room, has the same effect. It is not physically addictive, but over time users have to increase the amount they sniff to get the same results. Sometimes it is used as a sexual stimulant, and after a time users discover they cannot enjoy sex without it.

Although an inhalant high lasts only five minutes and the short-term physical effects of sniffing usually last about half an hour, long-term damage from inhalants can shorten a user's life span. This damage can result in lung, liver, and kidney disease as well as damage to bone marrow. Suffocation, choking, anemia, and stroke are other possible consequences, as is an electrolyte (salt) imbalance in the blood. Weight loss, fatigue, and mental impairment are other telltale signs of inhalant abuse.

Designer Drugs

Designer drugs are chemical imitations of narcotics (synthetic heroin, new heroin, and china white), amphetamines (MDMA,

Ecstasy, STP, and DMA), and PCP (PCE). Often these imitation drugs are as much as several hundred times stronger than the original drug.

Although Ecstasy, a designer drug manufactured illegally and usually sold in capsules on the street, is primarily meant to raise users' energy levels, it also causes hallucinations. Ecstasy produces a high that resembles that of a combination of speed and mescaline, a hallucinogen. The negative effects of Ecstasy and other speed imitations include nausea, blurred vision, chills, fainting, anxiety, depression, and paranoia. Because of Ecstasy's strength, users can face the possibility of brain damage with as little as one dose of the drug.

The strength of designer drugs that imitate narcotics can cause symptoms that are the same as those of Parkinson's disease: trembling, drooling, speech difficulties, paralysis, and irreversible brain damage.

Steroid Abuse

Anabolic steroids are a synthetic version of testosterone, the male hormone. First made in Europe during the 1930s, this drug helps the body rebuild muscle after dramatic weight loss caused by infection or injury. Steroids are prescribed by doctors to keep muscles from shrinking and weakening in people who are bed- or wheelchair-ridden for long periods of time. Sometimes they are given to male patients whose bodies do not produce enough testosterone.

Today the use of steroids by athletes is illegal in most sporting events. Still, the pressure to win continues, and experts believe that more athletes than ever are taking steroids and that they are taking the drugs at a younger age. As much as 70–80 percent of the anabolic steroids made by pharmaceutical companies in the United States are used illegally.

Their muscle-building ability has made steroids especially appealing because of the mistaken impression that this extra "edge" helps athletes perform better. Research done on male athletes shows, however, that steroids do not enhance athletic ability. Improved strength and performance are minor if they occur at all. Although steroids may somewhat improve a woman's athletic ability, the woman who takes them pays a price. She develops the secondary sex characteristics of a male: facial hair and a deep voice. Her menstrual periods may even stop.

Even though steroids do not work that well, many athletes still either ignore or do not know about the high risks of steroid use, and they take high doses, much higher than those a doctor would prescribe for medical purposes. Research shows that steroids, especially at high doses, raise the user's blood pressure and the amount of cholesterol in the bloodstream. Heart disease is just one of the possible long-term risks. Liver cancer has been associated by researchers with steroid use, as well as other liver problems such as internal bleeding caused by the rupture of blood-filled cysts and jaundice.

Men who abuse steroids may suffer from the enlargement of the prostate gland, which makes urination difficult and painful. This condition also raises a man's chances of getting prostate cancer. Ironically, when a man takes steroids his body slows down its own production of testosterone. His testicles may shrink and his sperm count may become low, so that he is infertile. In addition he may lose all sexual desire.

Teenagers face special risks when they decide to use anabolic steroids. The drug sometimes stops bone growth before users have grown to their full height. Adolescents who have acne soon discover that steroids make it much worse. Taking anabolic steroids is even more dangerous for both teens and adults because many of these physical effects do not go away when the athlete stops taking the drug. The harm that steroids do is in many cases irreversible.

Steroid users face a set of emotional hazards in addition to the physical problems. The drug can cause people to become short-tempered and aggressive, a syndrome sometimes referred to as roid rage. Sometimes it can cause psychosis. Although anabolic steroids are not physically addictive, those who take heavy doses of the drug may become psychologically hooked on it. When they stop using steroids, they become depressed to the point of having suicidal thoughts.

Prescription Drug Abuse

People do not need to take illegal drugs to qualify as drug abusers. Prescription and even over-the-counter drugs, such as cold capsules and allergy medications, have potential for abuse, as well, when they are taken at high dosages or in combination with other drugs.

The American Medical Association (AMA) estimates that over 30,000 prescription drugs are currently on the market. When consumed under a doctor's supervision, these drugs can be very beneficial. Even so, they sometimes have side effects. To make certain prescription drugs are used safely:

- Do not take anybody else's prescription
- Do not offer anyone your prescription

- Take prescription drugs only in the dosage your doctor recommends
- Get rid of old medicines
- Do not use drugs in combination without checking with your doctor first

Sometimes physicians prescribe mood-altering drugs, such as tranquilizers and antidepressants, to help patients cope with emotional problems and life stresses. Opiates are prescribed as pain-killers and barbiturates, as sleeping aids. It is important for patients to ask their doctors about the possible consequences of taking these drugs on a long-term basis and to be aware of the signs of addiction.

Over-the-counter medications for coughs and colds, motion sickness, and insomnia usually contain antihistamines. Antihistamines cause drowsiness, so it is important to take them only in the amount recommended and to avoid driving after taking them. It is very important, as well, not to combine drugs without a doctor's advice and not to drink and take prescription or over-the-counter drugs. Alcohol can interact with drugs to cause a deadly combination.

Prenatal Drug Abuse

One of the saddest tragedies of drug abuse and addiction in this country today is the burden it places on babies whose mothers used drugs during pregnancy. Both the legal and illegal drugs a pregnant woman takes reach her baby by way of the placenta, a fluid-filled organ that transfers nutrients from the mother's bloodstream to that of the unborn baby through the umbilical cord. Anything a pregnant woman puts in her mouth, her nose, or her veins is shared by the baby inside her. Sometimes a baby may be damaged by drug abuse before a woman even knows that she is pregnant.

The problems caused by drug use during pregnancy include

- Low birth weight and small-sized infants
- Miscarriages and stillbirths
- Premature births
- Sudden infant death syndrome (SIDS)
- Birth defects including deformities, seizures, strokes, mental retardation, and learning disabilities
- Infants who are addicted to drugs

Drug-dependent babies, through no fault of their own, have acquired a habit and must go through withdrawal, which may last for weeks. Symptoms of narcotics withdrawal can last for as long as six months. These babies are irritable, and they may shake and have seizures. They also may have fevers and eating and sleeping difficulties. Because hospitals currently tend to discharge new mothers and their babies very soon after childbirth and because infant withdrawal symptoms usually do not appear for two or three days, many of these addicted babies are never treated for their problems.

Although no long-term studies have been done, many drug abuse experts predict that babies who are born with drug addictions may suffer emotional and physical problems throughout their lives. In the future, society will need to find a way to deal with these problems.

Intravenous Drug Abuse and AIDS

Drug users who inject drugs into their veins run the risk of contracting the human immunodeficiency virus (HIV), the virus that causes the acquired immunodeficiency syndrome (AIDS), a fatal disease resulting from the failure of the immune system to protect a person from infections and other illnesses. In fact, drug users are the group of people among whom AIDS is spreading the fastest in the United States today. This is especially true in the inner cities. In some parts of the country, AIDS cases caused by the sharing of needles or syringes among intravenous (IV) drug users now outnumber those caused by unprotected (unsafe) sex with partners who carry HIV.

The AIDS virus is passed from person to person through the exchange of bodily fluids such as blood and semen. When an IV drug user injects himself or herself, the needle used to do this comes in contact with blood. Usually a tiny amount of blood remains in the needle. Sometimes a small amount of blood may be drawn back up into the syringe as well. Whether a user shoots up heroin, cocaine, amphetamines, steroids, or any other drug, if he or she shares needles or syringes with other IV drug users that person may soon become a statistic.

- By September of 1990, 150,000 AIDS cases had been reported in the United States (Stimmel, 257)
- AIDS spreads very rapidly among groups of IV drug users because 70–90 percent of them share needles and syringes when they shoot up (Stimmel, 262)

- IV drug users account for about 25 percent of the reported cases of AIDS in the United States (*Shooting, Sharing and AIDS*)
- In New York City in 1986, 61 percent of blood samples taken from IV drug users tested positive for HIV (Stimmel, 262)

Not everyone who is infected with HIV knows they have it, because people who have HIV often do not show any of the symptoms of AIDS for more than seven years. However, they can still transmit the virus to others. And not only IV drug users are at risk for contracting the disease; people who have sex with IV drug users are at risk as well. Because people who use drugs also tend to have multiple sex partners, they place themselves at double risk for contracting the disease. Female crack users, for instance, may trade sex for drugs in crack houses.

Currently there is no cure for AIDS, so it makes sense to think about prevention. Recently health departments throughout the country have been trying to educate addicts about the dangers of AIDS. If IV drug users do not kick their habits, they need to know never to share their "works" (hypodermic syringes, needles, and cookers) with others and never to borrow other people's works. If they do use equipment that has already been used, they need to learn to sterilize it with common household bleach, which kills the AIDS virus.

Teenagers and Drugs

Since 1979, drug use among teenagers 12 to 17 years old has begun to decline (*National Household Survey on Drug Abuse*, 11). However, drugs still remain a problem for many adolescents. As many as 5 percent of teenagers age 14 to 18 have drug addiction problems and require treatment (*Treatment Services for Adolescent Substance Abusers*, 1). Many more teens experiment with drugs. According to the 1987 Adolescent School Health Survey:

- Thirty-five percent of all tenth graders had tried marijuana. Of that number, more than half had tried it by the eighth grade.
- Almost one out of ten high school sophomores had tried cocaine, and one-third of these had experimented with crack.
- One in five tenth graders and the same number of eighth graders had experimented with inhaling solvents such as glue, gasses, and sprays.

- By the time they were high school seniors, half of the students in the United States had smoked marijuana and 15 percent had used cocaine. Six percent had tried smoking crack.

Teenagers use drugs for many reasons. In the first place, drugs are readily available to most adolescents. (According to the Adolescent School Health Survey, almost 60 percent of the students who responded said it would be very easy for them to get marijuana.) Many teens who ignore the frightening consequences of drugs see them as a fast, easy, and inexpensive way to feel good and escape their problems. Peer pressure is a big factor, too. Sometimes friends talk teenagers into using drugs in order to feel accepted or to belong. Other teenagers turn to drugs because they feel anxiety, depression, or stress. They mistakenly think that drugs are an effective way of coping with life's problems.

One major factor that researchers have found separates students who experiment with drugs from those who get into major drug difficulties is the teenager's family. Kids who find themselves in trouble with drugs tend to come from families where

- Parents are not happy with their children
- Parents are not very important in their teenagers' lives and are permissive about drug use
- Teenagers do not think their parents love them very much
- There is not much communication
- Authority and decision making are not shared

For these reasons, family therapy is especially important for adolescents in drug treatment programs.

Drug Treatment

In addition to drug abuse hotlines, which provide information, and hospital emergency rooms, which treat drug overdoses, a number of helpful sources exist for people who are addicted to drugs. They include therapeutic communities, inpatient programs, and outpatient programs.

In therapeutic communities, drug users live for half a year or more in a highly structured, drug-free environment. The daily schedule in such communities includes group therapy and individual counseling sessions, education classes, and hard work.

Inpatient programs are usually based in hospitals. These programs give drug users a chance for intensive counseling and space away from peer pressure for a month or two. Because they are located in hospitals, they provide medical support for drug detoxification. Because withdrawal symptoms for many drugs are dangerous, this medical back-up can be very important. Inpatient programs include medical and psychological testing along with individual and group therapy and often require that the drug abuser's family participate in family counseling sessions.

Outpatient programs—ranging from peer-counseling rap groups to individual, family, and group therapy—are the most popular form of drug abuse treatment today. In fact, over 80 percent of all recovering adolescent substance abusers undergo this form of treatment (*Treatment Services for Adolescent Substance Abusers*, 32). Often adults and adolescents who have gone through inpatient treatment graduate to outpatient groups for long-term aftercare. Outpatient providers may be independent therapists, community mental health centers, or drug abuse treatment centers.

The War on Drugs

The fact that many drugs are illegal means that they are imported or manufactured, bought, and sold secretly. Because of the high risks involved in drug dealing, people who sell illegal drugs can charge a great deal of money for them. The risks of being caught by drug enforcement agents or killed by other dealers are high, but so are the profits. For example, every year in the United States, the gross revenue for all drug sales is about $120 billion; $100 billion of that is pure profit. In addition, it is profit that dealers do not pay taxes on.

Because so many illegal substances are addictive, drug dealers are sure of a steady stream of customers who, as their tolerance increases, will buy more and more of the drugs. People addicted to substances such as heroin and cocaine sometimes turn to crimes such as embezzlement, robbery, and theft to get money to support their habits. Some addicts begin dealing drugs themselves.

Our government spends billions of dollars trying to stop illegal drug importing, manufacture, and use. In 1990, the government spent more than $10 billion. Some of the "drug war" efforts focus on convincing other countries to crack down on illegal drug growing and manufacturing within their borders, in order to cut down on the drug supply at the source. Other efforts are targeted at stopping illegal drugs from entering the United States at its borders. For drugs that do get inside or are produced inside this country, law enforcement officials are stepping up efforts to catch dealers and are trying to get stiffer laws passed so drug dealers will face longer sentences and bigger fines when they are caught. So far these attempts to reduce the supply of drugs have had little success.

Currently there is a debate about whether or not to just legalize all drugs, thereby lowering the profits dealers make and lowering the rate of crime now associated with illegal drug traffic. People for legalization argue that the money spent trying to stop the drug trade could be spent on educating people about the dangers of drugs and on drug treatment centers for those who are already addicted. People against legalization believe that once drugs were easy to obtain and legal to use, they would become as much a part of our culture as tobacco and alcohol. Yet another group of people focuses their efforts on cutting back the demand for drugs. Some are concentrating on educating the public, especially young people, to the dangers of drug use, whereas others advocate more treatment centers.

Drug testing in the workplace is gaining popularity as a possible solution as well. About one-quarter of the biggest U.S. companies now give potential and current employees drug tests as a basis for hiring new people and firing those who already work for the firm. Although people who want mandatory testing believe that being drug-free as a condition for employment will keep people from using drugs, many feel that such testing violates the rights of employees under the Fourth Amendment to the Constitution. In addition, many of the drug tests currently used in the workplace are inaccurate. One of the most sophisticated tests used today, the radioimmunoassay (RIA) screening, gives false positive results at a rate of 43 percent for cocaine, 51 percent for PCP, and 42 percent for barbiturates. Even so, the President's Commission on Organized Crime has recommended that all employers use drug tests. As the testing technology improves, chances are that workplace drug testing will become more widespread.

REFERENCES

Bach, Julie S., ed. *Drug Abuse: Opposing Viewpoints.* St. Paul, MN: Greenhaven Press, 1988.

Chasnoff, Ira. "Newborn Infants with Drug Withdrawal Symptoms." *Pediatrics in Review* (March 1988): 273–277.

Data from the Client Oriented Acquisition Process, series E, number 21. Rockville, MD: U.S. Department of Health and Human Services, National Institute on Drug Abuse, 1981.

Dobrin, Emanuela. "Who Cares about Drug Abuse?" *The Care Medic* (flyer). Minneapolis, MN: CompCare Publications, 1989.

Drug Prevention Curricula: A Guide to Selection and Implementation. Washington, DC: U.S. Department of Education, 1988.

Duncan, David, and Robert Gold. *Drugs and the Whole Person.* New York: John Wiley & Sons, 1982.

The Economic Costs of Alcohol, Drug Abuse and Mental Illness: 1985. Washington, DC: U.S. Department of Health and Human Services, 1990.

Facts about Your Baby and Drugs. Denver, CO: Mile High Council on Alcoholism and Drug Abuse.

Gordon, Alex, and Jules Saltman. *Know Your Medication: How To Use Over-the-Counter and Prescription Drugs.* New York: Public Affairs Committee, 1979.

HIV/AIDS. Atlanta, GA: Centers for Disease Control, October 1990.

Jennings, Chris. *Understanding and Preventing AIDS: A Book for Everyone,* 2d edition. Cambridge, MA: Health Alert Press, 1988.

Jones-Witters, Patricia, and Weldon Witters. *Drugs and Society: A Biological Perspective.* Monterey, CA: Wadsworth Health Sciences, 1983.

Julien, Robert M. *A Primer of Drug Action,* 3d edition. San Francisco: W. H. Freeman and Company, 1981.

National Household Survey on Drug Abuse: Highlights 1988. Washington, DC: U.S. Department of Health and Human Services, National Institute on Drug Abuse, 1990.

NIDA Capsules: Highlights of National Adolescent School Health Survey of Drug and Alcohol Use. Rockville, MD: U.S. Department of Health and Human Services, 1988.

Shooting, Sharing and AIDS. Denver: Colorado Department of Health.

Stimmel, Barry. *The Facts about Drug Use.* New York: Consumer Reports Books, 1991.

Treatment Services for Adolescent Substance Abusers. Rockville, MD: U.S. Department of Health and Human Services, 1989.

Youth and Drugs: Society's Mixed Messages. Rockville, MD: U.S. Department of Health and Human Services, Office for Substance Abuse Prevention, 1990.

Resources
for Finding Out about Drug Addiction

Fiction

Bridgers, Sue Ellen. **Permanent Connections.** New York: Harper & Row, 1987. 283p.

When Rob begins failing his high school classes and experimenting with drugs, his family sends him to live with eccentric relatives on the old family farm. He hates his exile, but that all changes when he falls in love.

Bunting, Anne Evelyn. **Face at the Edge of the World.** New York: Houghton Mifflin, 1985. 158p.

As 17-year-old Jed explores the reasons for his best friend's suicide, he stumbles into a mystery, and drug abuse is underneath it.

Corcoran, Barbara. **The Woman in Your Life.** New York: Atheneum, 1984. 159p.

When Anne goes to college, she falls in love with Aaron, a young man who grew up poor and has decided never to do without money again. His scheme for earning it involves smuggling drugs across the Mexican border. Out of love, she helps him and is caught and sentenced to jail. She waits in vain for him to come to her rescue by turning himself in.

DeClements, Barthe. **I Never Asked You To Understand Me.** New York: Viking Penguin, 1986. 138p.

Didi transfers to an alternative school and falls in with a group of kids who smoke grass. When her mother dies, she experiments with amphetamines. During the school year, she learns how to cope with peer pressure and with the stress in her life without relying on drugs.

DeVault, Christine, and Bryan Strong. **Christy's Chance.** Santa Cruz, CA: Network Publications, 1987. 84p.

During Christy's summer vacation, she meets many new people and has new and exciting experiences. She must decide whether trying marijuana will be a part of the summer. Readers of this book choose for Christy and then learn the consequences of those choices.

Gilmour, H. B. **Ask Me If I Care.** New York: Ballantine Books, 1985. 180p.

When Jenny and her mom cannot stand each other anymore, Jenny goes to live with her dad in New York, but life is just as unbearable there. Offered marijuana by a new acquaintance who sells drugs, Jenny accepts it and buys diet pills for an overweight friend. From there she goes to Quaaludes and cocaine. When she visits her mother for a week, she runs out of drugs and is desperate. Back in New York, her father confronts her about her habit. Even after this crisis, Jenny's life has to fall apart further before she is ready to seek treatment.

Halvorson, Marilyn. **Let It Go.** New York: Delacorte Press, 1985. 235p.

Fifteen-year-old Red's older brother began taking drugs when he was 17 and now lies in the hospital comatose and on life support from an angel dust (PCP) overdose. Red's dad does not accept the fact that his older son will never get better, and he is constantly suspicious that Red uses drugs, too. Eventually Red does start using, and it takes a crisis to change and resolve Red's relationship with his father.

Horowitz, Joshua. **Only Birds and Angels Fly.** New York: Harper & Row, 1985. 192p.

Danny, a college freshman, remembers his high school friendship with Chris, whose inner torment led him into drug addiction and finally death. This book portrays the good and the bad times in the boys' friendship.

Kerr, M. E. **Fell Back.** New York: Harper & Row, 1989. 192p.

John Fell finds himself investigating a prep school classmate's death. His attempts to solve the mystery uncover a drug ring, a murder, and a love affair.

————. **I Stay near You: 1 Story in 3.** New York: Harper & Row, 1985. 192p.

Three long stories detail the lives of one family living in a small town. It all starts when Mildred, awkward and from the wrong side of the tracks, falls in love with Powell Storm, Jr., the son of the richest man in town. Her son, Vincent, becomes a pop star and later is hooked on drugs. Years later, it is up to Vincent's troubled son to untangle the ill-fated loves and make a life of his own.

Kropp, Paul Stephan. **Snow Ghost.** St. Paul, MN: EMC Publishing, 1984. 93p.

Martin packs his grass as his survival kit when he goes to spend the week in a Canadian cabin with his teacher and the teacher's son. When their small plane crashes and only Martin is able to help the others, he longs for a joint but knows he has to stay clean to survive. This book is easy to read.

Levy, Marilyn. **Summer Snow.** New York: Fawcett Juniper, 1986. 176p.

During a trip to California, 16-year-old Leslie hangs out with kids who use cocaine. It takes time for her to learn that the drug and her friends, the users, both are more trouble than they are worth.

Meyer, Carolyn. **The Two Faces of Adam.** New York: Bantam, 1991. 176p.

Lan has never used drugs, and he thinks kids who do are fools. Nonetheless he volunteers to work a hotline so he can help kids in trouble. When he discovers that one of his friends has been calling the hotline about his brother's drug problem, Lan is shocked. He is even more shocked when the friend asks Lan to help him help his brother. Lan is forced to decide whether he can refuse to help another person just because he does not approve of that person's behavior.

Meyers, Walter Dean. **Motown and Didi: A Love Story.** New York: Viking, 1984. 174p.

Motown and his friend Didi live in Harlem. Down on their luck, they are both determined to better their lives. When Didi goes home to her apartment and discovers her brother is a heroin addict, she turns his pusher in to the police and faces grave danger. Death and danger from the drug underworld make this book gripping and suspenseful.

Orgel, Doris. **Crack in the Heart.** New York: Fawcett Juniper, 1989. 160p.

When Zanna's dad dies and her mother is caught up in her own grief, the teenager starts smoking pot. Soon she forms friendships with classmates who are into cocaine. Next she meets a musician who introduces her to yet more drugs. A disaster pushes Zanna to adapt to life without drugs, and eventually she learns that she can help others.

Snyder, Zilpha Keatley. **The Birds of Summer.** New York: Atheneum, 1983. 195p.

Summer's mom has been fired for coming to work stoned, and Summer is furious. She takes more and more responsibility as her family falls apart. Then she discovers a plot involving a marijuana farm, drug runners, and her mother. When her mother is arrested, Summer must make many decisions about her feelings for her mom and the course her own life will take.

Nonfiction

BOOKS

Asken, Michael J. **Dying To Win: The Athlete's Guide to Safe and Unsafe Drugs in Sports.** Washington, DC: Acropolis Books, 1988. 192p.

In *Dying to Win*, Asken covers why athletes use drugs, the myths and realities of drug use, a history of drugs and sports, and a values checklist. He also talks about prescription drugs used in sports medicine today.

Ball, Jacqueline. **Everything You Need To Know about Drug Abuse.** New York: Rosen Publishing Group, 1988. 64p.

Written at a fourth- to sixth-grade reading level, this is a good introduction to the basic facts teenagers need to know about drug use and abuse.

Baum, Joanne. **One Step over the Line: A No-Nonsense Guide to Recognizing and Treating Cocaine Dependency.** New York: Harper & Row, 1985. 314p.

This book focuses on recovery, including such topics as intervention, what to expect in therapy, and how Twelve Step groups can help break cocaine dependency.

Berger, Gilda. **Crack: The New Drug Epidemic!** New York: Franklin Watts, 1987. 128p.

Berger delves into how crack cocaine is made and why it is so dangerous. Information is included, as well, about possible solutions to the crack epidemic that have been tried since the drug was introduced in 1984. The book includes a good list of sources for further information and places to turn for help.

—————. **Drug Abuse: The Impact on Society.** New York: Franklin Watts, 1988. 144p.

The main focus of this book is a discussion of how major illegal drugs affect personality and behavior, thereby impacting all of us. Such current drug topics as the transmission of AIDS, street crime, families, and drugs in the workplace are all covered. In addition the author addresses issues about how far law enforcement officials should go in enforcing drug laws.

—————. **Drug Testing.** New York: Franklin Watts, 1987. 128p.

People who are against mandatory drug testing say that not only are their rights being violated but also the tests are inaccurate. Those for testing argue that because drugs affect work performance, employers have a right to screen out applicants and employees who are chemically dependent. This book covers the moral, legal, and medical arguments for and against drug testing.

—————. **Violence and Drugs.** New York: Franklin Watts, 1989. 112p.

Even though studies show that drug users are more prone to violence than other people, no one knows yet whether drugs actually cause the violence or tend to be used by people who are more violent to begin with. This book examines the link between drug use and violent acts.

Cohen, Sidney. **The Chemical Brain: The Neurochemistry of Addictive Disorders.** Minneapolis, MN: Care Institute, 1988. 132p.

Scientific advances during the 1980s unlocked the mysteries of addiction. This book examines those research breakthroughs, explaining how the brain's chemistry works to form addictions and how some addictions may have a genetic basis.

De Veaux, Alexis. **Don't Explain: A Song of Billie Holiday.** New York: Harper & Row, 1980. 160p.

Through words, illustrations, and pictures, this book depicts the rise and fall of jazz singer Billie Holiday, following her career and her addiction to heroin.

Dolan, Edward. **Drugs in Sports.** New York: Franklin Watts, 1986. 128p.

Even though they are not supposed to, some professional and amateur sports figures use illegal drugs. This book covers why these athletes take drugs and how those drugs impact both the individuals and the sports they play. The book also talks about steps taken by sports organizations to clean up athletics.

Edwards, Gabrielle. **Coping with Drug Abuse.** New York: Rosen Publishing Group, 1990. 168p.

This book provides a solid, basic understanding of the drug abuse problem as it applies to teenagers.

Ellis, Dan C. **Growing Up Stoned: Coming to Terms with Teenage Drug Abuse in America.** Deerfield Beach, FL: Health Communications, 1986. 154p.

This book separates the typical problems of adolescence from those involving drug abuse. This easy-to-read book is filled with practical advice.

Evans, Glen, Robert O'Brien, Sidney Cohen, and James Fine. **The Encyclopedia of Drug Abuse,** 2d edition. New York: Facts on File, 1990. 370p.

Over 500 entries in this reference book cover the research, facts, and statistics on all facets of drug abuse. Biological, legal, social, and medical aspects are covered on individual, national, and international levels. Hundreds of drug abuse treatment organizations are listed.

Gold, Mark. **800-Cocaine.** New York: Bantam, 1984. 108p.

From the history of cocaine use in the United States to the process of addiction in individuals, this book gives a broad overview of the drug. A medical doctor who specializes in cocaine addiction and founder of the national cocaine hotline, Gold is in a unique position to present the facts and debunk the myths about cocaine use and recovery.

Gordon, Barbara. **I'm Dancing As Fast As I Can.** New York: Harper & Row, 1979. 320p.

This classic story of Valium addiction and recovery discusses in a compelling way how Barbara Gordon got hooked and the nightmare life her addiction led to.

Johnson, Joan. **America's War on Drugs.** New York: Franklin Watts, 1990. 160p.

This book covers the other side of drug problems: stopping the manufacturing and distribution of illegal substances. Topics covered include U.S. efforts to prevent illegal drugs from crossing the borders and stopping marijuana growers in this country, as well as law enforcement attempts to stop dealers. Some new and creative community anti-drug programs are detailed.

Jones, Helen C., and Paul M. Lovinger. **The Marijuana Question.** New York: Dodd Mead, 1985. 552p.

This book takes a look at marijuana research up to 1984. There are stories from former users here as well. On the whole it presents a good overview of the issues surrounding the use of grass.

Kirsch, M. M. **Designer Drugs.** Minneapolis, MN: CompCare, 1986. 200p.

Designer drugs are the newest and most dangerous chemicals on the market. In this book, law enforcement personnel, users, and dealers give interviews about this underground industry, including crack cocaine, angel dust (PCP), crystal (an amphetamine), and china white (a narcotic). Use, prevention, and treatment are all covered.

McCormick, Michelle. **Designer Drug Abuse.** New York: Franklin Watts, 1989. 128p.

PCP, Ecstasy, and other designer drugs pose growing problems for society today. This book uses facts and case histories to point out the dangers of these drugs. Ways to get more information and sources of help are included in this comprehensive book.

Mann, Peggy. **Marijuana Alert.** New York: McGraw-Hill, 1985. 566p.

Written specifically for teenagers, this book is a comprehensive guide to the problems marijuana causes and what can be done about this drug. In addition to discussing the extent of the problem, it talks about physical and psychological consequences of marijuana use.

Mortner, Ira, and Alan Weitz. **How To Get Off Drugs.** New York: Fireside, 1984. 270p.

In addition to explaining why people take drugs and why they get addicted, this book gives practical advice about getting through the early stages of recovery. Chapters cover a variety of drugs, and each chapter offers a first step for getting off that particular drug. In addition, the authors offer helpful suggestions for family members of a person trying to get off and stay off drugs.

Nuwer, Hank. **Steroids.** New York: Franklin Watts, 1990. 144p.

Steroid use can cause both physical and emotional damage to those who try to bulk muscles synthetically. This book covers both organ damage and psychological disturbances that can occur when steroids are used.

O'Connell, Kathleen R. **End of the Line: Quitting Cocaine.** Louisville, KY: Westminster Press, 1985. 120p.

The informal and informative style of this book makes it ideal for people in the first few months of recovery from cocaine addiction. It is filled with practical strategies about quitting and staying off coke and offers hope and encouragement to recovering addicts.

Peluso, Emanuel, and Lucy Silvay Peluso. **Women and Drugs: Getting Hooked, Getting Clean.** Minneapolis, MN: CompCare, 1988. 238p.

This book chronicles the drug experiences of ten women from all walks of life who became dependent on legal or illegal drugs. The authors interweave facts about addiction and recovery with the stories, paying special attention to women's issues and how they relate to addiction.

Seymour, Richard B., and David E. Smith. **Drugfree: A Unique, Positive Approach to Staying Off Alcohol and Other Drugs.** New York: Facts on File, 1987. 271p.

In addition to the usual treatment suggestions offered in many books about dealing with drug addiction, the authors, who are affiliated with the Haight-Ashbury Free Medical Clinic, offer a number of positive alternatives to drugs. These include good nutrition, meditation, yoga, massage, acupuncture, and exercise.

Snyder, Solomon, ed. **The Encyclopedia of Psychoactive Drugs.** New York: Chelsea House, copyright date varies. 96–160p.

Titles in this comprehensive set of 50 reference books include *The Addictive Personality, Drugs & Civilization, Drugs & Pain, Drugs & Women, Drugs & the Law, Celebrity Drug Use,* and many more. Written for readers age 12 to adult, these books are a storehouse of current information and are well illustrated and indexed.

Staying Clean: Living without Drugs. Center City, MN: Hazelden Educational Materials, 1987. 76p.

This book lists and explores 33 proven methods for staying free from drugs. It provides both emotional and practical support for the newly recovering addict and covers everything from relationships to spirituality and therapy.

Terkel, Susan Neiburg. **Should Drugs Be Legalized?** New York: Franklin Watts, 1990. 160p.

How would the decriminalization of drugs affect society? That question is being hotly debated today. This book presents both sides of the issue from legal, moral, health, economic, and historical perspectives.

Trager, Oliver, ed. **Drugs in America: Crisis or Hysteria?** New York: Facts on File, 1987. 224p.

This book examines many sides of the drug issue. It explores the possibility of legalizing drugs; the notion that perhaps politicians and the media have exaggerated the drug problem; and the harm that legal substances, such as alcohol and nicotine, have caused Americans. These controversies are discussed by a number of authors in this compilation.

Weiss, Roger, and Steven M. Mirin. **Cocaine.** Washington, DC: American Psychiatric Association, 1986. 178p.

This book covers how cocaine is used and how it affects the brain and body. Affected families, cocaine and the workplace, and treatment are covered as well.

What Works: Schools without Drugs. Rockville, MD: National Clearinghouse on Alcohol and Drug Information, 1989. 87p.

Schools can be drug-free. This book gives information about alcohol and drug use among students as well as examples of school anti-drug programs that work.

PAMPHLETS

About Crack. Santa Cruz, CA: Network Publications, 1990. 5p.

Today crack is one of the fastest growing drugs of abuse. In fact, its use has reached epidemic proportions. This booklet tells teens about the physical effects of crack, how users become addicted, and the dangers of crack to unborn children.

About Ice. Santa Cruz, CA: Network Publications, 1990. 5p.

The facts about ice, a new version of methamphetamine, are presented in this booklet. Written in clear language, it covers just what ice is, how it affects the body, and why it is so dangerous.

About Marijuana. Santa Cruz, CA: Network Publications, 1990. 5p.

Marijuana's short-term and long-term effects on the body are covered in this leaflet, which also tells readers why people smoke grass and where to get more information about it.

About Steroids. Santa Cruz, CA: Network Publications, 1990. 5p.

This pamphlet details why doctors prescribe steroids and outlines the dangers of misusing this drug, including emotional side effects, physical injuries, and long-term damage.

Do You Know the Facts about Drugs? Deerfield Beach, FL: Health Communications, 1982. 30p.

This pamphlet is a complete guide to the facts about chemicals including alcohol, amphetamines, barbiturates, marijuana, cocaine, hallucinogens, opiates, solvents, tobacco, and tranquilizers.

Don't Lose a Friend to Drugs. Washington, DC: National Crime Prevention Council, 1986. 2p.

How to help a friend who is on drugs and how to begin community prevention programs are the focuses of this flyer.

Drug Abuse and AIDS. Rockville, MD: National Clearinghouse for Alcohol and Drug Information, 1989. 2p.

This leaflet explores the link between IV drug use and HIV transmission.

Drug Abuse and Pregnancy. Rockville, MD: National Clearinghouse for Alcohol and Drug Information, 1989. 4p.

Focusing on an overview of the scope of the problem, this leaflet also talks about the effects of drugs on the mother, the fetus, and the baby after it is born.

Drugs! Kim and Tran Talk to Teens. Santa Cruz, CA: Network Publications, 1990. 5p.

Kim and Tran, two teenagers, talk about their friends' experiences with marijuana and cocaine. The facts about these drugs and advice on how to stop using them are presented in a realistic and interesting way.

Dunn, Richard. **Relapse and the Addict.** Center City, MN: Hazelden Educational Materials, 1986. 24p.

Knowing the warning signs and stages of a relapse is important if recovering cocaine addicts are to remain drug-free. This booklet sets out these warning signs and relapse stages and tells readers what to do when they happen.

The Fact Is . . . The Use of Steroids in Sports Can Be Dangerous. Rockville, MD: National Clearinghouse for Alcohol and Drug Information, 1989. 5p.

This leaflet describes the negative effects of steroids on users and gives a list of resources for further information and help.

Gorski, Terence. **Managing Cocaine Craving.** Center City, MN: Hazelden Educational Materials, 1990. 36p.

Managing cravings for cocaine is one of the toughest parts of recovery for cocaine addicts. This pamphlet meets that challenge head-on and offers very practical suggestions about how to move beyond cravings.

Hewett, Paul. **Straight Talk about Drugs.** Minneapolis, MN: CompCare, 1990. 44p.

This easy-to-read booklet tells both teens and adults the basic facts about drugs. It is concise and fact-filled.

Hull-Mast, Nancy. **Living Drug-Free.** Center City, MN: Hazelden Educational Materials, 1989. 20p.

No matter what drug a chemically dependent person is trying to recover from, he or she faces the challenges of peer pressure, reluctance to attend meetings, and distorted thinking. This booklet covers those issues and provides help for dealing with them.

Meyers, Mark. **Compulsive Exercise and Steroid Abuse.** Park Ridge, IL: Parkside Publishing Corporation, 1990. 32p.

In the rush to fitness, some teens take steroids. Rather than being life-enhancing, exercise for these teens becomes life-threatening. This booklet looks at steroid abuse from several angles: how young people get started, what steroid abuse does to them, and how to recover.

Neely, William. **I Can't Be Addicted Because . . .** Center City, MN: Hazelden Educational Materials, 1986. 24p.

Denial is probably the biggest barrier that stops addicts from seeking treatment. This pamphlet explores the seven most common excuses addicts hang on to in order to keep using.

Nuckols, Cardwell. **Ice Storm: Methamphetamine Revisited.** Center City, MN: Hazelden Educational Materials, 1990. 26p.

Ice is cheap and very powerful, which is why it is becoming one of the most popular drugs in this country today. This booklet looks at the physical and psychological effects ice has on its users and talks about treatment as well.

Orange, Cynthia. **Addicts and Families in Recovery.** Center City, MN: Hazelden Educational Materials, 1986. 20p.

Drug abuse affects not only the addict but his or her family as well. This booklet looks at what Nar-Anon, a group for significant others of addicts, can do to help them solve their very real problems caused by living with and loving an addict.

Spence, W. R. **Marijuana: How Much of a Gamble?** Waco, TX: EDCO, 1987. 15p.

Many teens still believe grass is harmless. This book sets out to correct that myth by showing how dope affects both the body and the mind.

Washton, Arnold W. **Cocaine and the Family: Understanding Addiction and Recovery.** Center City, MN: Hazelden Educational Materials, 1990. 37p.

When family members are not knowledgeable about addiction, they often enable, or unintentionally help, the addict to continue using drugs. This booklet talks about how family members enable addicted loved ones and how family members can detach in order to start taking care of themselves.

————. **Crack: What You Need To Know.** Deerfield Beach, FL: Health Communications, 1986. 32p.

The basics about crack, addiction to it, and treatment are covered in this booklet.

Webster, Terry. **Needing Cocaine: Stories of Recovering Cocaine Addicts.** Center City, MN: Hazelden Educational Materials, 1985. 56p.

This moving collection of personal stories shows how cocaine addicts can benefit from self-help groups such as Narcotics Anonymous (N.A.).

When Cocaine Affects Someone You Love. Rockville, MD: National Clearinghouse for Alcohol and Drug Information, 1987. 12p.

This booklet answers the most frequently asked questions about cocaine and crack and offers lists of self-help groups, readings, and additional sources of help.

Why Eddie Murphy Won't Do Drugs. Rockville, MD: National Clearinghouse for Alcohol and Drug Information, 1985. 1p.

This one-page reprint from *Parade* magazine talks about how Eddie Murphy came to his anti-drug attitudes.

Nonprint Materials

AIDS: The Reality in the Dream
Type: VHS video
Length: 26 min.
Cost: Purchase $50
Distributor: Network Publications
               P.O. Box 1830
               Santa Cruz, CA 95061-1830
Date: 1988

This prevention video is aimed at teenage IV drug users and their sexual partners. It follows a young African-American woman as she finds out that she is HIV positive. Sexual transmission of the virus, the importance of not sharing needles or syringes, and the need for testing are all covered.

All My Tomorrows
Type: 16mm film, VHS video
Length: 17 min.
Cost: Rental $75, purchase $395 (film); rental $75,
               purchase $250 (video)
Distributor: Coronet/MTI Film and Video
               108 Wilmot Road
               Deerfield, IL 60015
Date: 1979

Peggy mixed barbiturates and alcohol, and the violent and instant reaction changed her life forever.

America Hurts: The Drug Epidemic
Type: 16mm film, VHS video
Length: 34 min.

Cost:	Rental $85, purchase $595 (film); rental $85, purchase $495 (video)
Distributor:	Coronet/MTI Film and Video 108 Wilmot Road Deerfield, IL 60015
Date:	1987

Interviews with addicts and reports of drug murders and corruption will shock viewers. This program focuses not only on how drug abuse affects users and families but also on how it can shatter communities and the entire nation. The economic costs of drug use to the country are covered as well.

Anabolic Steroids: Quest for Superman

Type:	VHS video
Length:	31 min.
Cost:	Purchase $149
Distributor:	Sunburst Communications 39 Washington Avenue Box 40 Pleasantville, NY 10570-9971
Date:	1991

Even though many young athletes know taking steroids is dangerous, about one-quarter of a million teens take these drugs anyway. This video mixes facts and statistics with interviews of professional athletes and physicians. It is aimed at both young males and females.

Angel Death

Type:	16mm film, VHS video
Length:	33 min.
Cost:	Rental $75, purchase $450 (film); rental $75, purchase $250 (video)
Distributor:	Coronet/MTI Film and Video 108 Wilmot Road Deerfield, IL 60015
Date:	1979

Paul Newman and Joanne Woodward narrate this award-winning film about the consequences of PCP use.

Benny and the 'Roids: A Story about Steroid Abuse

Type:	16mm film, VHS video
Length:	25 min.
Cost:	Rental $85, purchase $575 (film); rental $85, purchase $375 (video)

Distributor: Coronet/MTI Film and Video
                108 Wilmot Road
                Deerfield, IL 60015
Date: 1988

A starting linebacker for his high school team, Benny wants to play in the pros. He buys steroids to make his dream come true, but the drug's side effects turn his dream into a nightmare.

Beyond Body Building
Type: 16mm film, VHS video
Length: 29 min.
Cost: Rental $75, purchase $80
Distributor: Coronet/MTI Film and Video
                108 Wilmot Road
                Deerfield, IL 60015
Date: 1989

This show about steroids explains the physiological background of how muscles work and offers tips on how to naturally make them work better.

Cocaine: Athletes Speak Out
Type: VHS video
Length: 34 min.
Cost: Rental $28, purchase $189
Distributor: Britannica Educational Corporation
                310 South Michigan Avenue
                Chicago, IL 60604
Date: 1987

The sports figures in this video make the point that cocaine users do not control the drug; the drug controls them.

Cocaine and Crack: The Lost Years
Type: 16mm film, VHS video
Length: 23 min.
Cost: Rental $19, purchase $675 (film); rental $19,
                purchase $300 (video)
Distributor: Britannica Educational Corporation
                310 South Michigan Avenue
                Chicago, IL 60604
Date: 1987

Teenagers often use cocaine and crack to get a mental, emotional, and sexual high. This film explores these motives and looks at the pain drug use causes.

Cocaine and Human Physiology

Type:	16mm film, VHS video
Length:	20 min.
Cost:	Purchase $475 (film), $350 (video)
Distributor:	The Health Connection
	12501 Old Columbia Pike
	Silver Spring, MD 20904-6600
Date:	1987

Given an honorable mention by the National Council on Family Relations, this program documents the physical damage cocaine causes when it is snorted, injected, or smoked. The brain, heart, lungs, nose, eyes, vocal cords, gums, kidneys, liver, and intestines are among the organs covered, along with the damage that pregnant cocaine users do to their unborn babies.

Cocaine Babies Update: The Research Is In

Type:	VHS video
Length:	19 min.
Cost:	Purchase $249
Distributor:	Parkside Publishing Corporation
	205 West Touhy Avenue
	Park Ridge, IL 60068
Date:	1989

Twenty percent of all babies born in the urban United States are crack addicted. This video examines the research done since 1985, when this problem was first discovered.

Cocaine/Crack: A Teenager's Story

Type:	VHS video
Length:	28 min.
Cost:	Purchase $189
Distributor:	Sunburst Communications
	39 Washington Avenue
	Box 40
	Pleasantville, NY 10570-9971
Date:	1989

Matt thinks he is just experimenting when he takes his first snort of coke. Soon he is transformed into a paranoid and is willing to do anything, even steal, to buy more cocaine. During a high his heart temporarily stops beating, and Matt finally realizes he is hooked and he needs help. In the second half of this video, two psychiatrists explain the biological and psychological reasons for cocaine's addictive power.

Cocaine Kids: Their Problem Is Our Problem

Type:	VHS video
Length:	16 min.
Cost:	Purchase $249
Distributor:	Parkside Publishing Corporation
	205 West Touhy Avenue
	Park Ridge, IL 60068
Date:	1990

What happens to cocaine babies when they grow up? This video follows them to school and includes the insights of teachers, social workers, researchers, and mothers to explore the difficulties in coping with the problems of these children.

Cocaine Mothers: Beyond the Guilt

Type:	VHS video
Length:	25 min.
Cost:	Purchase $249
Distributor:	Parkside Publishing Corporation
	205 West Touhy Avenue
	Park Ridge, IL 60068
Date:	1990

Mothers who were crack addicts not only have a hard time with their own recovery; they also are faced with the consequences of and guilt over their crack use during pregnancy. Produced from the mother's point of view, this video looks at the disease concept of addiction and seeks ways to promote understanding and forgiveness.

Coke *Isn't* It: Hard Facts about Cocaine

Type:	VHS video
Length:	26 min.
Cost:	Purchase $139
Distributor:	Guidance Associates
	P.O. Box 1000
	Mount Kisco, NY 10549-0010
Date:	1987

Interviews with former cocaine users spell out the consequences of coke use. This video talks about how cocaine use is invading not only schools but also factories and businesses. Sources of help are also covered.

Count Me Out

Type:	16mm film, VHS video
Length:	16 min.

Cost: Purchase $495 (film), $375 (video)
Distributor: Perennial Education
                 930 Pitner Avenue
                 Evanston, IL 60202
Date: 1988

This film dramatically tells the story of a group of teenagers who decide to use alcohol and drugs, including crack, at a spur-of-the-moment party. Before the evening is over their fun turns into tragedy. Both *Booklist* and *Drug Abuse Update* have given excellent reviews to the film.

Crack!

Type: VHS video (available in open caption for the deaf)
Length: 15 min.
Cost: Purchase $119
Distributor: Sunburst Communications
                 39 Washington Avenue
                 Box 40
                 Pleasantville, NY 10570-9971
Date: 1986

People who use crack run a five times greater risk of addiction than those who use powder cocaine. Arnold Washton, Ph.D., an expert on the drug, talks about the facts and interviews six crack addicts in this award-winning video.

Crackdown II

Type: VHS video
Length: 49 min.
Cost: Purchase $159
Distributor: The Health Connection
                 12501 Old Columbia Pike
                 Silver Spring, MD 20904-6600
Date: 1990

This video uses dramatized stories and talks by both actor Scott Valentine and medical experts to motivate adolescents not to use crack. It also gives suggestions on how to get help for friends or family members who use this drug.

Crack Street, USA: First-Person Experiences with a New Killer Drug

Type: VHS video
Length: 29 min.
Cost: Purchase $139

Distributor: Guidance Associates
          P.O. Box 1000
          Mount Kisco, NY 10549-0010
Date: 1987

Former crack users tell what effects the drug had on their lives—socially, emotionally, and physically. Medical experts also are interviewed, as are social workers.

Death by Design
Type: VHS video
Length: 20 min.
Cost: Purchase $295
Distributor: New Dimension Media
          85803 Lorane Highway
          Eugene, OR 97405
Date: 1988

Covering the many new drugs invented by underground chemists during the 1980s, this video explains the dangers in their use.

Designer Drugs and Human Physiology: Crack, Cocaine, Methamphetamine
Type: 16mm film, VHS video
Length: 14 min.
Cost: Purchase $335 (film), $275 (video)
Distributor: The Health Connection
          12501 Old Columbia Pike
          Silver Spring, MD 20904-6600
Date: 1989

The damaging effects of crack and speed are covered in this video, which focuses on the permanent damage these drugs cause to users.

Designer Drugs and Human Physiology: PCP, Ecstasy, Fentanyl
Type: 16mm film, VHS video
Length: 30 min.
Cost: Purchase $445 (film), $375 (video)
Distributor: The Health Connection
          12501 Old Columbia Pike
          Silver Spring, MD 20904-6600
Date: 1989

Synthetic drugs are a big profit-maker for the chemists who manufacture them. But the poisons in these drugs can prove fatal to users, and this film explains why.

Drug Abuse: Meeting the Challenge

Type:	VHS video
Length:	23 min.
Cost:	Rental free, purchase $80
Distributor (rental):	National Clearinghouse for Alcohol and Drug Information
	P.O. Box 2345
	Rockville, MD 20852
Distributor (purchase):	National Archives and Records Administration
	Customer Service Section PZ
	8700 Edgeworth Drive
	Capitol Heights, MD 20743-3701
Date:	1987

After a short introduction by the director of the National Institute on Drug Abuse, this video gives an overview of the drug problem facing the United States today. Segments include prevention, research, drugs in the workplace, and IV drug use and the AIDS epidemic.

Drug Abuse: Sorting It Out

Type:	VHS video
Length:	20 min.
Cost:	Purchase $290
Distributor:	Britannica Educational Corporation
	310 South Michigan Avenue
	Chicago, IL 60604
Date:	1989

The focus of this film is on values clarification and decision making— things every teenager needs to know to cope with peer pressure.

Drug Abuse and AIDS: Getting the Message Out

Type:	VHS video
Length:	27 min.
Cost:	Rental free, purchase $80
Distributor (rental):	National Clearinghouse for Alcohol and Drug Information
	P.O. Box 2345
	Rockville, MD 20852
Distributor (purchase):	National Archives and Records Administration
	Customer Service Section PZ
	8700 Edgeworth Drive
	Capitol Heights, MD 20743-3701
Date:	1987

This documentary for adolescents and adults shows several very effective model programs from throughout the country that are getting out the message about the transmission, consequences, and treatment of AIDS. The ideas in this video are especially useful for teens and adults wanting to start AIDS information outreach programs in their communities.

The Drug Abuse Test

Type: 16mm film, VHS video
Length: 22 min.
Cost: Rental $75, purchase $475 (film); rental $75, purchase $415 (video)
Distributor: Coronet/MTI Film and Video
               108 Wilmot Road
               Deerfield, IL 60015
Date: 1983

In this program, which is presented in a quiz format, viewers are asked 14 questions. Then these questions are answered by experts.

Drug-Affected Children: The Price We Pay

Type: VHS video
Length: 18 min.
Cost: Purchase $249
Distributor: Parkside Publishing Corporation
               205 West Touhy Avenue
               Park Ridge, IL 60068
Date: 1990

The social and economic costs of crack babies are enormous. This video takes a look at who pays for the care of these children and where a parent can go for help. Hospitals, social health services, and foster parents all comment on their experiences.

The Drug Information Series

Type: 16mm film, VHS video
Length: 10 min. each
Cost: Rental $60, purchase $205 (each film); rental $60, purchase $185 (each video)
Distributor: Coronet/MTI Film and Video
               108 Wilmot Road
               Deerfield, IL 60015
Date: 1983

These seven ten-minute programs are narrated in a dramatic and fast-paced manner by emergency room personnel, doctors, and lab technicians. Covered are signs of drug use and abuse, resulting behavioral changes, and long- as well as short-term consequences. The titles of the individual programs are *Alcohol, Depressants, Hallucinogens, Inhalants, Marijuana, Narcotics,* and *Stimulants.*

Drug Problems in Sports

Type: VHS video
Length: 24 min.
Cost: Purchase $99
Distributor: Britannica Educational Corporation
                       310 South Michigan Avenue
                       Chicago, IL 60604
Date: 1982

Coaches and physicians talk about how drugs interfere with an athlete's goals in this training video that is appropriate for high school audiences.

Drug Testing: Handle with Care (employee version)

Type: VHS video
Length: 27 min.
Cost: Rental free
Distributor: National Clearinghouse for Alcohol and Drug
                       Information
                       P.O. Box 2345
                       Rockville, MD 20852
Date: 1989

This video explores the options available for establishing a drug-free workplace. Topics include specimen collection, laboratory analysis, accuracy of test results, and the needs of both employers and employees.

Drugs: Helpful and Harmful

Type: 16mm film, VHS video
Length: 15 min.
Cost: Rental $60, purchase $345 (film); rental $60,
                       purchase $260 (video)
Distributor: Churchill Films
                       12210 Nebraska Avenue
                       Los Angeles, CA 90025
Date: 1988

This film discusses the effects all kinds of drugs can have on the nervous system—even prescription and over-the-counter drugs. It is also available in Spanish.

Drugs and Drinks Don't Mix

Type:	16mm film, VHS video
Length:	19 min.
Cost:	Purchase $395 (film), $345 (video)
Distributor:	Perennial Education
	930 Pitner Avenue
	Evanston, IL 60202
Date:	1985

Anyone who takes medication, whether it is over-the-counter cold medicine or a prescription, can find the combination of medication and alcohol to be deadly. This film warns about the physiological and psychological side effects of stimulants and depressants when they are taken in combination with alcohol.

Drugs and the Nervous System

Type:	16mm film, VHS video
Length:	17 min.
Cost:	Rental $60, purchase $385 (film); rental $60, purchase $290 (video)
Distributor:	Churchill Films
	12210 Nebraska Avenue
	Los Angeles, CA 90025
Date:	1987

This film, which is also available in Spanish, talks about the many ways drugs upset the nervous system. It is narrated in part by recovering teenagers.

Drugs and Your Amazing Mind

Type:	16mm film, VHS video
Length:	18 min.
Cost:	Rental $60, purchase $395 (film); rental $60, purchase $355 (video)
Distributor:	Alfred Higgins Productions, Inc.
	6350 Laurel Canyon Boulevard
	North Hollywood, CA 91606
Date:	1989

This film, which covers many types of drugs, talks about how the mind works and how drugs interfere with those workings. Interviews with former drug users provide insight into why people use drugs and their reasons for stopping. This film is also available in Spanish.

Epidemic! Kids, Drugs and Alcohol

Type:	16mm film, VHS video
Length:	27 min.
Cost:	Rental $75, purchase $520 (film); rental $75, purchase $475 (video)
Distributor:	Coronet/MTI Film and Video
	108 Wilmot Road
	Deerfield, IL 60015
Date:	1982

The media, music, and peers all pressure kids to use drugs. This program produced by the Gannett Broadcast Group explores that pressure and the consequences of caving in.

Good Kids Die Too

Type:	16mm film, VHS video
Length:	25 min.
Cost:	Rental $75, purchase $550 (film); rental $75, purchase $250 (video)
Distributor:	Coronet/MTI Film and Video
	108 Wilmot Road
	Deerfield, IL 60015
Date:	1989

Many drug-related deaths happen to first-time drug users, kids who did nothing more than experiment. This dramatic film follows two kids from positive backgrounds as they experiment with crack and pay for it with their lives.

Heroin and Human Physiology

Type:	16mm film, VHS video
Length:	22 min.
Cost:	Purchase $495 (film), $395 (video)
Distributor:	The Health Connection
	12501 Old Columbia Pike
	Silver Spring, MD 20904-6600
Date:	1988

Not only does heroin affect users' minds but it damages the body, too. The medical consequences of this drug use are detailed in this video by experts and by former users. In addition to the damage the drug itself does, intravenous drug use spreads HIV, and this, too, is discussed.

Icy Death

Type:	VHS video
Length:	25 min.

Cost:	Purchase $49.95 (video)
Distributor:	The Health Connection
	12501 Old Columbia Pike
	Silver Spring, MD 20904-6600
Date:	1991

The basic facts about ice are covered in this video by dramatic scenarios and narration accompanied by a music score.

I'll Never Forget You

Type:	VHS video
Length:	14 min.
Cost:	Purchase $295
Distributor:	Perennial Education
	930 Pitner Avenue
	Evanston, IL 60202
Date:	1991

When college basketball star Len Bias was drafted by the Boston Celtics basketball team, that night he celebrated by doing cocaine, and he died. One of his former college rivals, Johnny Dawkins, is the narrator of this film about Len Bias. The message of saying no to drugs is clear and dramatic.

Inhalants: Tony's Choice

Type:	VHS video
Length:	18 min.
Cost:	Purchase $295
Distributor:	New Dimension Media
	85803 Lorane Highway
	Eugene, OR 97405
Date:	1990

Although this video is aimed at a middle school audience, it discusses a type of drug abuse often neglected in educational materials. The story of Tony dramatizes the dangers when kids inhale chemicals for a high.

Kids and Drugs: The Reasons Why

Type:	16mm film, VHS video
Length:	15 min.
Cost:	Rental $75, purchase $390 (film); rental $75, purchase $250 (video)
Distributor:	Coronet/MTI Film and Video
	108 Wilmot Road
	Deerfield, IL 60015
Date:	1984

This film helps empower teenagers to resist drug use without losing out on either fun or having friendships.

Marijuana: Myths and Misperceptions
Type: VHS video
Length: 90 min.
Cost: Purchase $400
Distributor: The Health Connection
                 12501 Old Columbia Pike
                 Silver Spring, MD 20904-6600
Date: 1986

This video comes in four parts and takes an in-depth look at how marijuana smoking disrupts the brain's functioning. It is narrated by a neuro-psychiatrist.

Marijuana: Waking Up from Dope
Type: VHS video
Length: 39 min.
Cost: Purchase $69.95
Distributor: The Health Connection
                 12501 Old Columbia Pike
                 Silver Spring, MD 20904-6600
Date: 1986

A former drug user and rock musician details the facts about dope smoking, using humor teenagers can relate to. This video includes tips on how to avoid giving in to peer pressure.

Marijuana and Human Physiology
Type: 16mm film, VHS video
Length: 21 min.
Cost: Purchase $475 (film), $375 (video)
Distributor: The Health Connection
                 12501 Old Columbia Pike
                 Silver Spring, MD 20904-6600
Date: 1986

Chronic coughing, impairment of memory and judgment, and loss of motivation are only a few of the things marijuana does to people who smoke it. This program also goes into doping and driving and the problems that come from mixing pot with alcohol.

Marijuana and Your Mind
Type: VHS video (available in open caption)
Length: 15 min.

Cost:	Purchase $119
Distributor:	Sunburst Communications
	39 Washington Avenue
	Box 40
	Pleasantville, NY 10570-9971
Date:	1982

This video, which won an award from the National Council on Family Relations, talks about what marijuana is and what it does to the body. The stories of two high school pot smokers are reenacted to demonstrate amotivational syndrome, memory impairment, and physical responses to grass both in the short and the long run.

Marijuana Facts: Myths and Decisions

Type:	VHS video
Length:	45 min.
Cost:	Purchase $209
Distributor:	Guidance Associates
	P.O. Box 1000
	Mount Kisco, NY 10549-0010
Date:	1981

Marijuana's effects on the mind and body are covered as well as the special impacts it can have on teenagers. Adolescents talk about how marijuana has impacted their lives. Legal aspects of dope smoking are covered, too.

New Crack Facts

Type:	VHS video
Length:	14 min.
Cost:	Purchase $295
Distributor:	Perennial Education
	930 Pitner Avenue
	Evanston, IL 60202
Date:	1991

Both teenagers and parents need to know the facts about crack. Personal stories, medical information, statistics, and illustrations in this video provide those facts. The program includes segments featuring a former crack user now dying from AIDS, a female former user and her children, and New York City police officers.

Night Journey into Crack

Type:	VHS video
Length:	28 min.
Cost:	Purchase $295

Distributor:	Perennial Education
	930 Pitner Avenue
	Evanston, IL 60202
Date:	1991

In this dramatic story, three teens leave a dull party to buy crack and experiment with it. The addictive potential of the drug is explored as is the peril of overdose.

Peer Pressure and Drugs

Type:	VHS video
Length:	20 min.
Cost:	Rental $75, purchase $395
Distributor:	Coronet/MTI Film and Video
	108 Wilmot Road
	Deerfield, IL 60015
Date:	1989

Dramatizations and discussions point out some reasons that teenagers turn to drugs: lack of self-esteem, a need to belong, and problems at home and at school. The actors in this program are real teenagers instead of professionals, and the scenes are dramatizations of their personal experiences.

Peer Pressure, Drugs . . . and You

Type:	VHS video
Length:	32 min.
Cost:	Purchase $189
Distributor:	Sunburst Communications
	39 Washington Avenue
	Box 40
	Pleasantville, NY 10570-9971
Date:	1990

Paul, a teenager who cannot say no, gets stoned at the urging of his friends and joins them in a drag race. Sam drives his friends for beer and later is angry at himself for giving in to the pressure. Gina allows her friends to bring liquor to her party and feels bad for doing it. Peer counselors discuss what peer pressure is and what teens can do about it without losing their friends. The video acknowledges that it is not easy to say no.

Real People: Meet a Teenage Drug Addict

Type:	VHS video
Length:	24 min.
Cost:	Purchase $169

Distributor: Sunburst Communications
                 39 Washington Avenue
                 Box 40
                 Pleasantville, NY 10570-9971
Date: 1988

When she was a young teenager, Wendy tried drinking, pills, and marijuana. After that she began using cocaine. Now drug- and alcohol-free, she tells how she turned to chemicals to fill her emptiness and how she was able to deceive her teachers and even her parents about her habit. Finally she talks about how she is rebuilding her life in recovery.

Speak Up, Speak Out: Learning To Say NO to Drugs
Type: VHS video
Length: 50 min.
Cost: Purchase $209
Distributor: Guidance Associates
                 P.O. Box 1000
                 Mount Kisco, NY 10549-0010
Date: 1988

Adolescents on a class trip to Washington, D.C., learn techniques that help them say no to drugs.

Steroids: Dream Drug or Nightmare?
Type: VHS video
Length: 18 min.
Cost: Purchase $295
Distributor: New Dimension Media
                 85803 Lorane Highway
                 Eugene, OR 97405
Date: 1990

This video overviews steroid use and the effect it has on the body. Students who used to take steroids are the narrators, and they go into detail about why they used the drug and what happened to them.

Steroids: Shortcut to Make-Believe Muscles
Type: VHS video
Length: 32 min.
Cost: Purchase $125
Distributor: The Health Connection
                 12501 Old Columbia Pike
                 Silver Spring, MD 20904-6600
Date: 1988

In this video, athletes and medical experts talk about the damage steroids do. They also explain an effective body-building program that does not involve drug use.

Stoned: An Anti-Drug Film
Type: 16mm film, VHS video
Length: 30 min.
Cost: Rental $75, purchase $500 (film); rental $75, purchase $250 (video)
Distributor: Coronet/MTI Film and Video
                 108 Wilmot Road
                 Deerfield, IL 60015
Date: 1981

In this award-winning film, actor Scott Baio plays a shy adolescent who uses marijuana so he can feel popular and more independent from his older brother's influence.

Straight Talk about Drugs: Psychedelics, PCP and Dangerous Combinations
Type: VHS video
Length: 40 min.
Cost: Purchase $209
Distributor: Guidance Associates
                 P.O. Box 1000
                 Mount Kisco, NY 10549-0010
Date: 1982

LSD, mescaline, psilocybin (mushrooms), and angel dust are explored in this film. The dangers of combining drugs are also talked about. This is a filmstrip on video.

Straight Talk about Drugs: Stimulants and Narcotics
Type: VHS video
Length: 48 min.
Cost: Purchase $209
Distributor: Guidance Associates
                 P.O. Box 1000
                 Mount Kisco, NY 10549-0010
Date: 1982

Xanthines, amphetamines, cocaine, morphine, and heroin are covered in this video. Treatment options are discussed in addition to the impact these drugs have on users' lives. This is a filmstrip on video.

Straight Talk about Drugs: Tranquilizers and Sedatives
Type: VHS video
Length: 40 min.
Cost: Purchase $209
Distributor: Guidance Associates
               P.O. Box 1000
               Mount Kisco, NY 10549-0010
Date: 1982

Valium, Thorazine, Stellazine, and Librium as well as barbiturates and Quaaludes are covered in this film that discusses their potential for both psychological and physical addictiveness. This is a filmstrip on video.

These Kids Are Tough: True Stories of Real Teens Resisting Drugs
Type: VHS video
Length: 30 min.
Cost: Purchase $189
Distributor: Sunburst Communications
               39 Washington Avenue
               Box 40
               Pleasantville, NY 10570-9971
Date: 1991

Choosing to be drug-free can be very difficult for teens, especially when friends and maybe even neighbors urge an adolescent to use or sell drugs. This video tells the true stories of kids who have overcome problems without using drugs. One of them is Davida, who was seven when her mom was killed and then she was sexually abused by her dad. She managed to work through her problems in a support group. The video ends with the Broadway performance of a song she composed.

Organizations

Cocaine Anonymous
P.O. Box 1367
Culver City, CA 90232
(213) 559-5833

This international fellowship of recovering cocaine addicts shares experiences and helps members recover from their addiction. Help is available for starting local groups.

Drugs Anonymous

P.O. Box 473
Ansonia Station
New York, NY 10023
(312) 874-0700

Formerly called Pills Anonymous, this self-help group uses a
Twelve Step approach for those who want to break the substance
abuse habit. It also publishes a monthly newsletter.

Marijuana Smokers Anonymous

135 South Cypress, B
Orange, CA 92666
(714) 997-2926

Based on Alcoholics Anonymous's Twelve Step formula, this
self-help recovery program is for people who want to stop using
marijuana and other mind-altering chemicals. It publishes
guidelines for starting new groups.

Narcotics Anonymous

P.O. Box 999
Van Nuys, CA 91409
(818) 780-3951

The largest of the Twelve Step self-help groups that deal with drug
abuse, Narcotics Anonymous has over 900 chapters around the
world. It offers a monthly magazine, a pen pal and telephone
network, audiotapes, and literature.

Pill Addicts Anonymous

P.O. Box 278
Reading, PA 19603
(215) 372-1128

This support group helps people who are seeking freedom from pills
and other drugs. In addition to helping people start local groups, it
offers a network of pen pals.

Potsmokers Anonymous

316 East Third Avenue
New York, NY 10009
(212) 254-1777

This nine-week program is for people who want to give up
marijuana. It is not based on the Twelve Steps of Alcoholics
Anonymous (A.A.) but is a class instead. People who attend weekly
sessions are given homework. There is a charge for this program.

Hotlines

Just Say No Kids Club
(800) 258-2766; (415) 939-6666 in California

This hotline helps kids age 7 to 14 start anti-drug clubs in their neighborhoods. The phone is answered from 8:30 A.M. until 4:30 P.M. Pacific Time.

National Cocaine Hotline
(800) COC-AINE (262-2463)

This 24-hour hotline provides answers about the health risks to users of cocaine and provides referrals to drug treatment centers.

National Parents' Resource Institute for Drug Education (PRIDE)
(800) 241-7946; (404) 658-2548 in Georgia

In addition to providing information on drug-related issues, this crisis line answers legal questions about drug and alcohol abuse. If they cannot answer a question, they will try to refer you to an organization that can. Their hours are from 8:30 A.M. until 5:30 P.M. Eastern Standard Time.

NIDA Hotline
(800) 662-HELP (622-4357)

The primary focus of the National Institute on Drug Abuse (NIDA) Hotline is to provide information about drug use in general and about intravenous drug use and AIDS. The hours are from 9:00 A.M. to 3:00 P.M. Eastern Standard Time on weekdays and from midnight until 3:00 A.M. on weekends.

Target Resource Center
(800) 366-6667

School programs, publications, videotapes, and referrals for both alcohol and drug abuse are the focus of this hotline, which is a service of the National Federation of State High School Associations. Their hours are 8:00 A.M. to 4:30 P.M. Central Time.

CHAPTER 4

Tobacco: Going Up in Smoke

Sarah smoked one more cigarette before she went to bed that night. The next day, she didn't smoke at brunch break as she usually did. By lunch time she really wanted a cigarette so she walked across the street from the school and smoked her second-to-last one. She saved the last for after school.

She walked home with Michelle and another girl, Shawna Rains. "Can I bum a cigarette off you?" Shawna asked.

"Sorry, this is my last one," said Sarah. She stopped to light it.

"Oh, okay. I've gotta get some anyway."

When they got to the Mini Market, Shawna bought cigarettes. Sarah stocked up on chewing gum.

"No cigarettes?" Shawna asked.

"Um, no. I've got some at home." It wasn't true, but she didn't want to tell anyone besides Danny and Michelle that she was trying to quit. That way, if she wasn't successful at it, she wouldn't have to explain it to a lot of people.

Danny's Dilemma by Christine DeVault and Bryan Strong (Santa Cruz, CA: ETR Associates, 1987), 21.

Tobacco, or nicotine, addiction, especially in the form of smoking, is one of the most prevalent chemical dependencies in the United States today, and, as Sarah found, it is also one of the most difficult to kick. In addition, it is one of the most deadly. According to the surgeon general tobacco is currently responsible for one out of every six U.S. deaths. In fact, this habit is the single most important preventable cause of death in this country today.

Facts about Smoking

- Smoking takes 7 years off the average smoker's life, according to the American Cancer Society.
- Each year cigarette smoking kills almost 400,000 Americans. Of these deaths, 136,000 die from cancer, 115,000 from heart disease, 60,000 from chronic lung disease, 27,000 from stroke, and the rest from other smoking-related diseases.
- Twenty-five percent of all smokers will die from smoking-related illness.
- Smoking is responsible for $22 billion in medical costs every year.
- A 2-pack-a-day smoker spends from 3 to 4 hours smoking every day and takes in as many as 1,000 milligrams of tar.
- Of all U.S. farm crops, tobacco ranks sixth as a source of income to farmers.
- In 1985 Americans spent over $30 billion to buy cigarettes.
- In 1987, 575 billion cigarettes were sold in the United States.
- Nine out of 10 smokers say they want to quit.

Tobacco History

The practice of tobacco use goes back very far in time. Archaeologists have found ancient Mayan stone carvings more than 2,500 years old that show people using tobacco. The habit did not spread, however, until early explorers of the Western Hemisphere observed indigenous peoples smoking and brought tobacco leaves back to Europe. There smoking spread quickly. Tobacco was expensive, sometimes worth its weight in silver, and there are stories of rich people spending fortunes on it and poor people buying tobacco leaves instead of food.

By World War I, smoking had become so acceptable to people living in the United States that cigarettes were handed out to soldiers along with their food as part of their rations. After World War II, tobacco companies began huge advertising campaigns designed to convince women and young people to smoke. By 1967 the industry was spending $250 million dollars annually on advertising.

Smoking was declared a health hazard by the U.S. surgeon general in 1964, and in 1970 the Congress passed a law banning cigarette advertising on television. In 1985 tobacco companies were required by law to print health warnings on cigarette packages. Since that time, cigarette smoking has declined, but even so, it continues to be a problem today.

According to a 1989 American Cancer Society report, an esti- mated 49 million people in this country over the age of 18, or 29 percent of the U.S. population, still smoke. And those who do smoke are smoking more than ever before. Sales of tobacco products in the United States have more than doubled since the 1960s. The average smoker goes through 1 pack, or 20 cigarettes, each day.

Forms of Tobacco Use

Tobacco is used in several forms: wet and dry snuff, chewing tobacco, cigarettes, pipes, and cigars. Dry snuff is made from tobacco leaves that have been ground into powder. When users sniff this powder, nicotine is absorbed through the mucous lining of the nose. Even though during several periods in history snuff has been popular in European countries, its use never caught on to any extent in the United States. Wet snuff, which is held between the cheek and gum, is a more common form of snuff.

Chewing tobacco, although used like wet snuff, is finer and is made by soaking finely shredded tobacco leaves in molasses. When this tobacco is "chewed," or held between the cheek and gum, nicotine is absorbed into the body through the mucous membranes of the mouth. Users do not swallow either the tobacco or the juice. Although chewing tobacco has declined in popularity in this country over the past 100 years, it is making a comeback today because of anti-smoking laws and aggressive advertising campaigns mounted by the tobacco companies.

People who smoke tobacco do so in the form of cigarettes, cigars, or pipes. Most tobacco users today smoke cigarettes, inhaling the smoke, unlike cigar or pipe smokers, who usually do not inhale. When cigarettes were first brought to this country by tourists from England before the Civil War, they soon replaced snuff and chewing tobacco in popularity because cigarette smokers absorb the most nicotine and absorb it the quickest.

Nicotine: An Addictive Drug

For years it was believed that tobacco was not addictive because when people use it they do not act as though they are intoxicated. Today, however, it is known that tobacco, especially when it is smoked, is extremely addictive. Nicotine is the colorless chemical that accounts for tobacco's addictive properties. It is so powerful that in one study drug users who were given an intravenous dose of nicotine thought it was cocaine. The surgeon general has declared that nicotine is an addicting drug just the same as heroin and cocaine.

The average U.S. cigarette contains 10 milligrams of nicotine. Nicotine is a poison. In fact, its only commercial use is for insecticides. An overdose of this toxin—60 milligrams taken into the body at one time—can send a person into convulsions and eventually death. Because smokers and those who chew tobacco take in the nicotine slowly, they do not overdose; they kill themselves a little at a time.

Nicotine's poisonous qualities are felt acutely the first few times a person tries cigarettes. Dizziness, faintness, clammy skin, and nausea are all side effects that wear off after tolerance is built up. As far as researchers have been able to find out, that tolerance, once it is established, lasts over a lifetime. An ex-smoker who takes only one or two puffs on a cigarette becomes easily hooked again and must go through the struggle of stopping smoking.

When it is absorbed into the body through the lungs or mucous membranes, nicotine speeds up breathing and the heartbeat. The blood vessels get smaller, raising blood pressure, and the heart must work harder to circulate blood through the body. Whether people smoke, chew, or sniff tobacco, it raises blood sugar levels and thereby decreases appetite. (When people stop smoking they often eat more and gain weight.) Smoking and chewing further affect appetite by making the taste buds less sensitive.

Nicotine starts working on the brain within seven seconds after a smoker takes a puff. It can act both as a depressant and as a stimulant on a user's nervous system, depending on how much is used. When people smoke, they act more alert because the drug stimulates the cerebral cortex. It also stimulates the adrenal glands to produce and release adrenaline, a hormone that causes further alertness. The more nicotine a user takes into his or her body, however, the more it tends to act as a depressant. In addition to nicotine, tobacco smoke contains acetaldehyde, a sedative chemical. This is the first substance the body makes as it metabolizes alcohol.

Smokers report that lighting up gives them pleasurable feelings, improves their memory, and helps them be more attentive as well as relaxes them. This last effect may be partially due to the fact that smokers tend to get nervous when their bodies are low on nicotine and taking in more of this drug relieves the withdrawal anxiety. Nicotine depresses muscle tone and, for many smokers, serves as a crutch to help them deal with life's stresses.

The altered mood that nicotine provides serves as a powerful reinforcer for the smoking habit. Each puff gives the smoker an almost instant burst of nicotine in his or her system with the speed of harder drugs. Given that the average cigarette requires about 10 puffs to smoke, a smoker who has a pack-a-day habit will have this mood-altering sensation reinforced about 70,000 times a year.

Like other addictive substances, nicotine causes users to have an increased tolerance for the unpleasant side effects new smokers experience as well as for the mood-altering effects. It is easier to increase the number of cigarettes a smoker lights up in a day than it is to cut back. Nicotine levels drop about 45 minutes after the smoker has finished a cigarette and the urge for more nicotine begins.

When users give up tobacco, they go through withdrawal. Symptoms of nicotine withdrawal include a craving for tobacco, restlessness, anxiety, problems with concentration, and appetite changes. In a study of people in treatment for other forms of chemical dependency, more than half of the subjects who smoked reported that quitting smoking would be harder than giving up alcohol or the other drugs they had become dependent upon.

Health Risks of Smoking

When a smoker lights up, nicotine is not the only thing he or she inhales. Cigarette smoke contains over 1,000 different gasses and vapors. Carbon monoxide is one of them. This gas cuts down on the blood's ability to carry oxygen. Other chemicals in cigarettes are cadmium, a metal that stays in the lungs and negatively affects the immune system; hydrogen cyanide, the gas used in gas chambers; and benzene, a solvent banned in paint thinners because it is so dangerous.

Eight percent of cigarette smoke is made up of tiny particles. When these particles, called tars, are collected in a filter or in the lungs, they appear brown and sticky. Tars contain over 4,000 different chemicals. Some of them are carcinogens, chemicals that either by themselves or in combination are known to cause cancer.

The short-term health consequences of smoking include coughing, which is triggered by irritation of the smoker's throat and lungs by the chemicals in the smoke he or she inhales. Smoker's cough, which happens when a smoker first wakes up, is caused by the paralyzing action of smoke on the cilia, tiny hairlike formations that sweep the air passages in the body free of pollution. When a smoker sleeps these cilia begin their cleaning action again, and in the morning, coughing brings up the results of their efforts.

Other almost immediate results of smoking include a low resistance to disease. This lowered resistance happens for two reasons. First, the paralyzed cilia cannot sweep out viruses and germs, so both organisms have more of a chance to breed in the lungs and cause upper respiratory infections. Second, smoking lowers the immune system's ability to respond to germs by fighting them. According to the U.S. Department of Health, smoking is responsible for 145 million days spent ill in bed and 81 million days missed from work each year.

Diminished lung volume caused by smoking means that those who smoke get less oxygen in their bloodstreams. They may experience shortness of breath and are more easily fatigued than nonsmokers. This effect combined with the decrease in muscle tone that smoking causes makes smokers less than physically fit. The more a person smokes, the more difficult it becomes to exercise. Long-term risks of smoking include lung and other cancers, emphysema, heart disease, and stroke.

LUNG AND OTHER CANCERS

Ninety percent of all lung cancer and 30 percent of all other cancers are directly related to smoking. In people over 35 years old, the chances of getting lung cancer are 22 times higher for male smokers and 12 times higher for female smokers than they are for people who have never smoked.

Not only are smokers at higher risk for lung cancer, but they are also susceptible to other cigarette-caused cancers, including cancers of the mouth, larynx, esophagus, bladder, kidney, and pancreas.

EMPHYSEMA

Most cases of emphysema, a chronic disease that obstructs the breathing passages, are caused by smoking. More than 2 million Americans suffer from emphysema, and about one-quarter of them are so affected that they cannot work or live by themselves.

HEART DISEASE AND STROKE

Smoking affects the heart and circulatory system by increasing blood clotting, speeding up the heart rate, shrinking the blood vessels, raising blood pressure, and irritating the electrical conducting system that signals the heart when to beat. Smokers die twice as often as nonsmokers from strokes and heart attacks.

OTHER HEALTH PROBLEMS

On top of the health problems listed above, smokers are at higher risk for stomach ulcers. They also have higher rates of gum disease than do nonsmokers. In addition, smokers face higher risk for being injured or dying in house fires. As many as 39 percent of all house fires are caused by careless cigarette smoking.

Health Risks of Smokeless Tobacco

About 12 million tobacco addicts in this country use smokeless tobacco—either dipping snuff or chewing tobacco. It is the most rapidly growing form of nicotine addiction among both adults and young children. Most people who use smokeless tobacco are men between 18 and 24 years old. Many of them began using it as early as grade school. Close to 1.7 million teenage boys have used some type of smokeless tobacco according to the American Cancer Society. Some boys chew tobacco or dip snuff because of peer pressure. Others see athletes they admire chewing tobacco and want to imitate them. Still others believe smoke-free tobacco is also risk-free. This belief is a myth.

Besides nicotine, smokeless tobacco contains ten times more nitrosamines, a cancer-causing substance, than do cigarettes. Because the nicotine and the nitrosamines are absorbed by the lining of the mouth and nose, chewing tobacco and snuff cause sores called leukoplakia, which may eventually lead to cancer. Tooth decay and tooth wear are other problems associated with smokeless tobacco.

Teenagers and Tobacco

More than 3,000 teenagers begin smoking each day, adding up to over 1 million every year. Smoking is on the increase for teenage girls;

more of them smoke than do boys. Today 20 percent of all high school–age girls and 16 percent of boys smoke. Research shows that the earlier a person starts smoking, the more difficult it is to deal with a nicotine addiction later in life when he or she decides to kick the habit.

According to experts who have studied smoking patterns, teenagers get hooked on nicotine in three stages, and it is important to know that they do not start out wanting to be hooked. First they experiment just to see what smoking is like. Seven out of 10 children have tried a cigarette. Many of them test out tobacco in grade school. Next teens begin smoking only occasionally—either on dates, at parties, or when they are around people who smoke. Finally some of them become confirmed smokers. This last stage is usually reached by the time a person is in his or her 20s.

Whether or not a teenager smokes is influenced by his or her parents' smoking. Three-quarters of all teenage smokers have parents who smoke. The decision to smoke or not is also influenced by peer pressure and advertising.

Women and Smoking

The good news about women and smoking is that fewer women than men smoke in the United States today: 27 percent of women as opposed to 32 percent of men. The bad news is that women seem to have a harder time quitting. Since 1965, when the harmful consequences of smoking began to be public knowledge, women have been able to decrease their percentage of smokers by only 5 percent. Male smoking, at the same time, dropped by 18 percent. As women continue to smoke, their rates of chronic lung disease have soared, increasing 2 to 3 times over what they were in the 1960s. Today more women die from lung cancer than from breast cancer.

Women also have some special health issues regarding addiction to cigarettes. If a woman takes oral contraceptives (birth control pills) and smokes, she is at a five times greater risk of having a heart attack than is a nonsmoking woman who takes the pill. The risks of blood clots and strokes are higher for these women as well.

Even if a woman is not taking oral contraceptives, she faces risks. The rate of cancer of the cervix is higher for smokers than it is for nonsmokers. Elderly women who have smoked have a greater chance of getting osteoporosis, a weakening of the bones. Another consequence of smoking that becomes evident with age is that smokers have more and deeper facial wrinkles than do nonsmokers.

Women who smoke sometimes have a difficult time getting pregnant, and when they do they put their unborn babies at risk if they continue to smoke during pregnancy. Both nicotine and carbon monoxide travel from the pregnant woman's blood to the baby. Risks of miscarriage and stillbirth are higher for smoking pregnant women, as is the risk of a premature birth.

Babies born to women who smoke do not weigh as much as those born to women who do not smoke. These babies also are more prone to develop health problems. Recent research has uncovered that many babies who die of sudden infant death syndrome (SIDS) had mothers who smoked during pregnancy.

Passive Smoking

People who do not smoke but who live or work around those who do incur health risks, as well. The damage done to passive smokers depends on the amount of second-hand smoke they breathe and on how long they are exposed to it. Sidestream smoke, which is given off when a smoker puts a cigarette down between puffs, contains more carbon monoxide than does mainstream smoke inhaled directly from the end of a cigarette. Because sidestream smoke is produced by tobacco burning at lower temperatures, it also contains more byproducts, including carcinogens. Environmental smoke, the smoke that drifts through smoke-filled rooms, is made up of about 85 percent sidestream smoke.

When people with bronchitis, asthma, or allergies are exposed to smoke, they often find their symptoms getting worse. Babies and children who live with parents who smoke catch upper respiratory infections such as colds twice as often as do those who live in a smoke-free environment. According to the U. S. Department of Health, 40 percent of smokers live with babies, thereby exposing these babies to the hazards of passive smoke.

The federal government does not allow people to smoke in its buildings. Most states and many cities and towns have made it illegal for smokers to light up in restaurants and other facilities open to the public. Many businesses are banning smoking by employees as well. Smoking is also banned on many airline flights. It is likely that in the future smokers will find more and more restrictions on smoking in public.

The Group Against Smoker's Pollution (G.A.S.P.), an activist organization trying to defend nonsmokers from the hazards of passive smoke, has come up with a bill of rights for nonsmokers. These rights include

1. The right to breathe clean air
2. The right to speak out, voicing objection when smokers light up without permission
3. The right to act to discourage smoking in public places through social pressure and legislation

Quitting

Because nicotine is so addictive, stopping cigarette smoking can be a very difficult thing to do. According to one study reported by the U.S. Department of Health and Human Services, one year after quitting cigarettes only one-quarter of all those who had tried were still smoke-free. This is the same relapse rate for heroin addiction. Alcoholics have a greater chance of staying on the wagon (35 percent) than do smokers of staying clean of nicotine.

Despite the difficulty of quitting, doing it is well worth the effort. When a smoker stops, his or her body immediately begins repairing itself. According to the American Cancer Society, after 10 years of not smoking an ex-smoker's risk for heart attack is about the same as it is for a person who never smoked. After 15 years, an ex-smoker's risk for lung cancer drops until it is close to the rates for people who never smoked.

In addition to decreased risks for health problems, people who quit smoking experience an energy boost, smell more appealing to others, and find that food tastes better.

The American Cancer Society reports that every year 17 million smokers try to quit. The vast majority of smokers who give up cigarettes do it on their own. They may go "cold turkey" (quit completely all at once) or slowly cut back on the number of cigarettes they smoke each day until they stop entirely. When smokers decide to get serious about quitting, a number of helps are available for them. Some of the most common aids for stopping smoking are smoking cessation programs, aversion therapy, nicotine gum, and hypnosis.

Smoking cessation programs, many of which are offered free or at inexpensive rates by groups such as the American Cancer Society and by hospitals, use education and positive peer support to help people kick the smoking habit.

Aversion therapy conditions smokers to associate negative feelings with lighting up. In these programs, smokers may receive a mild electric shock when they inhale or they may be forced to smoke so much at one time that they become ill.

Nicotine gum, which is obtained with a doctor's prescription, is a way for smokers to ease their physical withdrawal pangs while breaking their smoking rituals—lighting up, holding a cigarette, and inhaling. The reason this gum is used only under a doctor's supervision is that some former smokers have become addicted to it. People who are more physically than psychologically addicted to nicotine, such as people who need a cigarette first thing in the morning, have the highest success rates with the gum.

Hypnosis and subliminal suggestion, either from a hypnotist or from tapes, can reinforce motivation to quit smoking. Researchers are currently divided on whether these two techniques work on a long-term basis.

REFERENCES

Berger, Gilda. *Smoking Not Allowed: The Debate.* New York: Franklin Watts, 1987.

Cocores, James A. *The Clinical Management of Nicotine Dependence.* New York: Springer-Verlag, 1991.

Crowther, Richard L. *The Paradox of Smoking.* Denver, CO: Directions Publishers, 1983.

Facts on Lung Cancer. Atlanta, GA: American Cancer Society, 1987.

Ferguson, Tom. *The Smoker's Book of Health: How To Keep Yourself Healthier and Reduce Your Smoking Risks.* New York: G. P. Putnam's Sons, 1987.

The Most Asked Questions about Smoking, Tobacco, and Health and . . . the Answers. Atlanta, GA: American Cancer Society, 1982.

Smoking Tobacco & Health: A Fact Book. Washington, DC: U.S. Department of Health and Human Services, 1989.

Stimmel, Barry. *The Facts about Drug Use: Coping with Drugs and Alcohol in Your Family, at Work, in Your Community.* New York: Consumer Reports Books, 1991.

Yoder, Barbara. *The Recovery Resource Book.* New York: Fireside Books, 1991.

Resources
for Finding Out about Tobacco

Fiction

DeVault, Christine, and Bryan Strong. **Danny's Dilemma.** Santa Cruz, CA: ETR Associates, 1987. 84p. (For more information about other related materials, call 1-800-321-4407.)

Danny, a high school athlete, knows that smoking is bad for him, but he wants to be cool. The readers decide what he will choose in this interactive novel. Then they get to read about the consequences of his choices.

Nonfiction

BOOKS

Arkava, Morton, and John E. Russell. **Coping with Smoking.** New York: Rosen Publishing Group, 1985. 132p.

Arkava, a professor of social work at the University of Montana, and Russell, a technical writer, cover a history of tobacco use and the motivation people have when they begin to smoke. One chapter addresses options for smokers and, for those who want to stop, several chapters provide quitting techniques ranging from behavior modification to aversive methods and stress reduction techniques. Of special interest are sections of the book on how to assert your rights around nonsmokers. A resource list is included.

Berger, Gilda. **Smoking Not Allowed.** New York: Franklin Watts, 1987. 144p.

Even though the trend is toward banning smoking in public places, smokers complain that they have rights, too. This book examines the response to smoking bans enacted by governments and employers as well as the push to make smoking illegal and stop all tobacco advertising in response to studies on the effects of passive smoke.

Burton, Dee. **The American Cancer Society's "Fresh Start" 21 Days To Stop Smoking.** New York: Pocket Books, 1986. 159p.

If you are looking for a book to provide practical suggestions on how to quit smoking and stay smoke-free, this is it. The focus is on the first three weeks of tobacco abstinence, and daily checklists are provided.

Casey, Karen. **If Only I Could Quit: Recovering from Nicotine Addiction.** Center City, MN: Hazelden Educational Materials, 1987. 320p.

Twenty-four recovering smokers share their experiences in this book, which contains 90 meditations and a how-to-quit program based on the Twelve Steps. The book offers advice on how to break the tobacco habit and stay smoke-free. It is for people who are desperate to quit as well as for those who have tried and failed.

Keyishian, Elizabeth. **Everything You Need To Know about Smoking.** New York: Rosen Publishing Group, 1989. 64p.

People begin smoking because they think it is cool and often because they are pressured by peers and tobacco company advertising. Written at fourth- through sixth-grade reading level, this book helps teens make certain they make their own decisions about smoking. In addition it discusses why people begin smoking, the health risks involved with the habit, and how to quit smoking. Resources are listed to help teens who want to stop smoking.

Rogers, Jacqueline. **You Can Stop Smoking.** New York: Pocket Books, 1987. 286p.

A smoker for over 20 years, Jacqueline Rogers, the founder of SmokeEnders, knows what she is talking about when she says it can be tough to quit. This book explores the excuses smokers use to continue smoking and the nature of the addiction process. Rogers shares her own experiences with smoking and quitting to help readers change their own attitudes.

PAMPHLETS

Chew or Snuff Is Real Bad Stuff. Bethesda, MD: National Cancer Institute. 8p.

This booklet talks about the dangers of smokeless tobacco, focusing on cancer and other oral problems, heart effects, and blood pressure changes.

Cigarettes! Eriko and Nate Talk to Teens. Santa Cruz, CA: Network Publications, 1990. 7p.

The facts and the dangers of cigarette smoking are detailed in this pamphlet written in the words of two teens who talk about a friend who is a smoker. Included are reasons not to start smoking and ideas on how to stop.

Engleman, Jeanne. **Breathing Easy.** Center City, MN: Hazelden Educational Materials, 1990. 40p.

This is a collection of 40-page booklets that provide very practical techniques for stopping smoking. The titles include *Disarming Triggers, Managing Stress, Overcoming Cravings,* and *Staying Quit.*

Facts on Lung Cancer. Atlanta, GA: American Cancer Society, 1987. 12p.

Explaining the causes of lung cancer as well as the tests and treatments for it, this pamphlet provides a good introduction to one of the most frightening consequences of smoking.

Freedom from Smoking for You and Your Family. New York: American Lung Association, 1987. 56p.

This booklet offers practical strategies for anyone who wants to stop smoking. It covers issues such as weight control and how to avoid nicotine relapses.

How To Stop Smoking. Deerfield, MA: Channing L. Bete Co., 1987. 16p.

This booklet gives readers several ideas about how to quit smoking and how to stay off nicotine.

Making a Choice about Smoking. Deerfield, MA: Channing L. Bete Co., 1986. 16p.

Smoking's health risks and other drawbacks are presented in this cartoon booklet, which was written especially for teens.

The Most Often Asked Questions about Smoking, Tobacco, and Health and . . . the Answers. Atlanta, GA: American Cancer Society, 1982. 22p.

This easy-to-read booklet covers the basics about smoking.

Smokeless Tobacco: Check It Out, Think It Out, Take It Out, Throw It Out, Snuff It Out, Keep It Out. Atlanta, GA: American Cancer Society, 1991. 20p.

This how-to workbook helps people who use smokeless tobacco to kick that habit. It includes exercises, suggestions, and affirmations.

Smokeless Tobacco! Yolanda and Mark Talk to Teens. Santa Cruz, CA: Network Publications, 1990. 7p.

Chewing tobacco is just as dangerous as the kind that is smoked. The risks of this habit and the advantages of quitting are discussed in addition to suggestions about how to quit.

Smoking, Tobacco & Health: A Fact Book. Washington, DC: U.S. Department of Health and Human Services, 1989. 41p.

In addition to discussing the risks and health consequences of smoking, this booklet also explains the economics of the tobacco industry—all the way from farmers to manufacturers.

Nonprint Materials

The American Cancer Society's "Freshstart" 21 Days To Stop Smoking

Type:	VHS video
Length:	75 min.
Cost:	Purchase $9.95
Distributor:	Network Publications
	P.O. Box 1830
	Santa Cruz, CA 95061-1830
Date:	1986

This one-day-at-a-time program has helped many people to stop smoking through its guidance, counseling, and encouragement. It is hosted by comedian Robert Klein.

The Big Dipper

Type:	16mm film, VHS video
Length:	19 min.
Cost:	Purchase $375 (film), $195 (video)
Distributor:	The Health Connection
	12501 Old Columbia Pike
	Silver Spring, MD 20904-6600
Date:	1986

Music, clips from TV commercials, and narration by teenagers make this film about smokeless tobacco especially interesting.

Breathing Easy

Type:	16mm film, VHS video
Length:	30 min.
Cost:	Rental $75, purchase $520 (film); rental $75, purchase $250 (video)
Distributor:	Coronet/MTI Film and Video
	108 Wilmot Road
	Deerfield, IL 60015
Date:	1984

Breathing Easy features LeVar Burton, Mark Harmon, and Joan Van Ark in an upbeat format that demolishes the myth that smoking is cool. Self-identity, goal setting, values clarification, and decision making are all covered in this award-winning video.

Death in the West

Type:	VHS video
Length:	32 min.
Cost:	Purchase $99
Distributor:	Network Publications
	P.O. Box 1830
	Santa Cruz, CA 95061-1830
Date:	1976

This documentary takes a look at the image of the Marlboro man and contrasts it to the agony of six real cowboys who are battling lung cancer and emphysema caused by smoking. This technique points up the deception in tobacco advertising. A curriculum guide is also available for $8.

Dirty Business

Type:	VHS video
Length:	24 min.
Cost:	Purchase $99.95
Distributor:	Network Publications
	P.O. Box 1830
	Santa Cruz, CA 95061-1830
Date:	1988

This video, a tribute to a friend who died of lung cancer, provides an anti-smoking message in the form of award-winning commercials. The dangers and the consequences of smoking are both covered. This video is recommended by *Booklist* and *School Library Journal*.

The Feminine Mistake

Type:	16mm film, VHS video
Length:	25 min.
Cost:	Purchase $525 (film), $325 (video)
Distributor:	The Health Connection
	12501 Old Columbia Pike
	Silver Spring, MD 20904-6600
Date:	1989

Because tobacco companies are targeting women as potential consumers, it is important for young women to know both the facts about these ad campaigns and the harmful effects of smoking.

Fire without Smoke

Type:	VHS video
Length:	15 min.
Cost:	Purchase $29.95
Distributor:	Network Publications
	P.O. Box 1830
	Santa Cruz, CA 95061-1830
Date:	1983

This video provides information on the history of smokeless tobacco and on how its use is currently on the upswing. Developed by the School of Public Health at Loma Linda University, the program explains the health problems associated with this form of tobacco and talks about why some teenagers are tempted to use it.

Growing Up in Smoke

Type:	16mm film, VHS video
Length:	15 min.
Cost:	Rental $50, purchase $290 (film); rental $50, purchase $250 (video)
Distributor:	Coronet/MTI Film and Video
	108 Wilmot Road
	Deerfield, IL 60015
Date:	1984

The central theme of this film is the deceptive tactics the tobacco industry uses to convince young people to smoke. These tactics include free samples, posters, t-shirts, and movie theater ads. A sound analysis is presented of the profits to be gained by the tobacco companies if they convince teens to smoke.

No Butts

Type:	VHS video
Length:	30 min.

Cost:	Rental $75, purchase $80
Distributor:	Coronet/MTI Film and Video
	108 Wilmot Road
	Deerfield, IL 60015
Date:	1987

Featuring the anti-smoking commercial Yul Brynner made right before he died, this program discusses the pleasures behind smoking and presents hard-hitting evidence of the perils. There is a segment on smoking by pregnant women and one in which Mary Tyler Moore tells of her struggle to give up the habit.

Showdown on Tobacco Road

Type:	VHS video
Length:	57 min.
Cost:	Purchase $149.95
Distributor:	Network Publications
	P.O. Box 1830
	Santa Cruz, CA 95061-1830
Date:	1987

Smokers' versus nonsmokers' rights is the focus of this video, which includes opinions on all sides of the question. Interviews with experts and Hollywood film footage provide a history of smoking in the United States over the past 100 years.

Smoke Screens: Cigarettes and Advertising

Type:	VHS video
Length:	15 min.
Cost:	Purchase $280
Distributor:	New Dimension Media
	85803 Lorane Highway
	Eugene, OR 97405
Date:	1991

Teenagers have an easier time not starting smoking when they understand the tricks of the advertising trade used to convince them that smoking is the "in" thing to do. This video provides critical thinking ammunition that makes it easier to say no to tobacco and mean it.

Smokeless Tobacco: It Can Snuff You Out

Type:	16mm film, VHS video
Length:	22 min.
Cost:	Rental $50, purchase $295 (film); rental $50, purchase $265 (video)

Distributor: Alfred Higgins Productions, Inc.
                 6350 Laurel Canyon Boulevard
                 North Hollywood, CA 91606
Date: 1986

Many adolescents believe they can avoid the perils of cigarettes by using smokeless tobacco, also called chew or snuff. This film counters that myth by presenting the dangers of smokeless tobacco, and it discusses the advertising campaigns that tobacco companies design to encourage teens to use their products.

Smokeless Tobacco: The Sean Marsee Story
Type: 16mm film, VHS video
Length: 16 min.
Cost: Rental $75, purchase $420 (film); rental $75,
              purchase $315 (video)
Distributor: Coronet/MTI Film and Video
              108 Wilmot Road
              Deerfield, IL 60015
Date: 1986

Sean Marsee was a high school track star who was a habitual user of snuff and died of oral cancer when he was 19. The film dramatizes his story and includes an interview with a mouth and throat specialist who talks about the signs of oral cancer. Johnnie Johnson of the Los Angeles Rams football team also talks about athletes and smokeless tobacco.

Smoking: The Choice Is Yours
Type: 16mm film, VHS video
Length: 11 min.
Cost: Rental $75, purchase $290 (film); rental $75,
              purchase $220 (video)
Distributor: Coronet/MTI Film and Video
              108 Wilmot Road
              Deerfield, IL 60015
Date: 1981

The dangers of smoking are covered in this program as are the reasons smokers begin their habit. Humor makes this video especially appealing. It was produced by Disney Educational Products.

Smoking: It's Your Choice
Type: 16mm film, VHS video
Length: 17 min.

Cost: Rental $60, purchase $395 (film); rental $60,
                 purchase $355 (video)
Distributor: Alfred Higgins Productions, Inc.
                 6350 Laurel Canyon Boulevard
                 North Hollywood, CA 91606
Date: 1989

This film presents smoking facts so teenagers can make a wise
decision. Coverage includes information about the addictive nature
of smoking and its consequences to the respiratory system. Helpful
hints are also presented about how to deal with peer pressure.

Smoking: Personal Pollution
Type: 16mm film, VHS video
Length: 18 min.
Cost: Purchase $340 (film), $290 (video)
Distributor: Perennial Education
                 930 Pitner Avenue
                 Evanston, IL 60202
Date: 1980

This film asks teenagers to take a serious look at the reasons they
smoke. It also shows the consequences of smoking, not only on the
lungs but on blood pressure and the circulatory system as well.

Tobacco and Human Physiology
Type: 16mm film, VHS video
Length: 21 min.
Cost: Purchase $475 (film), $380 (video)
Distributor: The Health Connection
                 12501 Old Columbia Pike
                 Silver Spring, MD 20904-6600
Date: 1986

A doctor explains the physical damage tobacco causes to the human
body. The effects of smoking on unborn children are covered, as are
the effects of using chewing tobacco.

Up in Smoke: How Smoking Affects Your Health
Type: VHS video
Length: 38 min.
Cost: Purchase $209
Distributor: Guidance Associates
                 P.O. Box 1000
                 Mount Kisco, NY 10549-0010
Date: 1982

This video not only takes a look at why people smoke and the damage it does to their bodies, but it also examines how difficult it is to quit smoking.

You Don't Have To Smoke To Be Cool: Peer Pressure and Smoking

Type: VHS video
Length: 30 min.
Cost: Purchase $209
Distributor: Guidance Associates
P.O. Box 1000
Mount Kisco, NY 10549-0010
Date: 1990

Dramatizations, statistics, and interviews are all combined to make this video an interesting way to separate the facts about smoking from the myths. Included are tips about how to quit smoking and suggestions about where to go for help.

Organizations

American Cancer Society
4 West 35th Street
New York, NY 10001
(800) ACS-2345 (227-2345)

The American Cancer Society provides information and classes that help people stop smoking.

American Heart Association
7320 Greenville Avenue
Dallas, TX 75231
(214) 750-5300

The American Heart Association provides facts, statistics, and other information about how smoking is related to heart disease.

American Lung Association
Box 598
New York, NY 10001
(212) 315-8700

This group publishes information about smoking and lung disease. They also publish how-to-stop-smoking guides and videotapes.

Emphysema Anonymous

7976 Seminole Boulevard, Suite 6
Seminole, FL 33542
(813) 391-9977

Emphysema Anonymous is a self-help support group for people
with this disease and people with chronic bronchitis. Membership is
free. The group holds meetings and publishes both pamphlets and a
newsletter.

National Cancer Institute

U.S. Department of Health and Human Services
Building 31, Room 10A24
Bethesda, MD 20892

The National Cancer Institute is a research organization that
publishes the results of studies that link smoking to cancer.

Nic-Anon

511 Sir Francis Drake Boulevard, C-170
Greenbrae, CA 94904

Nic-Anon is a Twelve Step program for family members and friends
of people who smoke. At meetings members work on their own
codependency issues that revolve around being in a relationship
with a smoker. Although only a few chapters of this group exist at
present, they can provide information about how to start a chapter.

Office on Smoking and Health

Public Information Branch, Room 118
Park Building
5600 Fishers Lane
Rockville, MD 20857

This government agency, run by the Centers for Disease Control,
publishes the annual reports from the U.S. surgeon general as well as
other reports, pamphlets, and statistics.

Smokers Anonymous

2118 Greenwich Street
San Francisco, CA 94123
(415) 922-8575

Smokers Anonymous is a Twelve Step group for people who want to
quit smoking. It also publishes a newsletter. By calling the national
office in San Francisco, smokers can get referrals to meetings in their
area.

CHAPTER 5

Eating Disorders: The Battle with Body Image

When Kessa got to her room, she locked the door behind her. She wasn't going to have her mother barging in again. After taking off her robe, she lay down on the bed. Kessa always felt her cleanest and thinnest right after she had showered and tonight she felt especially good. True, she had been forced to eat dinner, but she had gotten rid of dinner. There was no food in her body. She was clean and pure and lean. Now for the test of how lean. Kessa ran her fingers over her stomach. Flat. But was it flat enough? Not quite. She still had some way to go. Just to be safe, she told herself. Still, it was nice the way her pelvic bones rose like sharp hills on either side of her stomach. I love bones. Bones are beautiful. She ran her hands up to her ribs and began to outline them carefully. One, two . . . the third was not sharp enough. There seemed to be a layer of tissue between her finger and the bone. There was no doubt about it. She still had a way to go. Kessa picked up her head and looked down at her breasts. Flatter, but still not flat enough. She lifted her left breast by the nipple and swayed it back and forth. Floppy, too floppy. She'd have to exercise more.

The Best Little Girl in the World by
Steven Levenkron (New York: Warner Books,
1978), 52–53.

Francesca demanded nothing less than perfection from herself. That meant being thin, and at 98 pounds this 5-foot-4 dance student still felt obese. Self-control became her weapon in her battle with hunger pangs as she starved herself until pound after pound fell away. She even changed her name to Kessa because it sounded thinner. Hating her body, she refused to eat. When her frantic parents sent her to see a psychiatrist, Francesca broke appointment after appointment and was finally hospitalized. It was only then that she could start to make peace with her weight and begin the long journey toward self-acceptance.

Francesca's jabbing hunger pangs, her obsession with not eating, her secret trips to the bathroom to vomit the meals her parents forced her to eat—all of this added up to the horrible ordeal of an eating disorder. Eating disorders are far too common today, especially among teenage women.

An estimated 1 out of 25 female college students suffers from anorexia, which is the refusal to eat, and as many as 15 percent are bulimic, which means they binge on food and then purge themselves by vomiting or taking laxatives. Some people have both of these conditions at the same time, so they alternate between gorging and starving. One set of researchers discovered that about half of their anorexic patients also periodically stuffed themselves with food, and over half of those who did used self-induced vomiting to avoid gaining weight (Clark, Parr, and Castelli, 232).

Although eating disorders are more prevalent among young women, they exist in the adult population as well. Both anorexia and bulimia usually begin before the age of 20, and the risk of succumbing to these two disorders decreases with age. Once these eating patterns begin, however, they may persist into midlife. Anorexia and bulimia are not limited only to women. Five percent of all people with eating disorders are male (*The Diagnostic and Statistical Manual III*, 66). Frequently males begin starving or binging and purging because of the rigid weight requirements for athletic events such as wrestling.

Compulsive eating, though it sometimes is not officially classified by the mental health community as an eating disorder but rather as an impulse control disorder, is a big problem in society today. A vicious cycle of eating, self-loathing, and eating even more to dull the emotional pain, compulsive eating leads to obesity, one of the major health problems in the United States.

It would be a mistake to assume that all anorexics and bulimics are underweight or that all compulsive eaters are grossly overweight. Eating problems are a matter of degree. Because of our culture's emphasis on how people look, many people with mild forms of eating disorders are never diagnosed.

An Obsession with Thinness

Eating disorders and compulsive eating, major disturbances in eating behavior, have been increasing in industrialized countries since the 1960s. At the same time, society's concern with weight has increased as well. Researchers studying the Miss America Pageant have discovered that over the years the winners have been getting thinner. Fashion models, too, have changed in shape over the past decades.

Overweight people are looked down upon in this nation today. In studies, when children are shown pictures of children with crutches, missing hands, in wheelchairs, with facial scars, and then a picture of an obese child, they consistently say they would least like to be friends with the child who is overweight. When asked why, they say that obesity is the child's fault.

This dislike and distrust of overweight people and tendency to blame them for their problem persists past adolescence. In one survey, college students judged overweight people as harshly as prostitutes and embezzlers. They said, too, that they would rather marry a cocaine user or a former mental patient than someone who weighed too much (Blinder, Chaitin, and Goldstein, 36).

As a result, many people, most of them women, are displeased with their weight or body size. Even though they may maintain a normal weight for their height, they remain convinced that they are fat. In the 1960s, studies of high school students revealed that 65–80 percent of them, even then, wanted to be more slender. Over half had dieted. From the 1960s to the 1970s the number of articles in women's magazines about how to lose weight doubled. In one study of college women, during the 12 months before they were questioned, nearly 30 percent of them had tried to lose weight by taking over-the-counter diet pills (Blinder, Chaitin, and Goldstein, 36). From fad diets to nearly nonstop exercising, U.S. society seems to sanction eating disorders, especially among young women.

Hooked on Food

It is obvious that compulsive eaters have a relationship to food that resembles an addiction. Less obvious is the fact that anorexics and bulimics are obsessed with thoughts of food even though they starve or purge themselves. Many anorexics insist on cooking elaborate, high-calorie meals, which they would not dream of eating themselves, for other people. Bulimics, too, often think about food, planning when they will have their next binge. Researchers have found that bulimics think about cooking or eating 38 percent of the time. People without eating disorders think about food only half that often (Blinder, Chaitin, and Goldstein, 308).

Mental health professionals are not certain exactly what causes eating disorders. The reasons two anorexics or compulsive eaters begin to starve or binge may be very different. The experts do know that anorexia, bulimia, and compulsive eating have nothing to do with hunger and little to do with food as a source of nutrition. People who suffer from these disorders use food as a way to either express or cover up emotions.

Anorexia

Anorexics constantly feel that their bodies are fat even though they may be severely underweight, so they restrict their intake of food—sometimes to the point of stopping eating entirely. Some anorexics who also suffer from bulimia take laxatives and diuretics or make themselves vomit what little food they do eat, believing that this will keep the calories from being absorbed into their bodies. They also may exercise excessively, trying to burn away fat they do not have. They literally can starve themselves to death unless they are treated.

According to the American Psychiatric Association, people who have anorexia

- Refuse to maintain body weight appropriate for their height and age (Their weight generally is at least 15 percent below the minimum for their height.)
- Are terrified of gaining weight
- Have a distorted body image, believing they are fat even when they are very much underweight (This fear does not go away, no matter how much weight they lose.)

Anorexics typically limit the refined carbohydrates and fats they eat as well as the protein. Instead they focus on fruits and vegetables in order to cut back on calories. Frequently they will only drink diet drinks. Anorexics cut what little food they allow themselves to eat into tiny pieces and push it around on their plates. They eat very slowly and chew for a very long time. Often they hide their food or throw it away.

Anorexia may start out as a concern about weighing too much or it may be triggered by stress. Sometimes the stress of adolescence, alone, is enough to trigger it. Many teenagers begin to feel that their lives and their bodies are out of control as they reach adolescence. If they have rigid and perfectionist parents or are perfectionists them-selves, the changes of adolescence can be especially frightening. Some of these teens decide to take control of the situation by setting weight goals and restricting the amount of food they will eat. As this need to control escalates, they eat less and less.

Psychologists also have found that most anorexics come from families who are overprotective and overly controlling. Family members are enmeshed, not respecting one another's emotional boundaries. Self-starvation may be, at least in part, the anorexic's declaration of emotional independence from the family unit.

Anorexia tends to run in families. Mothers and sisters of anorexics suffer from this eating disorder at a higher rate than the general population (*The Diagnostic and Statistical Manual III*, 66). Some researchers believe there may exist a genetic predisposition toward anorexia that is somehow tied to bipolar disorder, which is also called manic-depression. A higher number of anorexics have close relatives who suffer from manic-depression than do non-anorexics. At this point, researchers are still exploring the link, and no genetic cause-effect relationship has yet been proven (Pope and Hudson, 1857).

Because of society's fixation on thinness, for whatever reason, once an anorexic begins to lose weight, he or she is often compli-mented by friends, parents, and teachers or coaches. About one-third of all anorexics are slightly overweight to begin with, and this initial stamp of approval can be a powerful reinforcement to cut down even further on food intake.

PHYSICAL CONSEQUENCES OF ANOREXIA

Anorexia is a dangerous disease. In fact, over 15 percent of anorexics die from their self-imposed starvation (Sacker and Zimmer, 19). Many of the physical symptoms of anorexia are the body's response to starvation. To conserve energy and to stay alive, the bones stop growing and sometimes become fragile. The anorexic's blood pres-sure lowers, and the beating of the heart is affected by the electrolyte imbalance in the bloodstream caused by dehydration.

Starving shrinks the heart because it causes the heart to lose muscle mass and reduces the amount it can work during exer-cise. Sometimes the heart rate slows down. Many anorexics have irregular heartbeats. Other symptoms from starvation include ane-mia, light-headedness, fatigue, kidney problems, and even brain damage. Often these problems can become so severe they are life-threatening.

Another physical consequence of such severe calorie cutbacks is amenorrhea, the stopping of a woman's menstrual period. A big mystery about anorexia for researchers is that about one-third of all women with this eating disorder stop having their periods before they lose any weight (Clark, Parr, and Castelli, 231). Some psychologists who specialize in treating eating disorders believe that these women might develop anorexia because they have difficulty accepting their bodies. During treatment, when weight is regained, an anorexic's periods usually begin again. Young men are not immune to sexual consequences of anorexia. When they refuse to eat, their testosterone levels drop. Sex drive, the ability to have erections, and the size of the testicles all decrease as well.

Because of vitamin deficiencies, an anorexic's skin becomes dry and flaky. A condition called lanugo develops in which a light layer of hair grows over the cheeks and back. An anorexic's hair on her or his head may fall out. Vitamin deficiencies also cause hypercarotinemia, which is yellow-colored skin. Usually this begins on the palms of the hands and the soles of the feet. Although the yellowish skin tinge eventually goes away as the anorexic recovers, it can last for weeks or months.

The body's ability to regulate temperature is severely affected by anorexia. People with this eating disorder often feel cold and have to wear sweaters. Part of the reason they feel chilly is because the fat layer beneath the skin is what insulates the body. Anorexics also may experience hypothermia, in which their bodies are unable to adjust internal temperature in response to temperature changes in the external environment.

Constipation is frequently a problem for anorexics because of the small amounts of food they ingest. Because they typically cut down on carbohydrates to lose weight, there is little fiber in their intestinal tracts. Even though anorexics are not eating anything to eliminate, they may decide that they need to have regular bowel movements and strain when they attempt to do so, causing hemorrhoids and tears in the anus.

TREATMENT

Because anorexics really believe that they are fat and do not want to do anything that would cause them to gain even an ounce of weight, they resist seeking help on their own. Usually it is concerned friends, family members, or even school personnel who confront them about their problems and urge them to get treatment. Often anorexics must be hospitalized as a life-saving measure, sometimes being "force fed" through tubes in order to save their lives. Once an anorexic's physical condition is stabilized, therapy begins.

For anorexics desperately clinging to their eating disorder, the most effective treatment often takes place in hospitals on eating disorder wards with specially trained staff. Here the anorexic's eating patterns can be closely monitored. During inpatient treatment, anorexics undergo behavioral therapy aimed at getting them to change their eating habits. They may participate in therapy groups as well. Usually family therapy is part of the treatment, too. Although sometimes mood-regulating drugs, such as tranquilizers and lithium, are prescribed, researchers still are not certain just how much these drugs help.

Bulimia

Bulimia was not officially recognized as an eating disorder by the mental health community until 1980. One reason for this oversight is that many bulimics maintain normal weight. Except in advanced stages of their eating disorder, they do not appear to have a problem. Whereas anorexics tend be anxious, timid, and withdrawn, bulimics seem to adapt better to the world. Friends and even family may believe the bulimic is happy and successful and often do not have a clue about what is going on behind the closed bathroom door or inside the bulimic's mind.

According to the American Psychiatric Association, bulimics

- Frequently binge on food (at least twice a week for a period of three months), gorging on enormous amounts of it in a short time
- Feel out of control during their eating binges
- Make themselves vomit, take laxatives, go on strict diets, or exercise compulsively so they will not gain weight
- Are extremely concerned with their body image and their weight

It is important to note that the American Psychiatric Association is very conservative about confining a diagnosis of bulimia to those who binge at least twice a week. Many mental health professionals believe that those who binge and purge less frequently are also bulimic and that they constitute a significant percentage of the U.S. population.

Bulimics have uncontrollable food cravings, often for "junk food," items that are high in sugar, refined carbohydrates, and fats such as cakes and cookies, ice cream, and potato chips. These binges are not triggered by hunger, but by an out-of-control urge to eat. Most of the time bulimics diet and avoid these foods, viewing them as dangerous, forbidden, and fattening. During a binge all that changes.

On a food binge, bulimics eat very rapidly, not paying much attention to the texture or even the taste of what they eat, consuming as much as 5,000 to 10,000 or more calories at one sitting. They take big bites, shoveling their food in. Often they just swallow, hardly chewing at all. The main difference between the occasional overeating many people indulge in and a bulimic binge is that bulimics know they have eaten too much, feel horrible about it, and are fully aware that they feel they have no control over their eating. These binges may happen several times a day or less frequently. More often than not, binges happen during the evenings and on weekends, when the bulimic's time is not structured by school or work.

Bulimia is a secret eating disorder. People who have it tend to binge alone so others will not discover them. Afterward they feel shame. Sometimes, like an alcoholic hiding liquor, bulimics hoard their binge foods, concealing them from other people. After a binge, most bulimics purge by self-induced vomiting. This is done in secret, as well, and is accompanied by feelings of self-disgust.

Bulimics are so tied to this binge/purge cycle that sometimes they will choose the food they eat based on how easy it will be for them to regurgitate it. A bulimic on a food binge may drink large amounts of liquid, too, to make throwing up easier.

Even though self-induced vomiting disgusts the bulimic, it can become habit-forming. Quickly getting rid of all the food consumed relieves stomach pains and discomfort that come with overeating. This instant relief becomes rewarding. Some researchers even believe that vomiting triggers the release of endorphins, the brain's natural opiates, so that vomiters may actually feel a kind of "high." In addition, vomiting may become a habit because bulimics mistakenly think that by almost immediately getting rid of the food they have eaten, they stop their bodies from absorbing any of the calories from that food. This notion is a myth according to doctors.

Some bulimics use laxatives to rid themselves of the large amounts of food they have eaten. Like vomiting, laxatives can be habit-forming. When habitual laxative users stop taking these over-the-counter drugs, they retain water, sometimes gaining as much as ten pounds in a very short period of time. They may become constipated, too, and set up a pattern in which they must rely on laxatives to have regular bowel movements. Enemas, diuretics, and diet pills are other methods bulimics use in an attempt to rid their bodies of calories.

Like anorexia, bulimia can begin when someone is overly concerned with weight gain. It has been found that as teenagers many bulimics were overweight and that bulimics tend to have obese parents (*The Diagnostic and Statistical Manual III*, 66). They do not want to become emaciated as the anorexic does, but they do set rigid ideal weights for themselves and will do nearly anything to maintain that weight.

According to a study done on bulimics and body image, 86 percent had an extreme fear of gaining weight, and over half were extremely sensitive about gaining weight (Blinder, Chaitin, and Goldstein, 394). Some bulimics weigh themselves several times a day. Others are very concerned about the shape of their bodies, especially their waists, hips, breasts, and thighs. Other bulimics react in the opposite way and avoid scales and mirrors at all costs out of fear that they will discover they have gained weight.

Although bulimics tend to be more outgoing than anorexics, they share the qualities of perfectionism and a need to achieve. Up to twice as many bulimics are depressed than are people in the general population. They are also more prone to self-mutilation—burning, cutting, and scratching themselves—and to suicide attempts than are other people (Clark, Parr, and Castelli, 239). Bulimics in addition have higher rates of alcohol and drug abuse than do others. Some shoplift, focusing their stealing on food (*The Diagnostic and Statistical Manual III*, 67).

PHYSICAL CONSEQUENCES OF BULIMIA

The methods bulimics use to rid their bodies of food cause a number of medical problems. They feel bloated and have abdominal pain and constipation. Often they feel weak, anxious, and tired, as well, possibly as a consequence of hypoglycemia (low blood sugar). When massive amounts of sugar are consumed, the pancreas releases extra insulin into the bloodstream to deal with it, and blood sugar plummets to levels far below normal. Low blood sugar causes people to crave and eat even more sugar, setting up a vicious cycle.

Self-induced vomiting can cause a sore throat and bleeding from the esophagus. Sometimes the esophagus tears during food binges from the repeated vomiting. Repeated vomiting can also cause the stomach to push through the diaphragm. This is called a hiatal hernia and leads to persistent heartburn. In extreme cases the stomach can rupture from being filled with too much food. Tooth enamel is eroded by hydrochloric acid from the stomach, so that bulimics may have more cavities than usual. The teeth also can lose calcium and become discolored.

Many bulimics use ipecac to make themselves vomit. Ipecac is a poison that triggers the vomiting center in the brain, and it is sometimes used as an antidote to other poisons. If a person takes ipecac and does not vomit, he or she will experience chest pains, an increased heart rate, and shortness of breath. When a bulimic abuses ipecac regularly, this drug builds up in the system, leading to poisoning and eventual shock and death.

About one-third of all bulimics use diet pills, diuretics, or laxatives. These methods are easier than vomiting and are more easily hidden (Boskind-White and White, 144). Abuse of diet pills to suppress the appetite may cause hypertension, seizures, and brain hemorrhages as well as kidney failure. Diuretics can make bulimics lose so much water they become dehydrated.

Laxatives are just as dangerous because they, too, produce dehydration from chronic diarrhea. Some laxatives work by stimulating the intestinal tract to contract. When abused, they destroy the mucous lining of the intestines and cause ulcers in the colon. Intestinal blockage may occur from fiber laxatives. Abuse of laxatives also can cause vomiting, chronic diarrhea, and even poisoning.

Whether a bulimic vomits or uses laxatives or diuretics, he or she loses fluid from the body, as well as potassium, sodium, magnesium, and other minerals. This leads to electrolyte imbalance in the bloodstream, which can cause dizziness, weakness, fainting, and irregular heartbeats. Seizures and kidney failure that may even require a transplant also can be results of electrolyte imbalances. Sometimes electrolyte imbalance causes death.

TREATMENT

Bulimia often continues undetected on and off over a period of years. Unlike anorexics, bulimics know they have a problem and often desperately want help, so once they seek out and find treatment, they tend to cooperate with their therapists. For the most part, when a bulimic seeks treatment, he or she can receive it on an outpatient basis. Therapy may be individual or within a group. Both the eating behavior and the underlying reasons for it are dealt with in either setting. Because most bulimics understand they are out of control and work hard to recover, their recovery rates are high.

Even so, like alcoholics, bulimics may have relapses, occasionally binging and purging even after treatment.

Compulsive Eating

Compulsive eaters binge without the purging. They are obsessed with thoughts of food. At the same time, they, like bulimics, have nearly constant thoughts about their weight and how they look. Gorging and hating themselves for their uncontrollable cravings for food, they are trapped in a vicious cycle of food binges and then dieting— only to go off the diet and on yet another binge.

Compulsive eating shares many of the characteristics of an addiction. People who eat compulsively are out of control. They eat to alter their moods, and they often deny that they have a problem. Technically, compulsive eating is not a true addiction because people who have developed this pattern of eating are not physically dependent on large amounts of cake or corn chips for their survival. Instead compulsive eating is more properly considered a compulsion or a psychological dependency.

There are many patterns of compulsive eating, but most people who have lost control of their ability to stop eating tend to be overweight. Research done at Duke and Stanford universities shows independently that at least once a week people who are obese go on food binges (Boskind-White and White, 134).

Ironically, strict dieting is one of the factors that may lead to compulsive eating. Research done at the University of Toronto indicates that, regardless of their weight, all dieters are prone to binge (Hirschmann and Munter, 20). One reason for this is that after being deprived of food they like for so long, they overindulge when they go off their diets.

Other studies show that most dieters who lose weight regain that weight along with a few extra pounds. Every time a dieter cuts back on food, his or her metabolism slows down to conserve energy. As a result, when people stop dieting, their metabolism is lower and their bodies burn calories more slowly than before. After years of on-and-off dieting, they may gain weight without eating large quantities of food.

Hunger has little to do with compulsive food binges. Most compulsive eaters have low self-esteem and they are unhappy with their lives. Often they eat to temporarily numb their painful feelings or to escape from their problems. Others eat to excess in order to insulate themselves from the world or to feel big and powerful. Their eating can be triggered, too, by unhappy childhoods. According to one study of adult children of alcoholics, over one-third were bulimic, and two-thirds binged on food.

Because food is so often associated with love when people are growing up, adolescents and adults who feel unloved or unlovable may eat compulsively to reassure and comfort themselves. Of course, that comfort and reassurance is only temporary. With its focus on slimness and fitness, society is often extremely critical of the compulsive eater. The more a compulsive eater eats, the more unlovable he or she feels, and the more that person feels driven to eat.

PHYSICAL CONSEQUENCES OF COMPULSIVE EATING

The compulsive eating cycle leads to obesity. People who are obese often experience shortness of breath and become exhausted after very little exercise. Because fat insulates the body, people who are grossly obese sweat more than others and may suffer from heat exhaustion. Because it is so difficult for them to move, severely overweight people's metabolisms are lowered even further, and they gain weight more readily than people at normal weight.

The heart also is affected by overeating. Obese people sometimes suffer angina pectoris, which is sharp pains in the chest and shoulder, because of an insufficient flow of blood to the heart muscle. This reduction of blood flow through the coronary arteries to the heart is an indication of heart disease. Sometimes a part of the heart muscle actually dies as a result of this condition. The outcome can be heart attack and even death. Because people who are overweight have high levels of cholesterol in the blood, their arteries may get clogged with fatty deposits. In some people who are overweight, the heart enlarges because it must work harder to pump blood to all parts of the body. This enlargement can lead to weakness of the heart muscle.

People who overeat are at greater risk for diabetes than are those who maintain normal weight. This may be because cells that are filled with fat may develop resistance to insulin. They also tend to have low blood sugar (hypoglycemia), for the same reasons bulimics do.

TREATMENT

Disgusted by their own eating habits, compulsive eaters are often too ashamed to reach out for help, and when they do they are often unrealistically certain that everything would be better as if by magic if they just weighed less. Only about 30 percent seek help, and most of them go to a weight loss program rather than into therapy.

Weight loss may be a good plan from a medical standpoint, but therapy is critical to deal with the underlying issues that caused the compulsive eating in the first place. Unlike alcoholics, drug addicts, or smokers, compulsive eaters cannot go cold turkey. They must still eat in order to live. For this reason they need to relearn healthy eating patterns and to heal their low self-esteem and feelings of unworthiness.

More and more eating disorder units in hospitals are starting programs to deal both with the obesity and the reasons compulsive eaters eat. In nearly every city, as well, there are now support groups for compulsive eaters that help them gain both self-esteem and a healthier relationship to food.

REFERENCES

Anderson, Arnold. *Males with Eating Disorders*. New York: Brunner/Mazel Publishers, 1990.

Blinder, Barton, Barry Chaitin, and Renee Goldstein. *The Eating Disorders: Medical and Psychological Bases of Diagnosis and Treatment*. New York: PMA Publishing Corporation, 1988.

Boskind-White, Marlene, and William C. White. *Bulimarexia: The Binge/Purge Cycle*. New York: Norton, 1987.

Brownell, Kelly, and John P. Foreyt. *Handbook of Eating Disorders: Physiology, Psychology and Treatment of Obesity, Anorexia, and Bulimia*. New York: Basic Books, 1988.

Clark, Christine, Richard Parr, and William Castelli, eds. *Evaluation and Management of Eating Disorders: Anorexia, Bulimia and Obesity*. Champaign, IL: Life Enhancement Publications, 1988.

The Diagnostic and Statistical Manual III (DSM III), revised. Washington, DC: American Psychiatric Association Press, 1987.

Hirschmann, Jane, and Carol Munter. *Overcoming Overeating: Living Free in a World of Food*. New York: Addison-Wesley, 1988.

Kolodny, Nancy J. *When Food's a Foe: How to Confront and Conquer Eating Disorders*. Boston: Little, Brown, 1987.

Pope, Harrison G., Jr., and James I. Hudson. "Eating Disorders," in *The Comprehensive Textbook of Psychiatry*, 5th edition, Harold I. Kaplan and Benjamin J. Sadock, eds. Baltimore, MD: Williams & Wilkins, 1989.

Sacker, Ira M., and Marc A. Zimmer. *Dying To Be Thin: Understanding and Defeating Anorexia Nervosa and Bulimia—a Practical, Lifesaving Guide.* New York: Warner Books, 1987.

Valette, Brett. *A Parent's Guide to Eating Disorders: Prevention and Treatment of Anorexia and Bulimia.* New York: Avon, 1988.

Yoder, Barbara. *The Recovery Resource Book.* New York: Fireside, 1990.

Resources
for Finding Out about Eating Disorders

Fiction

Benjamin, Carol Lea. **Nobody's Baby Now.** New York: Macmillan Publishing Company, 1984. 157p.

Liz Singer at 15 feels too fat and unattractive for anyone to love her, but she has devised a plan to lose weight. Her scheme gets sidetracked when her grandmother, who is depressed, comes to live with the family. Liz must devote most of her time and attention to caring for her elderly relative. That relationship becomes a mutually nurturing one and Liz discovers she has lost weight without trying.

Cavallaro, Ann. **Blimp.** New York: E. P. Dutton & Company, 1983. 166p.

Kim, who is called "Blimp" by her fellow juniors, keeps being nagged by her family to lose weight. She falls for Gary, a senior who is new at school, and begins losing weight—66 pounds. In the meantime Gary, who is suicidal, depressed, and lives with an alcoholic mother, gives her mixed messages about the romance. Kim is able to be supportive to him while gaining insights into her own problem and to learn that, although sometimes she is tempted to overeat, she never wants to be fat again.

Hamilton, Virginia. **A Little Love.** New York: Philomel Books, 1984. 207p.

Seventeen-year-old Sheema has found a boy, Forrest, who loves her for who she is inside and does not care about her obese body. The two of them set out to find Sheema's father, who abandoned her to her grandparents when she was an infant. Through that meeting, she discovers that she cannot fill her emptiness with other people. This book provides insights about how it feels to be overweight.

Hautzig, Deborah. **Second Star to the Right.** New York: Knopf, 1988.

To attractive New York teenager Leslie Hiller, being happy is the same as being thin. After all, she believes thin is perfect. And so she diets . . . to the point where she must be hospitalized and confront the reasons that she has been trying to starve herself to death.

Holland, Isabelle. **Jenny Kiss'd Me.** New York: Ballantine Books, 1985. 201p.

Seventeen-year-old Jill and her dad have made a deal. She will not talk about his drinking if he does not talk about the fact that she is fat. A set of circumstances causes them to break their truce, and Jill must decide whether she will continue to feel self-pity or instead begin to take charge of her life and her weight.

Kerr, M. E. **Dinky Hocker Shoots Smack!** New York: Harper & Row, 1972. 204p.

Dinky does not really use heroin, but she is fat. When her parents do not listen to her needs, she finds a way to make them hear her. This book about compulsive eating uses humor to make its point.

Levenkron, Steven. **The Best Little Girl in the World.** New York: Warner Books, 1978. 253p.

Francesca is devoted to studying ballet and to losing weight. She is a perfectionist, her mother's favorite child, and a good daughter. This fast-moving story of her struggle to starve herself for her art and then of her recovery is a classic. It provides rare and chilling insights into the thought processes that underlie anorexia nervosa as well as how pressures from adults can trigger the disorder.

————. **Kessa.** New York: Popular Library, 1986. 245p.

Released from the hospital where she was treated for anorexia, Francesca (Kessa) is faced with the struggle to build not only a new life but also a new self. It is not as easy as she thought it would be. She is not completely cured and absolutely happy. In fact, she does not want to live. This novel deals with the ongoing work involved in overcoming eating disorders.

Lipsyte, Robert. **One Fat Summer.** New York: Harper & Row, 1977. 160p.

Fourteen-year-old Bobby Marks is overweight. During the summer he learns to accept himself the way he is by sticking to a tough job and standing up to the kids who tease him about his weight.

Rabinowich, Ellen. **Underneath I'm Different.** New York: Dell
Publishing Company, 1983. 180p.

Amy, who is shy and overweight, has a friendship with one of the
most attractive girls at school. When Ansel, a sculptor, asks Amy out
on a date, she is surprised to find that all of his work is of overweight
women. She becomes his model and from that experience learns to
see herself in a new light. Although the relationship breaks up, Amy
loses weight and uses her newfound confidence to help introduce
more books by women into the curriculum at her school.

Ruckman, Ivy. **The Hunger Scream.** New York: Walker & Company,
1983. 188p.

Lily's father has always seemed to love her little sister best, and her
mother is emotionally distant. Lily is determined to start a
relationship with her next-door neighbor who is home from college,
but even though she is thin already, she resolves to lose more weight
before she talks with him. Although she has lost 42 pounds in 8
months and is seeing a psychiatrist, her father believes she is just
spoiled. Finally hospitalized, Lily learns to confront her parents in
family counseling and ask that her needs be met.

Sinykin, Sheri Cooper. **Apart at the Seams.** Center City, MN:
Hazelden Educational Materials, 1990. 120p.

Jessi is in the eighth grade when her big sister dies in a car accident.
All of a sudden her family starts to fall apart at the seams. Her
brother gets in trouble at school. Wrapped up in their grief, her
parents ignore her. Jessi is left trying to fill her sister's shoes, to be
the perfect daughter and the perfect ballerina. In the process she
becomes bulimic.

Stren, Patti. **I Was a Fifteen-Year-Old Blimp.** New York: Harper &
Row, 1985. 185p.

When the boys at school rank girls in terms of their attractiveness,
15-year-old Gabby gets a big, fat zero. She goes on a crash diet, but
her mother insists she quit because it will ruin her health. Then a
friend who is a dancer introduces Gabby to laxatives and vomiting.
Gabby's misguided efforts to control her weight soon push her out of
control. In the end, she seeks counseling and begins to put her
relationship to food back into a healthier perspective.

Wersba, Barbara. **Fat: A Love Story.** New York: Harper & Row, 1987.
128p.

Rita Formica at 16 weighs in at 200 pounds, and she has been to every diet counselor and psychologist on Long Island. She falls in love with Robert, who is athletic and handsome—so handsome that Rita fears he will never notice her. When she confides her fears to her employer, she is astonished to find that he is intelligent and compassionate and that the two of them were meant for each other.

Willey, Margaret. **The Bigger Book of Lydia.** New York: Harper & Row, 1983. 215p.

Michelle hates being large. She hates it so much that she has become anorexic to shrink herself. Her friend Wanda has the opposite problem: She despises being petite and wants to gain weight. Together they learn to be open about their fears and feelings, and they help each other overcome their problems and poor self-esteem so that, in the end, they both begin to feel comfortable about their size.

Nonfiction

BOOKS

Alexander, Elliot. **Sick and Tired of Being Fat.** Center City, MN: Hazelden Educational Materials, 1991. 154p.

After Elliot Alexander failed on diet after diet, he examined the underlying causes of his addiction to food. His recovery started when he began attending Overeaters Anonymous meetings. This candid recounting of Alexander's struggle and healing will appeal to young men with eating disorders.

B., Bill. **Compulsive Overeater: The Basic Text for Compulsive Overeaters.** Minneapolis, MN: CompCare, 1980. 372p.

Based on his own experiences of overeating and his subsequent recovery, the author explains the basics of getting well through the Twelve Step program that forms the basis of Overeaters Anonymous. One of the few books on eating disorders written by a man, it not only provides information and practical suggestions but is inspirational as well.

Brandon, Carla Willis. **Eat Like a Lady.** Deerfield Beach, FL: Health Communications, 1989. 129p.

Beginning with how the families we grew up in can affect our feelings toward food, Brandon takes a look at how bulimia starts, how this disease of binging and purging progresses, and the steps bulimics can take to recover.

Chernin, Kim. **The Hungry Self: Women, Eating and Identity.** New York: Harper & Row, 1981. 214p.

In this book Chernin examines how the mother-daughter relationship can encourage women to overeat. The reasons women eat, other than to satisfy hunger, are explored as the author examines the root causes of eating disorders in women.

Claypool, Jane, and Cheryl Diane Nelson. **Food Trips and Traps.** New York: Franklin Watts, 1990. 90p.

Written especially for adolescents, this book explains the symptoms of compulsive overeating, bulimia, and anorexia. In addition, it talks about the causes and treatments of these disorders. Personal stories and easy-to-understand language make this a good introductory book.

Ebbitt, Joan. **Tomorrow, Monday or New Year's Day: Emerging Issues in Eating Disorder Recovery.** Park Ridge, IL: Parkside Publishing Corporation, 1989. 103p.

Once a person with an eating disorder begins working through the addiction, all sorts of other issues come to the foreground. This helpful book deals with self-esteem, sexuality, emotional intimacy, and spirituality. Suggestions are offered about how to cope with these issues as they arise and how to reap the rewards of recovery.

Gelinas, Paul. **Coping with Weight Problems.** New York: Rosen Publishing Company, 1983. 131p.

Why do people eat compulsively? Gelinas explains the roles of frustration, anxiety, and despair in compulsive eating. Eating to escape these feelings does not help for long. In the second half of this book, which deals with solutions, the author covers how to cope with the needs to belong and to achieve, fear, guilt, love, and emerging sexual feelings. The book also includes a chapter for readers who are underweight.

Hall, Lindsey, and Leigh Cohn. **Bulimia: A Guide to Recovery.** Carlsbad, CA: Gurze Books, 1986. 160p.

Detailing a two-week program for recovery from bulimia, this book draws on the authors' personal experiences as well as on those of 217 other women. There are lists of things to do besides binging as well as resources and suggestions for family members of bulimics.

Hampshire, Elizabeth. **Freedom from Food: The Secret Lives of Dieters and Compulsive Eaters.** Park Ridge, IL: Parkside Publishing Corporation, 1988. 138p.

A compelling picture of what it is like to have an eating disorder is created through six stories. In addition to talking about food addiction, this book deals with recovery.

Hollis, Judi. **Fat Is a Family Affair.** Center City, MN: Hazelden Educational Materials, 1985. 80p.

Based on the philosophy of Overeaters Anonymous, this book helps readers learn to emotionally nurture themselves rather than self-medicating their psychological pain with food. It covers how eating disorders begin and talks about recovery as well.

Kane, June Kozak. **Coping with Diet Fads.** New York: Rosen Publishing Group, 1990. 162p.

A registered dietician, Kane lays to rest many myths about dieting and includes profiles of several different dieting patterns that teens fall prey to when they want to lose weight. She discusses the yo-yo syndrome of gaining and losing and regaining weight and offers sound tips about how to start thinking sensibly about food rather than obsessing over it. This is a good starting point for any adolescent who wants to lose weight and keep it off.

Kano, Susan. **Making Peace with Food: A Step-by-Step Guide to Freedom from Diet-Weight Conflict.** New York: Harper Collins, 1991. 256p.

This workbook helps readers sift through anxieties about their weight, dieting, and eating disorders in a gentle, thought-provoking way. It contains exercises and resources to more fully explore personal reasons behind an individual's struggle with food.

L., Elizabeth. **Listen to the Hunger: Why We Overeat.** Center City, MN: Hazelden Educational Materials, 1989. 85p.

This book helps those who overeat examine the hidden motivations that are behind their eating disorder, such as anger, fear, and boredom. Written by a member of Overeaters Anonymous, it also addresses the spiritual issues involved in recovery through a Twelve Step program.

LeBlanc, Donna. **You Can't Quit 'til You Know What's Eating You.** Deerfield Beach, FL: Health Communications, 1990. 130p.

A book for people who are chronic dieters, bulimics, or compulsive eaters, this title approaches the topic from a permanent weight-loss perspective. The author asserts that understanding, not starvation and self-denial, is what really works in the long run. Included is an exercise to help readers learn the extent of their eating problems.

McFarland, Barbara. **Feeding the Empty Heart: Adult Children and Compulsive Eating.** Center City, MN: Hazelden Educational Materials, 1988. 106p.

More often than not eating disorders have their roots in childhood. This book takes a close look at how emotional repression in childhood leads to low self-esteem and lays the groundwork for eating disorders. Several treatment options are discussed.

McFarland, Barbara, and Tyeis Baumann. **Shame and Body Image: Culture and the Compulsive Eater.** Deerfield Beach, FL: Health Communications, 1990. 204p.

Shame and Body Image probes the shame-promoting roles society teaches women, roles that push many women into compulsive eating. Physical and mental exercises help readers recognize these roles and begin to transcend them to develop more realistic attitudes about their body image.

Roth, Geneen. **Breaking Free from Compulsive Eating.** New York: Signet, 1991. 256p.

Breaking Free includes tips on how to recognize hunger and how to know when to stop eating. The practical techniques are unique and useful. The material is based on the author's very successful seminars and workshops.

————. **Feeding the Hungry Heart: The Experience of Compulsive Eating.** New York: New American Library, 1982. 212p.

The message in this upbeat book is that complusive eating has very little to do with physical hunger and that it is a struggle that can have a positive outcome.

Sandbek, Terence J. **The Deadly Diet: Recovering from Anorexia and Bulimia.** Oakland, CA: New Harbinger, 1986. 264p.

This book provides a tried and true, step-by-step process for fighting the inner voices that urge anorexics and bulimics to practice their eating disorders. Based on cognitive techniques, this process helps readers move toward self-enhancing eating patterns and away from self-destructive ones.

Sheppard, Kay. **Food Addiction: The Body Knows.** Deerfield Beach, FL: Health Communications, 1989. 128p.

A look at the physical component of food addiction is provided in this book. Much of the focus is on nutrition, and the author suggests that one step toward recovery is to avoid highly refined food and other additive chemicals.

Valette, Brett. **Surviving an Eating Disorder: Perspectives and Strategies for Family and Friends.** New York: Avon Books, 1988. 222p.

If a close friend or family member suffers from anorexia, bulimia, or compulsive eating, this book gives suggestions not only for helping that person but for helping yourself as well. In addition to discussing causes, the book gives practical suggestions about how to deal with anger and denial and how to relate to the eating-disordered person on a daily basis.

Waldrup, Heidi. **Showing Up for Life: A Recovering Overeater's Triumph over Compulsion.** Center City, MN: Hazelden Educational Materials, 1991. 252p.

Heidi Waldrup recounts her own story of conquering food addiction. Overweight since the age of 12, by 29 she weighed over 300 pounds. This book chronicles her recovery through the Overeaters Anonymous Twelve Step program.

Weiss, Lillie, Sharlene Wolchik, and Melanie Kauffman. **You Can't Have Your Cake and Eat It Too: A Program for Controlling Bulimia.** Saratoga, CA: R&E Publishers, 1986. 103p.

This seven-chapter workbook for bulimics details a seven-week program for boosting self-esteem. It includes exercises, homework, readings, and a binge-purge diary.

PAMPHLETS

Cowan, Sally, and Steven P. Dingfelder. **A Practical Guide to Anorexia and Bulimia.** Deerfield Beach, FL: Health Communications, 1987. 32p.

Both anorexia and bulimia are defined in this pamplet that presents the facts and, at the same time, takes a personal approach to addressing the emotional issues of eating disorders.

Ebbitt, Joan. **The Eating Illness Workbook.** Park Ridge, IL: Parkside Publishing Corporation, 1987. 61p.

This booklet presents the facts about eating disorders. In addition, Ebbitt, a counselor and eating disorder program manager, provides readers with a series of exercises, activities, and suggested readings.

————. **Spinning: Thought Patterns of Compulsive Eaters.** Park Ridge, IL: Parkside Publishing Corporation, 1987. 10p.

Focusing on the thought patterns that underlie food addiction, this pamphlet probes beneath the symptoms of overeaters to explore the issues underneath this addiction.

Nonprint Materials

Dark Secrets, Bright Victory: One Woman's Recovery from Bulimia

Type: VHS video
Length: 13 min.
Cost: Purchase $150
Distributor: Hazelden Educational Materials
               P.O. Box 176
               Center City, MN 55012-0176
Date: 1988

During the course of a family therapy session, Heidi and her family examine their secrets. As Heidi honestly reveals her feelings about herself and her parents, she moves toward recovery. This award-winning video, which includes a study guide, is narrated by actor Leslie Neilsen and includes comments by Judi Hollis, Ph.D., the founder of an eating disorder program.

Faces of Recovery

Type: VHS video
Length: 35 min.
Cost: Purchase $29.95
Distributor: Gurze Books
               P.O. Box 2238
               Carlsbad, CA 92008
Date: 1990

Cathy Rigby, the former Olympic gymnast, narrates this overview of anorexia and bulimia, weaving together the stories of several women who suffered from these eating disorders and information from professionals who specialize in the field. A bulimic herself for 12 years, Rigby tells her own story as well. Individual, family, and group therapy sessions also are shown.

Fear of Fat: Dieting and Eating Disorders

Type:	16mm film, VHS video
Length:	26 min.
Cost:	Rental $60, purchase $465 (film); rental $60, purchase $350 (video)
Distributor:	Churchill Films 12210 Nebraska Avenue Los Angeles, CA 90025
Date:	1987

When women become overly concerned with food and have other psychological problems, the stage for an eating disorder is set. Five women discuss their eating disorders in this program that urges women to accept their bodies as they are rather than try to fit some media ideal.

Learning about Eating Disorders

Type:	VHS video
Length:	16 min. each
Cost:	Rental $60 each; purchase $494 for the set of six, $150 each
Distributor:	Churchill Films 12210 Nebraska Avenue Los Angeles, CA 90025
Date:	1989

This series of videos is aimed at people with eating disorders and their families and friends. Titles include *Starving and Binging, Anorexia Nervosa, Bulimia, Getting Help,* and *Changing Behavior.*

Portraits of Anorexia

Type:	16mm film, VHS video
Length:	28 min.
Cost:	Rental $60, purchase $490 (film); rental $60, purchase $370 (video)
Distributor:	Churchill Films 12210 Nebraska Avenue Los Angeles, CA 90025
Date:	1987

Seven anorexics, both currently eating-disordered and recovering ones, talk about the expectations and relationships that surround their eating problem.

Real People: Coping with Eating Disorders
Type:	VHS video
Length:	27 min.
Cost:	Purchase $169
Distributor:	Sunburst Communications
	39 Washington Avenue
	Box 40
	Pleasantville, NY 10570-3496
Date:	1989

Why do teenagers have such a high incidence of eating disorders? This video works to answer that problem as narrator Kay Pitsenberger, director of the Center for Medical Treatment at Santa Ana Community Hospital, pulls together the stories of three teens who have problems in their relationships to food: Staci, an anorexic; Shauna, a bulimic; and Mike, a compulsive eater.

Real People: Meet a Teenage Anorexic
Type:	VHS video
Length:	18 min.
Cost:	Purchase $149
Distributor:	Sunburst Communications
	39 Washington Avenue
	Box 40
	Pleasantville, NY 10570-3496
Date:	1989

In this video, 17-year-old Staci expands on what it was like for her to suffer from anorexia. In her own words, she talks about how her obsession with being thin controlled her life and left her near starvation. The causes and consequences of self-starvation are thoroughly explored in this video.

Organizations

American Anorexia and Bulimia Association, Inc.
133 Cedar Lane
Teaneck, NJ 07666
(201) 836-1800

In addition to providing referrals and information, this group runs annual conferences for people with eating disorders and their families. It also publishes a newsletter and has guidelines available for starting your own group.

Anorexia Nervosa and Associated Disorders, Inc.
Box 5102
Eugene, OR 97405
(503) 686-7372

This group provides information and referrals about self-help groups and therapists who specialize in eating disorders. It has over 200 chapters throughout the country. Each local group has as its sponsor a professional in the field of eating disorders. The organization publishes some pamphlets and booklets and a newsletter as well.

Anorexics/Bulimics Anonymous
Box 112214
San Diego, CA 92111

This Twelve Step recovery program focuses on methods of coping with eating disorders that do not have to do with controlling food intake. For this reason diets and abstinence from particular foods are not discussed at meetings. Currently it operates in the San Diego area but will help individuals start groups in their own parts of the country.

Bulimia Anorexia Self-Help (BASH)
6125 Clayton Avenue
Suite 215
St. Louis, MO 63139
(314) 991-BASH (991-2274)

This self-help organization runs groups for people with eating disorders and for their families. It has free literature and sponsors discussion groups led by a trained peer facilitator. It publishes a monthly newsletter and sponsors an annual conference. The organization also has written a facilitator's manual for people wishing to start their own local groups.

National Anorexic Aid Society, Inc.
5796 Karl Road
Columbus, OH 43229
(614) 436-1112

This group provides both a support network and information for people with eating disorders. It publishes a quarterly newsletter, makes referrals to treatment professionals and self-help groups across the country, and has a list of films and videotapes about anorexia, bulimia, and other related eating disorders.

National Association to Aid Fat Americans (NAAFA)
P.O. Box 43
Bellerose, NY 11426
(516) 352-3120

There are 25 local chapters of this group, which focuses on helping members to raise their self-esteem and to accept themselves as they are. The group's services include a newsletter, a telephone support network, pen pal referrals, and a convention. It also will help people wanting to start their own local chapters.

O-Anon
P.O. Box 4305
San Pedro, CA 90731

A group for the family members of people who eat compulsively, O-Anon follows a Twelve Step program and in many ways is like Alcoholics Anonymous.

Overeaters Anonymous
P.O. Box 72870
Los Angeles, CA 90009
(213) 320-9741

This group has been in existence for 30 years and has over 7,000 local chapters throughout the United States. Its self-help program is based on the Twelve Steps of Alcoholics Anonymous. In addition to groups for adults, it sponsors groups for teenagers. It publishes a monthly magazine and can provide information about how to start your own group if none exists in your area.

Hotline

Food Addiction Hotline
(800) USA-0088 (872-0088)

This hotline, sponsored by the School of Psychology at the Florida Institute of Technology, refers callers to eating disorder professionals in their area and to chapters of Overeaters Anonymous. It also sends out a packet of information on request.

CHAPTER 6

Obsessive-Compulsive Disorder and Impulse Control Disorders: Hooked on Self-Defeating Behaviors

> I suffer from obsessive-compulsive disorder. I cannot remember ever not being an obsessive-compulsive. I cannot imagine life free of obsessive-compulsive behavior. It is as much a part of me as my blue eyes. It is as if I had been born with a birth defect, like the baby that cannot hear that knows no life of sound. . . .
>
> My first memories of obsessive-compulsive behavior center on the age of seven. I was playing with a group of children in front of my house. We were playing a variation of a game called "It." We called it "Cooties." One person "had the cooties" and all of the others tried to avoid being tagged and "getting the cooties," being contaminated. I remember the feeling. It was more than just a game. It was a matter of desperation for me. I just could not allow myself to be tagged, to have all the contamination flow into me. I ran very fast to escape.
>
> *The Boy Who Couldn't Stop Washing: The Experience and Treatment of Obsessive-Compulsive Disorder* by Judith Rapoport (New York: Plume Books, 1989), 51–52.

People do not only become hooked on substances, such as alcohol, drugs, or food. Like Zach, the man who tells his story in Dr. Rapoport's book, they also can become hooked on behaviors, such as repeating particular words or engaging in other rituals. They can become hooked on things such as gambling, having sex, or working as well. Although these acts are not physically addictive, as many chemical substances are, they can become compulsions or impulse disorders—things people do over and over again uncontrollably, even though the rest of their lives may suffer because of it.

In the Middle Ages it was thought that people who repeated strange behaviors were witches or were possessed by devils. Today it is known that usually the acts such people perform happen in response to thoughts, ideas, and urges that these people just cannot get out of their minds. These thoughts are called obsessions and are often accompanied by shame and anxiety. Because such ideas and feelings cause discomfort, the person who experiences them acts out to relieve the tension the thoughts cause.

Obsessive-Compulsive Disorder

According to psychologists, compulsions are repeated acts that cause either physical or emotional pain for the person who does them in an attempt to rid themself of anxiety. Sometimes a compulsion seems to logically follow an uncontrollable thought as a way to relieve the anxiety or shame a person feels or a way to get rid of the thought. For example, a person who is obsessed with catching diseases from germs may wash his or her hands over and over again, or someone who is terrified of being evil may repeatedly recite Bible verses.

At other times, the way the obsessive thought and the compulsive habit are connected may not make much sense to anyone but the compulsive person. Even so, counting all the squares in a sidewalk or reciting the alphabet, at least momentarily, relieves the anxiety that results from the obsessive thought and makes the person feel a little safer. That relief provides motivation for continuing the behavior, and obsessive-compulsive disorder (OCD) is begun.

Uncontrollable thoughts and urges often begin to occur when obsessive-compulsives are children or teenagers. Sometimes compulsive behaviors begin to be evident then as well. The symptoms may not be constant throughout a person's life but rather may come and go in cycles, sometimes seeming to disappear and then returning. Although psychiatrists formerly thought that such problems were very rare, now it is believed that mild compulsions are common. It is also believed that they may be caused in part by biological factors, problems with either the brain's chemicals or its structure.

Compulsive behavior takes up a great deal of time. To qualify as a true compulsion, according to the American Psychiatric Association, the behavior must take up more than one hour a day and must interefere with social life or relationships with others. Even so, many compulsives are able to survive undetected. Compulsives are often loners, and many do not marry. They tend to be of above average intelligence and hide their symptoms. In effect, they lead secret lives.

On the surface people with compulsions seem to share several traits with alcoholics and drug addicts. They cannot stop doing the behavior even though they suffer from negative consequences. Many compulsive people are depressed and anxious, just as addicts are. There is a major difference, though, beyond the fact that compulsive acts are not physically addicting. That difference is that, often from the very start of their disorder, people who are compulsive know that they have a problem. They are aware that their behavior is out of their control, and they do not want to behave the way they do. They understand that what they are doing is irrational, and they try to stop themselves, but such attempts fail. They are not in self-denial about what is going on in their lives, even though they may hide their problems from the outside world.

Treatment for obsessive-compulsive disorder can take many forms. Currently the most popular is therapy, which includes examining why the disorder began and using behavior modification techniques to stop compulsive routines. Recently psychiatrists have begun treating OCD with clomipramine, a tricyclic antidepressant medication, to stop the obsessions that trigger compulsive behaviors. Fluoxetine, also known as Prozac, is another drug used to treat this disorder.

Impulse Control Disorders

Repeated activities from which people gain initial pleasure, such as eating or having sex, are not true compulsions according to psychiatrists. Instead, they are classified as impulse control disorders. Sometimes, within the addiction treatment field, they are called process disorders or process addictions.

Unlike OCD, impulse control disorders have not been linked to biological causes within the brain, although pleasure-providing activities do cause the brain to produce endorphins, natural opiates. The resulting natural high may reinforce the behavior that caused it, but it is unlikely that endorphins alone compel people to spend or have sex or work uncontrollably.

Instead it is believed that the vicious cycle of impulse control disorders is brought on by a person's need to feel better emotionally.

We, as human beings, tend to learn to do things that make us feel better. The more pleasure we feel right after we do something, the more we want to do it again, especially if the negative consequences of our behavior do not happen right away.

For example, if people feel depressed and discover that buying themselves a present with a credit card cheers them up, they will be tempted to repeat that behavior. Giving in to such impulse shopping is especially tempting because the bill does not come due until the end of the month. Therefore, in the immediate moment, it seems as if this mood-booster is absolutely free. For some people, over time this can become a pattern and then a habit.

Finally, this behavior may become a ritual that the person does every time he or she is down in the dumps. A person with an impulse disorder may spend beyond the amount he or she can comfortably afford. Then getting the credit card bill at the end of the month causes anxiety, which in turn pushes the person to shop even more to calm down. Once such a vicious cycle has been set in motion, it can be extremely difficult to break.

Anything that can temporarily relieve anxiety or make us feel good can become the "quick fix" basis for impulse control disorders. Some possible behaviors that can become part of the vicious cycle of impulse control disorders are shopping, going into debt, work, exercise, love, and sex. When done in moderation many of these things are socially acceptable and even good for us, such as eating, exercising, or falling in love. In fact, they are often a natural and necessary part of life. Once the vicious cycle is started, however, these acts are performed too many times or inappropriately—at the wrong time or in the wrong place.

Shopaholics, even when they are pressed for time and do not have that much money, feel pushed to shop—often for things they do not need. Whether they cruise store sales or frequent garage sales, they cannot resist a bargain, and if something interferes with a shopping trip they become anxious. While shopaholics are buying things they get excited, and some even say they feel a high, but later they usually feel regretful about what they have bought and may even try to return their purchases. Sometimes they hide the things they have bought, and they may have closets filled with items they never use.

Compulsive debtors are often but not always also compulsive shoppers. They live on credit and borrow money from friends and relatives in order to live beyond their means. Often they have difficulty paying back the money they have borrowed.

Workaholics devote their lives to their jobs and feel terribly guilty about taking time away from work to relax. They have a tough time delegating responsibility and believe that if they want the job done they need to do it themselves. Often they approach their work with a frenzied, frantic attitude, and the more they dislike their job, the harder they will work at it because they believe it is good for them. They are often perfectionists. Workaholics typically suffer from burnout and stress-related disorders such as headaches, ulcers, and muscle aches.

Compulsive exercisers carry the workaholic mentality into their recreational pursuits. Whether they run or go to aerobics classes, they do it to excess. Even though maximum physical benefit is obtained from about an hour of exercise three times a week, these folks just cannot quit. They set unreasonably high fitness goals for themselves and often train harder than professional athletes. When they develop muscle pulls and knee injuries, they tend to tough out the pain and continue their workouts even though they may cause permanent damage to muscles and ligaments because they cannot bear the thought of getting off schedule. Sometimes people who are hooked on exercise also have eating disorders and are trying to burn as many calories as possible to lose weight.

Love "addicts" share many characteristics with codependents because they look to other people to fill the empty space inside of them where their self-esteem should be. Whereas codependents look to all their relationships with other people to fill their needs, love addicts tend to focus more on romantic relationships. The highs and lows of romance often make their lives as chaotic as that of any drug addict.

The consequences of impulse control disorders on people's lives in many ways resemble those of chemical addiction. People who have these disorders focus everything around their quick fix, eventually excluding many other activities. They no longer believe they have a choice to do or not to do that particular behavior. Their relationships with family and friends suffer, as may their ability to work. Often they try to hide their problem from people around them, and just as often they deny, especially to themselves, that they have a problem at all.

Treatment for impulse control disorders includes therapy and self-help groups that provide emotional support and offer practical suggestions about how to break these habits. In the past few years, some addiction treatment centers have also begun setting up special units to deal with impulse control disorders.

Pathological Gambling

Pathological gambling is placed in a category of its own by the American Psychiatric Association. People who are commonly called compulsive gamblers are preoccupied with gambling, and they get edgy and nervous if they cannot place bets. Compulsive gamblers believe money is both the solution to and the cause of all of the problems in their lives.

Often they bet larger amounts of money than they intended to, and these amounts grow even larger over time. Not surprisingly these people usually lose their money, but that does not stop them; frequently they return the next day to try to win back their losses. In time gambling becomes a bigger and bigger part of their lives, interfering with work, relationships, and other interests. Often at this point compulsive gamblers try to stop gambling, but they cannot, even though they may have to borrow money to support the habit. Sometimes they even break the law to obtain money so they can gamble.

An estimated 2–3 percent of the adult population in the United States are compulsive gamblers (*The Diagnostic and Statistical Manual III*, 324). Male compulsive gamblers often begin when they are teenagers, but women usually start to gamble later in life. By the time a compulsive gambler seeks help, he or she usually has debts running from $55,000 to $92,000.

Pathological gambling usually occurs along with other problems. About three-quarters of compulsive gamblers in one study had suffered from attention-deficit disorder, also called hyperactivity, and about half said they had trouble controlling the amount of alcohol they drank. Some researchers believe that compulsive gamblers place bets as self-medicating behavior because gambling temporarily makes them feel better.

As is the case with people who have impulse control disorders, compulsive gamblers can recover through therapy and regular attendance at self-help group meetings. In addition, some residential treatment centers now exist for those who suffer from this problem.

REFERENCES

Brister, Phyllis, and David Brister. *The Vicious Circle Phenomenon, Our Battle for Self-Control: How To Win the War.* Birmingham, AL: Diadem Publishing, 1987.

The Diagnostic and Statistical Manual III (DSM III), revised. Washington, DC: American Psychiatric Association Press, 1987.

Jenike, Michael, Lee Baer, and William Minichiello. *Obsessive-Compulsive Disorders: Theory and Management*, 2d edition. Chicago: Yearbook Medical Publishers, 1990.

Nemiah, John, and Thomas Uhde. "Obsessive-Compulsive Disorder," in *The Comprehensive Textbook of Psychiatry*, 5th edition, Harold I. Kaplan and Benjamin J. Sadock, eds. Baltimore, MD: Williams & Wilkins, 1989.

Rapoport, Judith. *The Boy Who Couldn't Stop Washing: The Experience and Treatment of Obsessive-Compulsive Disorder*. New York: New American Library, 1989.

Witkin, Georgia. *Beyond Quick Fixes: Control Your Irresistible Urges before They Control You*. New York: Berkeley Books, 1988.

Yaryura, Tobias and Fugen Neziroglu. *Obsessive Compulsive Disorders: Pathogenesis, Diagnosis, Treatment*. New York: Marcel Dekker, 1983.

Resources
for Finding Out about Self-Defeating Behaviors

Nonfiction

BOOKS

Booth, Father Leo. **Breaking the Chains: Understanding Religious Addiction and Religious Abuse.** Long Beach, CA: Emmaus Publications, 1989. 269p.

With chapters on the TV evangelist scandal and who is at risk regarding this problem, Father Booth makes a convincing argument that people can be addicted to religion. That addiction shares many parallels with alcoholism and drug abuse. This book outlines the stages of religious addiction and offers help not only for the religious addict but for his or her family members as well.

Carnes, Patrick. **Out of the Shadows: Understanding Sexual Addiction.** Minneapolis, MN: CompCare, 1983. 196p.

Unraveling the web of love, sex, hate, fear, and compulsion, Carnes, who runs a sexual addiction treatment program, helps readers take a look at a major problem in the United States today. This book is considered a classic in the field.

Damon, Janet. **Shopaholics: Serious Help for Addicted Spenders.** New York: Price Stern Sloan, 1988. 240p.

Out-of-control spending is the topic here as Damon tells exactly what compulsive shopping is and offers suggestions about how to deal with it. She also includes a chapter for families and friends of compulsive shoppers.

Kasl, Charlotte Davis. **Women, Sex and Addiction: A Search for Love and Power.** New York: Ticknor & Fields, 1989. 416p.

Many women in our culture believe sex is the price they have to pay for love. Some women turn to sex because they feel it gives them power, or they use it to escape. For them, sex becomes as much of a drug as alcohol. This book tells women how to begin to meet their needs for approval and love themselves so that their sexuality is healthy rather than dependent.

Kaye, Yvonne. **Credit, Cash and Co-Dependency.** Deerfield Beach, FL: Health Communications, 1991. 112p.

Compulsive spending is something that can profoundly affect codependents. This book explains how to break through the denial that often surrounds this behavior and talks about how compulsive spenders—and compulsive savers—can reclaim their self-worth.

Lasater, Lane. **Recovery from Compulsive Behavior: How To Transcend Your Troubled Family.** Deerfield Beach, FL: Health Communications, 1988. 132p.

In this book Lasater tells how compulsive behavior patterns can be healed. In addition to providing material on substance abuse, Lasater delves into sexual addiction and compulsive spending, gambling, and overeating. The key points here are that compulsiveness underlies a number of addictions and that, if that compulsiveness is not healed, an addict will recover from one addiction only to trade it for another.

Miller, Joy. **Addictive Relationships: Reclaiming Your Boundaries.** Deerfield Beach, FL: Health Communications, 1989. 128p.

People who form addictive relationships give themselves away to other people—they do not know where they leave off and the person they love begins. This book helps readers start establishing boundaries by looking at who they are and where they want to go. Readers also learn to love themselves rather than to always be dependent on outside sources for validation and affection.

Robinson, Bryan E. **Work Addiction: Hidden Legacies of Adult Children.** Deerfield Beach, FL: Health Communications, 1989. 179p.

Because society generally praises workaholics, their compulsion to overachieve, often at the expense of other areas of their lives, is a hidden problem. This book explores the connection between growing up in a dysfunctional family and later suffering from work addiction.

Schaef, Anne Wilson. **Escape from Intimacy: Untangling the "Love" Addictions: Sex, Romance, Relationships.** New York: Harper & Row, 1989. 176p.

Schaef takes a long, hard look at love addiction and how U.S. society fosters it. She also offers a Twelve Step program for recovering from it.

Smith, Ann W. **Overcoming Perfectionism: The Key to a Balanced Recovery.** Deerfield Beach, FL: Health Communications, 1990. 174p.

Compulsive perfectionism prevents people from living full lives and from having close relationships. It stems from low self-esteem and often causes self-esteem to drop even further. This book is about learning to lighten up and enjoy life rather than always having to be perfect. It includes tips about "learning to live in the middle."

Witkin, Georgia. **Beyond Quick Fixes: Control Your Irresistible Urges Before They Control You.** New York: Berkeley Books, 1988. 216p.

When Witkin interviewed women for her book, she found that eating and shopping are the most prevalent ways women try to escape from their pain. Gambling, sexual fixes, and a number of other compulsive behaviors are covered in this book that helps women recognize the symptoms of compulsive behavior and then do something about it. A resource list is included in the back of the book.

PAMPHLETS

B., Patricia. **Me? A Sexual Addict?** Park Ridge, IL: Parkside Publishing Corporation, 1991. 17p.

Figuring out whether or not you have a sexual addiction can be one of the toughest parts of recovery according to this author. In this introductory pamphlet, she tells the stories of several sex addicts and tells readers what it is like to attend a Twelve Step recovery meeting.

Heineman, Mary. **When Someone You Love Gambles.** Center City, MN: Hazelden Educational Materials, 1988. 28p.

This booklet provides help for family members of compulsive gamblers.

Lorenz, Valerie C. **Releasing Guilt.** Center City, MN: Hazelden Educational Materials, 1988. 32p.

Compulsive gamblers deal with a great deal of guilt during the recovery process. Lorenz tells how to release this guilt and build positive self-esteem.

Nonprint Materials

Crush

Type:	VHS video
Length:	18 min.
Cost:	Purchase $75
Distributor:	Network Publications
	P.O. Box 1830
	Santa Cruz, CA 95061-1830
Date:	1989

This video, which was produced by the YWCA, provides an in-depth look at what it means to be an adolescent girl and infatuated. It assists viewers in looking at their own feelings of dependency centering on love and shows how to have healthy relationships.

Lovesick

Type:	VHS video
Length:	16 min.
Cost:	Purchase $75
Distributor:	Network Publications
	P.O. Box 1830
	Santa Cruz, CA 95061-1830
Date:	1989

A companion to *Crush*, in this video boys and young men talk about their experiences and about pressures society places on them regarding love relationships.

Organizations

Debtors Anonymous
General Service Board
P.O. Box 20322
New York, NY 10025-9992
(212) 969-0710

Debtors Anonymous helps compulsive spenders beat their habits and get their finances in order. Its work is based on a Twelve Step program, and it also publishes a newsletter as well as offering phone support.

Gam-Anon Family Groups
P.O. Box 157
Whitestone, NY 11357
(718) 352-1671

Gam-Anon is an organization for the families and friends of compulsive gamblers. It uses a Twelve Step recovery plan and has chapters throughout the country, including groups for teenagers. A newsletter, pamphlets, and guidelines for starting groups are also offered.

Gamblers Anonymous
National Service Office
P.O. Box 17173
Los Angeles, CA 90017
(213) 386-8789

Gamblers Anonymous is a Twelve Step program designed to help people stop gambling. It publishes a monthly newsletter and offers guidelines for starting local chapters.

Sex and Love Addicts Anonymous
Fellowship-Wide Services, Inc.
P.O. Box 119, New Town Branch
Boston, MA 02258
(617) 332-1845

This group, founded 15 years ago, has over 500 chapters throughout the country. It publishes literature and can offer advice about starting local chapters.

Workaholics Anonymous
511 Sir Francis Drake Boulevard, C-170
Greenbrae, CA 94904

Workaholics Anonymous is a new Twelve Step group for people who feel unable to take a break from work. The California chapter, whose address is listed above, can tell you whether a group exists in your area or provide a starter kit. Include a self-addressed, stamped envelope when you write to this organization.

Hotline

New Jersey Council on Compulsive Gambling
(800) GAMBLER (426-2537)

This hotline operates 24 hours a day.

CHAPTER 7

Codependents: Addiction's Other Victims

The truck didn't stop in the driveway. Dad drove it half-way across the lawn. Then I knew. Before he even got out of the truck, I knew.

He opened the door and almost fell out. Then he staggered over to the steps and grabbed the railing to keep from falling. I'd seen him drunk a lot of times. But never this drunk. He could hardly even talk.

"Hey there, boy! What yu doin' up here when your old man's lookin' for yu? Come on. We gotta get home and pack your shtuff. We're hittin' the road."

I couldn't think. My mind felt the same way your jaw does when the dentist pumps it full of freezing. "What?" was all I could say.

Cowboys Don't Cry by Marilyn Halvorson
(New York: Dell/Laurel Leaf, 1984), 122.

Shane's father was drinking and driving the night of the car wreck that killed the 14-year-old's mother. Since that time, the situation for Shane and his dad has gone from bad to worse. When Shane's dad, who travels with the rodeo, gets a chance to settle down, the teenager hopes against hope that finally he will have a chance to live a normal life. But having an alcoholic for a father, an irresponsible parent who embarrasses him in front of his friends and is never there when Shane needs him, means Shane's life cannot be normal. Angry at his dad and still grieving his mom's death, Shane learns to "stuff" his feelings deep inside himself. After all, cowboys do not cry.

Shane's confusion, numbness, and determination to survive at all costs are traits shared by children whose parents are chemically dependent. Codependents, who are members of families that include an addicted or compulsive parent or sibling, often feel alone, but they are not. A surprisingly high number of teenagers today live with a mother or father who is addicted to drugs, alcohol, or a behavior.

Addiction: A Family Disease

- An estimated 28 million Americans have at least 1 alcoholic parent, according to the National Association of Children of Alcoholics.
- Over 7 million children of alcoholics are under the age of 20.
- One in 4 families has a relative who is currently abusing alcohol, according to a 1987 Gallup Poll.
- Fifteen to 18 percent of the people in this country will, at sometime during their lives, become dependent on alcohol or another drug. Many of these people have children (Robins et al. and Meyers et al.).
- Some family therapists believe that if the definition of dysfunctional families is broadened to include those with battering, incest, emotional abuse, and compulsive behaviors, as many as 94 percent of all families in this country foster codependency.

When people are dependent on alcohol or drugs or on a behavior pattern such as overeating or gambling, their problem profoundly affects the people who love them most—their relatives. In these families or in families where incest or battering is present, every member becomes "addicted" in a sense to keeping the secret from outsiders. Problems arise no matter who is addicted, but children are most profoundly affected when the family addict is a parent, rather than a grandparent or a sibling.

Addicted or compulsive parents try to protect their habits, keeping their behavior secret at all costs because they are convinced they could not survive if they quit abusing their substance or engaging in their behavior of choice. The more deeply dependent they become on the chemical or the activity, the less time and energy they have to be a husband, a wife, or a parent. As addiction progresses, problem parents may lose their jobs, become suicidal, or get in trouble with the law. Consequently, families start to fall apart at the seams.

- In as many as 90 percent of child abuse cases, alcohol is a significant factor, according to the National Association of Children of Alcoholics.
- Sixty-three percent of women victims of domestic violence, in one study reported by the National Institute on Alcohol and Addiction, said their husbands had been drinking at the time the beatings occurred.

Even when domestic violence or sexual abuse is not part of the family picture, emotional abuse and neglect often go hand in hand with addiction. Parents caught up in addictions or compulsive behaviors cannot give their children the time and attention necessary to enable them to grow up to be emotionally healthy adults. These parents are too busy obsessing about their next drink or fix or food binge to show up at the softball game they promised to attend or to listen to their child's problems or concerns.

Often the other parent, the one who is not an alcoholic, drug addict, or overeater, is so wrapped up in trying to control the addict's behavior that he or she also has little time to be a good parent. Children may be left to fend for themselves. Quite frequently the children are even blamed for being the source of the family's unhappiness. As a result they develop feelings that there is something wrong with them and that they are not okay people.

Many of these children falsely believe that if only they could be better than or different from who they really are, or that maybe if they had never been born, their addicted parent would be fine again and the family would live happily ever after. After spending months and years blaming themselves and trying to be perfect, children of dysfunctional families start to second-guess their addicted parent in order to either control his or her behavior or avoid its consequences. This attempt to make life more predictable leads codependents to live outside of themselves. What other people feel and think and do seems more important to them than what is going on inside of them or their own needs.

To survive in a family with chemical dependency or compulsion problems, spouses and children must adapt to the unpredictable and sometimes dangerous lifestyle of the addict. Even though they may have started out as emotionally healthy, people who have learned to cope with an addicted or compulsive parent eventually develop emotional problems. They may not be hooked on a chemical or a compulsive behavior, but they are hooked into a harmful, dysfunctional relationship with the addicted person they love. The results can be very damaging.

The negative effects of growing up in a dysfunctional family—of learning to live outside one's own skin in order to emotionally, and sometimes physically, survive—can last for years if they are not faced and treated. If the codependent does not receive counseling, these problems can even persist when the alcoholic, drug abusing, or compulsive parent recovers.

Life with an Addict

Whether a parent drinks too much, takes drugs, is hooked on tranquilizers, or obsesses constantly about work, the family life he or she creates shares certain common characteristics. Dysfunctional families tend to be

- Unpredictable places to live
- Turned upside-down
- Centered around the problem family member
- Caught up in illusions
- Shame-filled
- Secretive and isolated
- Often perfectly normal in appearance to outsiders

Dysfunctional families are unpredictable places to live because there is no way of knowing from one minute to the next what an addicted parent's mood will be or whether he or she will follow through on promises. Family members learn not to trust the addict and the world in general.

These families are turned upside-down, with even young children often asked to serve as parents to their troubled parents. Children may do most of the work around the house, and sometimes teenagers must take nearly full-time jobs to help support the family. Many times children of chemically dependent or compulsive parents are expected to take responsibility for and provide emotional support and nurturing to both parents. These children are forced to act like adults long before they are ready to do so.

The dysfunctional family typically centers around the problem family member. Most decisions are made based on the addiction. Family members may consciously avoid doing things that they think would upset their chemically dependent or compulsive relative. At other times family members rebel against the addict. People who live with addicts spend most of their time caretaking and trying not to cause more trouble than the family already has. Because talking about feelings rocks the boat, dysfunctional family members learn to stuff emotions deep inside. Eventually they may lose the ability to know within themselves what they are feeling.

The dysfunctional family also is caught up in illusions. People who grow up in dysfunctional families do not just have their feelings and their needs ignored, but also they are often told that what they see and hear did not happen or does not exist. When Mom eats two boxes of donuts and a quart of ice cream and then throws up, she is not bulimic; she simply has the flu. Dad did not spend all of his paycheck at the racetrack; he was mugged. After repeatedly being labeled wrong, bad, or crazy for telling the truth, children learn not to trust their own perceptions. Eventually they begin to lie to themselves, denying that the problem exists.

Shame is another characteristic of dysfunctional families. Although people who live in dysfunctional families usually do not talk about their emotions even within the walls of their home, they constantly carry a crippling burden of shame because of the addict's behavior and their own self-blame. Quite justifiably, they feel outraged at the unfairness of living with an addict and sad that their lives are not better. As a result, they feel even more shame about their sadness and anger. Feeling worthless and unlovable, many codependents will do anything to get other people to love them, in an attempt to fill the empty ache inside where self-esteem should be.

Dysfunctional families also tend to be secretive and isolated. Because they are so ashamed of their family and because they often believe they are the cause of their parent's problems, codependents make every effort to keep what goes on inside the family a secret from other people. This involves not talking about the family problem to outsiders and keeping friends at a distance. When they are confronted by teachers, counselors, or social workers, children of addicted or compulsive parents sometimes lie, afraid that if anyone knew the truth about what their family was really like, the consequences would be unbearable.

Ironically, dysfunctional families often appear perfectly normal to outsiders. Despite the fact that they have difficulty forming and maintaining close relationships with people outside their families, people from families with addicts are experts at looking good. Over the years they learn to be compliant people-pleasers even though they may secretly want to cry or blow up. Because of their ability to get by without drawing attention to themselves, many codependents seem okay on the surface to people who do not know them very well. That characteristic often means they do not get the help they need.

Family Roles

The price for keeping a dysfunctional family together while protecting the addiction or compulsion is a high one. Family members are forced to play rigid roles within the dysfunctional family system in order to remain a part of the group. As long as everyone plays his or her role without question, the family sticks together as a unit, even though it is an unhealthy one.

Although adult members of chemically dependent or compulsive families may have a choice about whether to stay and play their roles or leave the family unit, children and teenagers do not have that choice. They need to be part of a family in order to be fed, clothed, and sheltered. Even in families where little actual love exists, physical survival requirements keep children from rebelling too much against family expectations.

Not surprisingly, the dysfunctional roles that children must play if they are to remain in the family can be as restrictive as prisons. Instead of being valued for the unique individuals they are, people who are part of a family with an addicted or compulsive member are valued solely for the skill with which they act out their parts. When children try to break out of the mold and work to create their own definition of who they are, they run the risk of being disowned or abandoned.

After years of work with chemically dependent families, substance abuse counselors discovered that the following roles happen repeatedly. Because no two families are alike, some variations may occur. As a general rule, though, once he or she has learned a script in order to survive growing up, the child of an addict clings to that way of relating to the world, even outside of the family.

FAMILY HERO

Usually the oldest child, the Family Hero works hard to be a success, to always do what is right, and to gain approval. He or she tries to "make up" for the family problem by becoming a high achiever. A Family Hero may do this by getting good grades, participating in many extracurricular activities, and excelling in sports. Heros are the children who take on a heavy burden of responsibility around the house in addition to their outside accomplishments. On the negative side, Family Heroes tend to boss others around and to always believe they are right.

Rather than taking joy in their achievements, however, Family Heroes often feel disappointed in themselves. Perfectionists, they think they should always be doing more and doing it better. Some Family Heroes work doubly hard at achieving because they feel sure that if they can just win one more award or get one more scholarship, their dysfunctional family will change for the better. When this does not happen, the Hero tries even harder and may eventually use work like a drug to numb out feelings.

SCAPEGOAT

Because the Hero role is already taken, the next child born into a dysfunctional family tends to enact the role of Scapegoat. Because it would be too hard to compete with the superachieving star of the family, this child becomes the antihero. Defiant and angry on the outside, the Scapegoat feels hurt and guilty inside. A troublemaker, this child will do anything for attention, and most of the attention he or she receives is negative. Scapegoats have problems with authority figures, including teachers and sometimes even the law. Scapegoats may even fail school or get pregnant very young.

They are rebels with a cause. Even though the Scapegoat may not know it, he or she has a mission in life—to draw the family's attention away from the addict. Dysfunctional families get so caught up in the trouble this child causes that they "forget" about the chemically dependent or compulsive parent. More often than not, the Scapegoat is directly blamed for all of the family problems, not just those he or she provokes.

LOST CHILD

The Lost Child in a dysfunctional family cannot hope to compete with the "good" child or the "bad" one, so he or she tries to be invisible, giving up, becoming a loner and withdrawing from the family as far as possible. Although the family member who plays this role may give the appearance that he or she does not care about anything, inside this child feels incredibly lonely and unimportant.

Because the Lost Child is usually very little trouble, his or her parents are grateful for the vacation. But even though the Lost Child's quiet exterior causes very few problems for the family, Lost Children suffer a host of problems silently. They may be depressed or live in a fantasy world, eventually escaping into drugs. Lost Children are isolated and have few friends. They are very sensitive to peer pressure and tend to be easily swayed by others when they do form relationships outside their families. It is difficult for them to think for themselves or to make their own decisions and get motivated to carry them out. Sometimes it seems as though the Lost Child is not really there.

MASCOT

The last child to be born into a dysfunctional family usually takes on the Mascot role. This child is the family baby and sometimes remains so even through adulthood. Emotionally fragile and slow to mature, Mascots like to clown. By playing family fool, they take people's minds off the family problem in a fairly positive way. Older family members protect them, often to the point of keeping them completely in the dark about the family problem.

Although Mascots get taken care of in exchange for making people laugh, inside they are often afraid. They are able to manipulate other people in the family into taking over their responsibilities, but Mascots pay a high price for their immaturity. Because they do not learn the skills they need to be able to become even partially independent, they must rely on their families to completely care for them. Nobody takes them seriously, and they are often prone to learning disabilities and hyperactivity—they simply cannot sit still. Often they get into trouble in school for being disruptive.

Early Signs of Codependency

Because denial of the addicted parent's problem is such an important part of the addiction and compulsion process, even when a family is in deep trouble, it is still often difficult for them to acknowledge that they have a problem, too. This makes even more sense given the fact that children form their notions of what it means to be a family from their own families. Many people who grow up in a chemically dependent or compulsive home do not have a clear sense that their lifestyle is neither normal nor healthy. After all, they have not seen many, or possibly even any, alternatives, so they may believe that all homes are just as chaotic and shame-filled as their own.

People who think they may be a part of a dysfunctional family can ask themselves the following questions to make a decision about whether their parent's problem is harming them. The more of these questions that can be answered with a yes, the higher the chances a parent's substance abuse or addiction to a compulsive behavior has deeply affected you and your family.

- Do you hide your parent's behavior from outsiders and even family members?
- Do you try to protect your parent from the consequences of his or her behavior?
- Do you lie and make excuses to other people for the things your parent does?
- Do you feel responsible for your parent and ashamed of him or her?
- Do you try to ignore your parent's behavior by pretending that it is not happening?
- Do you make attempts to control your parent's use of chemical substances or his or her compulsive behaviors?
- Do you take over your parent's duties around the house?
- Do you worry a great deal about the problem?
- Do you experience severe mood swings from high to low?
- Do you feel resentful and disappointed?
- Do you feel self-doubt and fear?
- Do you have difficulty concentrating on school work because you nearly constantly think about your parent's problem?
- Do you have a hard time making plans because you never know what your parent will do next?
- Do you get headaches, feel sick to your stomach, or have a hard time sleeping because of your parent's behavior?

Adult Children

Adult children of alcoholics and other dysfunctional families, the term professionals sometimes use to describe codependents, is an appropriate one. When people grow up in a household that revolves around an addiction or a compulsion, they often do not get to experience a childhood, let alone a happy one. Not only does the constant stress take an emotional toll, but also many adult children have never been truly parented. They have not had a chance to go through developmental stages and learn the healthy coping skills necessary to become emotionally whole adults. Because their needs for love, security, acceptance, control, guidance, independence, and faith were never met by their parents, a part of them remains stuck in childhood.

Therapists refer to that part as the inner child or authentic self—the inner part of people that most truly reflects who they are as opposed to the persona they adopt or the roles they play. Even though an adult who grew up in a dysfunctional family can have children of his or her own, a house and a car, and even gray hair, without help he or she may remain an emotionally needy little child inside, afraid and unable to cope with the demands of parenting. An obvious addiction or compulsion does not need to be present in the family the adult child creates; this codependent parent still cannot provide a home where children can experience love, trust, guidance, and all the other necessities for emotional growth. Not only does the adult child not know how to parent, but also his or her inner child often demands nurturing from the actual children in the family. Another dysfunctional family is born, and the cycle continues.

In addition to childhood neglect, learning is a factor in this process as well. After years of adapting to life with a chemically dependent or compulsive family member, codependents have been schooled in their old family roles so well that they forget that in the world outside, they do not have to play by the old rules and roles. Without help they may grow up and leave their dysfunctional homes and still continue to act as if there were a chemically dependent or compulsive parent standing over their shoulder. In adulthood, those who grew up in chemically dependent families

- Have a high risk of developing chemical dependency themselves. Children of alcoholics have a four times greater risk of becoming alcoholics than others do (National Council on Alcoholism and Drug Dependence).
- Have a higher risk for marrying someone with a chemical dependency problem or other addiction (National Association for Children of Alcoholics).
- Suffer from a number of psychological difficulties such as suicide attempts, anxiety, eating disorders, and compulsive achieving (National Association for Children of Alcoholics).

The extent to which an adult child's family of origin affects his or her coping skills in later life is determined generally by the following factors:

- The point in an adult child's life when the parent's addiction or compulsive behavior started. Codependents who cannot remember having a healthy family have a very difficult time determining what is normal in later life.
- The severity of the addiction or compulsion. If a parent has an extreme problem, the children will be under more stress than if that parent is in the early stages of the problem.
- The parent's behavior. All addicts and compulsive people are not alike. For example, one chemically dependent parent may explode in rage when he or she is under the influence of a substance, whereas another parent will withdraw. As a rule,

the more bizarre and abusive the parent's behavior, the more negative the impact on the children.

- The family's stability. Some families with an addicted or compulsive parent manage to survive without major crises. House payments are made; food is on the table; the police do not knock at the door. Other families are torn apart by violence, sexual abuse, and financial or legal problems. Severe disruptions tend to cause more emotional trauma than do mild ones.
- The child's support systems. In some addicted and compulsive families, other relatives such as aunts and uncles or grandparents step in to fill the gaps in love and nurturing left by parents. Even when this does not happen, children may be able to form a support network of teachers and friends that helps them survive their growing-up years. In most instances, the more isolated a child from a dysfunctional family remains while growing up, the more severe his or her problems will be in adult life.

Characteristics of Codependency

The legacy of growing up in a dysfunctional family, adult codependency, can range from mild to so severe that the ability to function in later life is severely hampered. According to Codependents Anonymous (CoDA), a self-help group for those who grew up in dysfunctional families, codependence is the inability to form and maintain healthy relationships. Others have defined the problem as people addiction. No matter which definition one chooses to use, the basis of a codependent's many problems is that person's inability to form a healthy relationship with himself or herself. Because codependents spent most of their childhoods out of touch with their own feelings and needs, they have little sense of who they really are and as adults still rely on others to define them. Some of the most prevalent symptoms of adult codependency are shame, living through others, difficulty recognizing and sharing feelings, inability to trust, and dependency.

SHAME

Codependents tend to be perfectionists and to judge themselves harshly. If they make a mistake, they believe it has more to do with who they are inside rather than what they have done. Because they feel sure that they are deeply flawed people and that there is nothing they can do to change, they often feel helpless and depressed. They have difficulty taking charge of their own lives because they grew up passively reacting to situations that seemed out of control instead of learning to act from a solid sense of self-esteem.

Because codependents never received the parenting they needed as children, when they become adults they often seek out others to provide that parenting for them. When they are not taking care of people, they are demanding that others care for them. Childhood left them feeling so worthless and unlovable that adult codependents are terrified of abandonment and will do anything to hold on to a relationship. As long as another person loves them, they can believe they must be worth something.

LIVING THROUGH OTHERS

To keep another person in their lives, codependents become people-pleasers, putting the needs of others before their own. They try never to disagree or even to want things their friend or partner does not want. By always giving in to other people and rarely taking from them, codependents not only temporarily feel better about themselves, but they also are able to control other people by making them feel obligated.

Because approval from other people is one of the few methods codependents have for feeling that they are worthy of being alive, they often fall into the trap of approval seeking. Adult codependents take on the habits and the beliefs of the people they are with in order to fit into the crowd. Belonging, even to a group of people they do not really like, gives codependents a sense of family.

DIFFICULTY RECOGNIZING AND SHARING FEELINGS

To survive their traumatic childhoods, codependents had to stuff their feelings deep inside. As adults they still hide how they feel, even from themselves. Much of the time what they feel, besides shame, is resentment, because they have put their needs below the needs of the people around them. Masters at acting pleasant, codependents can smile and talk softly even when they are seething with hidden anger.

Having grown up with angry and unpredictable parents, as adults codependents remain terrified of anger, conflict, and criticism. They will agree to almost anything just to avoid an argument. Because expressing feelings was a taboo for them in their families of origin, they often have difficulty being open about even their positive emotions. It is possible to know a codependent for years, even to live with one, and still never know what he or she is really thinking or feeling.

INABILITY TO TRUST

Even though codependents need other people in their lives to provide them the nurturing they never received as children, they do not trust others. Living for so long in a home where everything seemed totally out of their control, codependents as adults always expect the worst from other people. To avoid what they consider to be inevitable—betrayal and hurt feelings—they learn to manipulate and control those with whom they enter into relationships.

Often they do this with a subtle kind of bossiness, telling others what is good for them or using third parties as go-between. Because these tactics usually result in just what the codependent tries to avoid—being hurt—they only reinforce the codependent's distrust of others. Many codependents react to crumbled relationships by isolating themselves, withdrawing from people completely until they need another self-esteem fix.

DEPENDENCY

Often codependents try to escape the painful reality of their own shame by looking to things outside themselves to make them feel better. For many codependents, relationships become the drug of choice. In recovery circles a current joke has it that codependents do not have relationships; they take hostages.

Because of the roles they played growing up, people from dysfunctional families are especially attracted to friendships and love relationships with addicts or other codependents. They tend to confuse pity with love and to bond with people they can rescue. After all, caretaking is what they know how to do best. Even though their alliances with others are troubled ones, there is some comfort in living out the familiar patterns learned while growing up, right down to the chaos.

Other codependents try to escape the harsh reality of their low self-esteem by taking drugs, using alcohol, or locking into behaviors such as eating disorders or compulsive spending. Although these strategies give the illusion of providing temporary escape, on a long-term basis they only compound the codependent's problems.

Healing from Codependency

Often codependents find it difficult to reach out for help. They have been taking care of other people for so long that they have forgotten how to take care of and to care about themselves. Once they get past their initial reluctance, they discover that healing from a life of codependency takes time and effort. Building a solid sense of self, learning to acknowledge and express feelings, and discovering how to relate to others in positive ways are complex tasks that are very difficult to accomplish alone. Yet it is a very worthwhile struggle, one that leads to self-esteem and positive relationships. Recovery is the only way to break the cycle of addiction and abuse in families.

In recent years available help for codependents has increased dramatically. Today most large cities have several therapists who specialize in issues common to people who grew up with an addicted or compulsive parent or who were raised in another type of dysfunctional family. A good way to find a qualified professional counselor is to call chemical dependency treatment centers in your area and ask for referrals.

Self-help groups can be a good option, too, because they offer recovering codependents a place to practice their newfound people skills. Simply discovering that others grew up in severely troubled families can help alleviate some of the shame and isolation many codependents have felt for most of their lives. Self-help recovery groups teach how to trust and how to recognize and express feelings honestly. They are safe places where the codependent can discover who he or she really is, rather than playing an old role.

Finally, scores of books have been written for codependents that provide both information and moral support for the road to recovery. A sampling of those materials is listed at the end of this chapter.

Coping with Adolescent Codependency

Adolescents who are old enough to begin recognizing that the families they live in are not healthy but who still depend on their parents for financial support face a difficult dilemma. If they rock the boat too much during their own recovery, they risk being put out of their family before they are emotionally or financially ready to be independent. Living with a parent who is compulsive or chemically dependent while working on one's own recovery requires a special set of coping skills. The following list contains some of the positive things teenagers who find themselves in this situation can do.

- Know that it is okay to feel. It is perfectly normal for those who live with a problem parent to be confused, angry, and sad. It is also perfectly normal for teenagers from dysfunctional families to love their parents and hate the addiction or compulsive behavior.
- Share feelings about the family problem with a close friend or a trusted adult. Talking about your emotions is not betraying the family, and it is a way to feel less alone. Everyone needs emotional support.
- Meet emotional needs by getting involved in activities that are fun to do and that provide a break from the problem parent. Hobbies, clubs, sports, and after-school activities expand people's horizons beyond the confines of the dysfunctional family.
- Get help by getting involved with Alateen or an Adult Children of Alcoholics (ACA) support group.
- Avoid riding in a car driven by anyone, even a parent, who is under the influence of alcohol or drugs.
- Try not to feel ashamed about the situation at home. A parent's addiction or compulsion is *not* the child's fault.
- Avoid taking responsibility for, protecting, and enabling the addicted parent.
- Remember that it is useless to try to talk sensibly to a parent about his or her habit when he or she is under the influence of alcohol or drugs. When people are drunk or drugged, they cannot listen to logic.
- Understand that teenagers have no control over a parent's addiction or compulsion. Whether or not the parent gets treatment is his or her decision. Teenagers need to detach and respect their parent's dignity, letting him or her take responsibility for himself or herself. Adolescents from dysfunctional families have enough to do taking care of themselves.
- Be realistic about the future. When an addicted or compulsive parent recovers, all of his or her children's problems do not automatically go away. Besides, there is no guarantee that a parent will ever get better. Codependents need to take care of themselves in the here and now by living one day at a time.

REFERENCES

Balis, S. "Illusion and Reality: Issues in the Treatment of Adult Children of Alcoholics." *Alcoholism Treatment Quarterly,* 1986, 3(4): 67–91.

Beattie, Melody. *Beyond Codependency—and Getting Better All the Time.* San Francisco: Harper/Hazelden, 1989.

————. *Codependent No More*. San Francisco: Harper/Hazelden, 1987.

Berkowitz, A., and H. W. Perkins. "Personality Characteristics of Children of Alcoholics." *Journal of Consulting and Clinical Psychology*, 1988, 56(2): 206–209.

Berry, Carmen Renee. *When Helping You Is Hurting Me: Escaping the Messiah Trap*. San Francisco: Harper & Row, 1988.

Black, Claudia. *It Will Never Happen to Me: Children of Alcoholics as Youngsters, Adolescents and Adults*. Denver, CO: M.A.C. Publishing, 1982.

Black, Claudia, S. Bucky, and S. Wilder Padilla. "The Interpersonal and Emotional Consequences of Being an Adult Child of an Alcoholic." *International Journal of the Addictions*, 1986, 21(2): 213–231.

Bradshaw, John. *Bradshaw on the Family*. Deerfield Beach, FL: Health Communications, 1988.

————. *Healing the Shame That Binds You*. Deerfield Beach, FL: Health Communications, 1988.

Bratton, M., and C. Galvin. "Inside the House of Mirrors: Blurred Boundaries and Identity Confusion in the Alcoholic Family." *Focus on Chemically Dependent Families*, 1988, 11(4): 24–25.

Brown, S. *Treating Adult Children of Alcoholics: A Developmental Perspective*. New York: John Wiley, 1988.

Codependency. Pompano Beach, FL: Health Communications, 1984.

Hibbard, S. "The Diagnosis and Treatment of Adult Children of Alcoholics as a Specialized Therapeutic Population." *Psychotherapy*, 1987, 24(4): 779–785.

Mellody, Pia. *Facing Codependence: What It Is, Where It Comes from and How It Sabotages Our Lives*. San Francisco: Harper & Row, 1989.

Merryman, R. *Broken Promises, Mended Dreams*. Boston: Little, Brown, 1984.

Porterfield, Kay Marie. *Coping with an Alcoholic Parent*. New York: Rosen Press, 1990.

————. *Coping with Codependency*. New York: Rosen Press, 1991.

Robins et al., 1984, and Meyers et al., 1984, both summarized in "Epidemiologic Bulletin No. 16." *Alcohol Health and Research World*, Summer 1987.

Wegschieder-Cruse, Sharon. *Another Chance: Hope and Health for the Alcoholic Family*. Palo Alto, CA: Science and Behavior Books, 1989.

————. *Choicemaking*. Pompano Beach, FL: Health Communications, 1985.

Wotitz, Janet. *Adult Children of Alcoholics*. Pompano Beach, FL: Health Communications, 1983.

Resources
for Finding Out about Codependency

Many of the materials listed in this section have to do with alcoholic parents because this is the type of dysfunctional family that has been researched the most. Both the problems and solutions discussed in these materials, however, apply to dysfunctional families in general, whether the problem they suffer from is chemical dependency or compulsions. Because emotional, physical, or sexual abuse often occurs in dysfunctional families where there is an alcohol or drug problem, these issues are dealt with in many of these materials as well.

Fiction

Brooks, Bruce. **No Kidding.** New York: Harper & Row, 1989. 224p.

In this science fiction novel set in the twenty-first century, alcoholism of epidemic proportions has caused society to collapse. Sam, a 14-year-old, finds himself placed in a position where he has to look out for his younger brother and his recovering mom.

Conrad, Pam. **Holding Me Here.** New York: Harper & Row, 1986. 192p.

You would think 14-year-old Robin would have enough problems of her own coping with her parents' divorce. When her mother takes in a boarder, a woman who has run away from her children and an abusively alcoholic husband, Robin begins to meddle. This book has been recommended for reluctant readers by the American Library Association.

————. **Taking the Ferry Home.** New York: Harper & Row, 1988. 224p.

Sixteen-year-old Ali has felt loved and understood ever since her dad started recovering from his alcoholism. But the family of Ali's best friend, Simone, is actively alcoholic, so Simone feels horrible and insecure. This book details the growing friendship between the two girls and how they deal with the tragedies that touch their lives.

Erika, Tamar. **Blues for Silk Garcia.** New York: Knopf/Borzoi Sprinter, 1991. 160p.

Linda is a born musician. This rising young rock musician knows she got her musical talent from her dad, a deceased jazz star. Compelled to find out more about him, she discovers that not only was he a thief but a junkie as well. She despairs that she has inherited her father's selfishness as well as his talent.

Fox, Paula. **The Moonlight Man.** New York: Bradbury Press, 1986. 179p.

Paula's father is a charmer despite the fact that he is three weeks late picking her up for their summer vacation together. Even though her time with him is a fun-filled adventure, she worries about his drinking. When she confronts him, he promises he will quit, but he does not. Paula is tormented by the conflict between her love for him and her anger at his drinking.

Greenberg, Jan. **Exercises of the Heart.** New York: Farrar, Straus & Giroux, 1986. 153p.

Roxie Baskowitz, whose mother is disabled and whose father is dead, feels sorry for herself until she becomes best friends with Glo, a girl whose mom is an alcoholic. A crisis brings Glo's mother's problem out into the open, and she is taken to a treatment center. This book explores the denial, caretaking, and covering up that children of alcoholics do for their drinking parent.

Halvorson, Marilyn. **Cowboys Don't Cry.** New York: Dell/Laurel Leaf, 1984. 160p.

Shane, a 14-year-old who follows the rodeo circuit with his father, is still grieving his mother's death of 4 years before. He is sure his dad was responsible for the accident that killed her because he knows his dad was driving under the influence of alcohol. Because his father has dealt with his own grief by drinking, Shane has a double problem. He wants his dad to quit traveling and stop drinking, but he is not sure how much impact his needs have on his father.

Likhanov, Albert. **Shadows across the Sun.** New York: Harper & Row, 1983. 150p.

Set in Russia and translated into English by Richard Lourie, this book tells of the friendship between Lena, a girl confined to a wheelchair, and Feyda, the neighbor boy whose father is an alcoholic. The two nurture each other through their difficulties and although, by the end, they know it is not wise to continue seeing each other, they are grateful for the emotional support they were able to give each other.

Lindquist, Marie. **In a Perfect World.** Center City, MN: Hazelden Educational Materials, 1991. 120p.

Kevin's buddies admire him for being such an outspoken freshman with a good sense of humor. He hides the fact that his dad is an alcoholic and admires his friend Mindy's family, which seems perfect. He is reluctant to go to Alateen meetings but finally discovers that the group can give him the support he needs to look inside.

Levy, Marilyn. **Touching.** New York: Fawcett Juniper, 1988. 176p.

Eve, who is 16, cannot stand her alcoholic dad, who shames her in front of her teachers and friends and a boy she really likes. When she helps an alcoholic classmate, she realizes that her dad is not humiliating her on purpose. She understands that he has a disease and that maybe she can help him, too.

Mazer, Harry. **War on Villa Street.** New York: Dell, 1979. 128p.

Willis's world falls apart when his alcoholic father beats him up and a local gang comes after him because he refused to join. When he defends a retarded boy against the gang, a whole series of explosive events is triggered.

Ryan, Jeanette Mines. **Reckless.** New York: Flare Books, 1983. 176p.

Jeannie, a top student, falls in love with Sam, a hunk from the wrong part of town. Sixteen-year-old Jeannie's family is horrified because Sam is cruel and moody, he drives too fast, and he drinks too much. Jeannie resents her parents' intrusion into her romantic life. Her relationship with Sam becomes dangerous to the point that it is almost too late to save either of them.

Wersba, Barbara. **Crazy Vanilla.** New York: Harper & Row, 1986. 184p.

Tyler's mother is an alcoholic, and his father is a workaholic. Depressed and confused, he becomes friends with a girl who shows him how to take care of his own emotional needs and how to make his own decisions. Although Tyler leaves Alcoholics Anonymous (A.A.) pamphlets for his mom to read and he knows she has read them, at the end of the book she is still drinking, and Tyler must learn to accept the fact that he cannot change her.

Zindel, Paul. **Pardon Me, You're Stepping on My Eyeball!** New York: Harper & Row, 1976. 272p.

This classic about how a boy with an alcoholic mother finds self-acceptance blends comedy and tragedy. It is an award-winning, page-turning read.

Nonfiction

BOOKS

Alateen: Hope for Children of Alcoholics. New York: Al-Anon Family Group Headquarters, 1980. 120p.

Twenty-one personal stories form the core of this book written for teenagers who are living with an alcoholic. In addition, material about the disease of alcoholism and information about the Alateen Twelve Step program are provided. Of special interest are chapters on how to start a group on your own and on being a lone member.

Alateen—One Day at a Time. New York: Al-Anon Family Group Headquarters, 1983. 379p.

This hardcover meditation book written just for adolescents offers both inspiration and concrete suggestions for living with an alcoholic parent—one day at a time.

Beattie, Melody. **Beyond Codependency—And Getting Better All the Time.** San Francisco: Harper/Hazelden, 1989. 268p.

A sequel to *Codependent No More*, Beattie's second book offers tips on raising self-esteem and on advanced coping skills for codependency recovery. Revealing her own struggle with codependency, she offers a long-term strategy for recovery.

———. **Codependent No More.** San Francisco: Harper/Hazelden, 1987. 237p.

This groundbreaking book about the causes and consequences of codependency remains one of the most popular on the topic. Beattie's style is warm, sensitive, and easy to read. In addition to providing an extensive description of the symptoms of codependency, she suggests strategies for overcoming people-pleasing and other problems. Each chapter ends with an exercise.

Berry, Carmen Renee. **When Helping You Is Hurting Me: Escaping the Messiah Trap.** San Francisco: Harper & Row, 1988. 128p.

Berry focuses on the caretaking role that codependents play, first with a dysfunctional parent and then often with friends and eventually marriage partners. This book helps codependents to go beyond the guilt they feel when they say no and to learn how to establish limits on what they will do for others. It also offers suggestions for raising self-esteem so readers can avoid falling into the needing-to-be-needed trap of enabling in their relationships.

Black, Claudia. **It Will Never Happen to Me: Children of Alcoholics as Youngsters, Adolescents and Adults.** Denver, CO: M.A.C. Publishing, 1982. 191p. Also available in Spanish, German, and Japanese. New York: Ballantine Books, 1987. 154p.

One of the first books written on what it means to grow up with alcoholic parents, *It Will Never Happen to Me* talks about how teenagers often endure family trauma unnoticed because they are so skillful at presenting a good appearance. Black discusses family roles and how codependents carry those roles into adulthood. This is a good book for someone first finding out about dysfunctional family issues. Although Black focuses on alcoholism, what she says is true for any chemically dependent family.

————. **Repeat after Me.** Center City, MN: Hazelden Educational Materials, 1988. 154p.

Filled with 75 exercises, this workbook helps readers explore dysfunctional family rules and roles. This hands-on exploration can provide readers insight into the issues of denial, setting boundaries and limits, family rituals, and overachieving in order to look good.

Bradshaw, John. **Bradshaw on the Family.** Deerfield Beach, FL: Health Communications, 1988. 252p.

Based on the TV series of the same name, this book examines the hows and whys of dysfunctional families, focusing on unhealthy rules handed down from generation to generation and the emotional harm they cause. Most important, this book points the way to recovery by showing how to uncover negative patterns learned early in life and then how to change them.

————. **Healing the Shame That Binds You.** Deerfield Beach, FL: Health Communications, 1988. 254p.

Toxic shame is at the core of addictions, compulsions, and codependency. In addition to information about shame, this book offers exercises, visualizations, and meditations to help readers beat the shame game.

Friel, John, and Linda Friel. **The Adult Child's Guide to What's "Normal."** Deerfield Beach, FL: Health Communications, 1991. 192p.

Often codependents have a tough time with their own recovery because they do not have a clear idea of what normal behavior is. After all, they were not raised around normal people. This book looks at the traps codependents fall into as they recover and gives strategies for avoiding those traps.

Homil-Beer, Edith. **A Teenager's Guide to Living with an Alcoholic Parent.** Center City, MN: Hazelden Educational Materials, 1984. 93p.

This question-and-answer format book provides easy-to-read answers to the basic questions children of alcoholics most often ask. Subject matter runs the gamut from how to tell whether a parent is an alcoholic to what to do about broken promises and inconsistent discipline.

Hull-Mast, Nancy, and Diane Purcell. **SIBS: The Forgotten Family Members.** Park Ridge, IL: Parkside Publishing Corporation, 1984. 64p.

Too often when a brother or sister has an addiction problem, the emotional needs of siblings are ignored. This book is written for these siblings. It talks about how chemical dependency affects siblings and how they can take control of their lives by communicating and meeting their own needs. Exercises are included.

Leite, Evelyn, and Pamela Espeland. **Different Like Me: A Book for Teens Who Worry about Their Parents' Use of Alcohol/Drugs.** Minneapolis, MN: Johnson Institute, 1987. 118p.

If there is one thing that bothers teenagers, it is being different from their peers. Living with an alcoholic parent can make teenagers feel unfairly singled out. *Different Like Me* helps teens grow beyond asking "Why me?" into making plans to live and enjoy their own lives in spite of family difficulties. This book is illustrated with cartoons and is a real mood-booster. It is easy to read and does not talk down to teenagers.

Mellody, Pia. **Facing Codependence: What It Is, Where It Comes from and How It Sabotages Our Lives.** San Francisco: Harper & Row, 1989. 224p.

Facing Codependence examines the childhood roots of codependency and describes emotional, spiritual, physical, sexual, and mental abuses that can cause people problems later in life. Because Mellody defines abuse as any behavior by parents that is less than nurturing, her book also helps teens whose parents have problems other than chemical dependency to identify their issues and begin the road to recovery through self-nurturing.

Owen, Lonny. **What's Wrong with Me? Breaking the Chain of Adolescent Codependency.** Minneapolis, MN: Deaconness Press, 1991. 128p.

A number of the problems teenagers fall victim to—depression, suicide, chemical dependency, sexual addiction, and criminal behavior—are set up by codependency. This book examines how families work and how teenagers can take control of their lives by changing codependent behaviors.

Porterfield, Kay Marie. **Coping with an Alcoholic Parent.** New York: Rosen Publishing Group, 1985, 1990. 134p.

This book helps teenagers look at the ways they have learned to adapt to living with an alcoholic parent and helps them break old codependent habits. Healthy emotional coping skills are discussed, and sources for additional help are listed.

———. **Coping with Codependency.** New York: Rosen Publishing Group, 1991. 146p.

Shame, low self-esteem, and difficulties relating to others can all result from growing up in a dysfunctional family. This book talks about ways to beat the shame game for teenagers who live with a chemically dependent parent or in a family turned upside-down by other long-term problems.

Ryerson, Eric. **When Your Parent Drinks Too Much: A Book for Teenagers.** New York: Facts on File, 1987. 144p.

Ryerson addresses the deep feelings of shame and isolation that children of alcoholics feel and tells how to connect with other children of alcoholics through support groups. He shows the steps teens can take to make their own lives better based on the precepts of Al-Anon, Alateen, and his own experience as an adult child of an alcoholic.

Scales, Cynthia. **Potato Chips for Breakfast: An Autobiography.** New York: Bantam, 1989. 189p.

Teenagers with a chemically dependent parent can easily relate to this painfully honest, true story of what it is like to grow up in a home where a mother's alcoholism causes neglect and abuse and where potato chips for breakfast are the rule rather than the exception. In this gripping and immediate account, the author takes a hard look at denial, confusion, and chaos.

Seaxis, Judith, and Geraldine Youcha. **Living with a Parent Who Drinks Too Much.** New York: Greenway Books, 1979. 128p.

Teens who want to know their rights and how to protect themselves in the sometimes dangerous environment of a substance abusing family can gain practical insights from this book. Pulling no punches, Seaxis and Youcha directly confront issues that many adolescents have trouble openly discussing: filth, medical emergencies, suicide, sexual abuse, and the alcoholic's loss of bladder control.

Shuker, Nancy. **Everything You Need To Know about an Alcoholic Parent.** New York: Rosen Publishing Company, 1985. 64p.

This easy-to-read book helps readers determine whether or not a parent is an alcoholic. It discusses how alcoholism makes an entire family sick and provides resources for getting help. In addition to talking about how to help an alcoholic parent, the authors tell how the child of an alcoholic parent can get help for himself or herself.

Taylor, Paul, and Diane Taylor. **Coping with a Dysfunctional Family.** New York: Rosen Publishing Group, 1990. 129p.

This upbeat and informative book has chapters on many of the problems that can cause a family to be dysfunctional. These problems include alcohol abuse, drug abuse, sexual abuse, physical abuse, and emotional neglect. If you cannot save your parents and siblings, the Taylors advise, save yourself, and they provide suggestions about how to reach out for help in order to do just that. They also cover in detail the positive consequences of reaching out and offer hope for those growing up in dysfunctional families that their emotional pain will not last forever.

The Twelve Steps, A Way Out: A Working Guide for Adult Children of Alcoholic and Other Dysfunctional Families. San Diego, CA: Recovery Publications, 1987. 107p.

Written by a group of people in an Adult Children of Alcoholics self-help group, this workbook gives readers many written exercises to help them work the Twelve Steps as part of a recovery program. In the few years since it was published, it has become a classic.

Wegschieder-Cruse, Sharon. **Another Chance: Hope and Health for the Alcoholic Family.** Palo Alto, CA: Science and Behavior Books, 1989. 356p.

One of the first family recovery books to explore the rigid roles family members of the chemically dependent play, this remains a classic in the field. Despite the fact that this book is written for counselors, it is easy to understand and provides a clear explanation of how substance abuse can turn families upside-down.

PAMPHLETS

Brooks, Cathleen. **The Secret Everyone Knows.** Center City, MN: Hazelden/Kroc Foundation, 1981. 40p.

Brooks, a survivor of early life in an alcoholic home, has written this book from the heart. Not only does she give readers emotional support, but she also offers practical advice about what to do when a parent is chemically dependent. This easy-to-read book can be a teenager's first step in forming a support network.

Chemical Dependence: Yes, You Can Do Something. Minneapolis, MN: Johnson Institute, 1987. 19p.

This leaflet includes a 30-point questionnaire to help readers determine whether or not someone they know is a chemical dependent. It also offers suggestions about what to do to help.

Chemical Dependence and Recovery: A Family Affair. Minneapolis, MN: Johnson Institute, 1987. 31p.

This booklet concentrates on how it feels to live with a chemically dependent person as well as discussing enabling, codependency, intervention, and recovery. It is a good introduction to many of the issues codependents face.

The Family Enablers. Minneapolis, MN: Johnson Institute, 1987. 15p.

Sometimes family members who want to help a chemically dependent person recover instead wind up helping that person continue his or her addiction. This booklet points the way out of this trap.

Hope for Young People with Alcoholic Parents. Center City, MN: Hazelden Educational Materials, 1981. 20p.

Offering practical suggestions for kids who live in an alcoholic home, this booklet helps teens take the necessary steps to detach.

If Your Parents Drink Too Much. New York: Al-Anon Family Group Headquarters, 1974. 24p.

This little comic book is filled with the stories of three teenagers whose parents drank too much. It covers positive as well as negative ways that teenagers respond to chronic family crisis and provides information about the Alateen program.

It's a Teenage Affair. New York: Al-Anon Family Group Headquarters, 1964. 4p.

This leaflet covers some of the problems teenagers who live with a chemically dependent parent face and explains how some teenagers are solving those problems.

Leite, Evelyn. **Detachment: The Art of Letting Go While Living with an Alcoholic.** Minneapolis, MN: Johnson Institute, 1987. 22p.

People who live with alcoholics often feel guilty, unworthy, angry, helpless, and hopeless. This pamphlet deals with those uncomfortable feelings and shows readers how they can begin taking responsibility for their own lives rather than being the caretaker for the alcoholic.

Operation Alateen: For Young People Affected by Someone's Drinking. New York: Al-Anon Family Group Headquarters, 1980. 7p.

This leaflet tells teenagers how to start their own Alateen group and includes a meeting plan as well as suggestions about how to build membership.

Recovery of Chemically Dependent Families. Minneapolis, MN: Johnson Institute, 1987. 11p.

When a family member stops drinking or using drugs, the people who love that person may expect family life to change overnight. However, recovery can be a slow and sometimes painful process for everyone involved. This booklet shares communication tips and ideas about how the whole family can recover together.

When Your Parent Drinks Too Much. Rockville, MD: National Clearinghouse for Alcohol and Drug Information, 1985. 4p.

Reprinted from an article in *Seventeen* magazine, this flyer is filled with coping strategies that work.

Youth and the Alcoholic Parent. New York: Al-Anon Family Group Headquarters, 1960 (updated periodically). 14p.

This booklet explains what Alateen is all about and answers some of the questions teenagers ask most often about coping with an alcoholic parent, including "Why can't my parent stop drinking?" and "What should I do if the alcoholic becomes violent?"

PERIODICAL

Changes: For and about Adult Children
Health Communications, Inc.
Enterprise Center
3201 Southwest 15th Street
Deerfield Beach, FL 33442-8190
Bimonthly; $18 per year

Every two months, *Changes* prints a variety of articles of interest to people who grew up in dysfunctional families. Some recent topics have been how recovery affects environmental issues, Native American therapeutic techniques, men's issues, and interviews with famous people. Besides articles by professionals, *Changes* has a monthly column written by readers.

Nonprint Materials

Alateen Tells It Like It Is
Type: VHS video
Length: 16 min.
Cost: Purchase $30
Distributor: Al-Anon Family Groups
                P.O. Box 862, Midtown Station
                New York, NY 10018-0862
Date: 1987

Three teenagers talk about what it is like growing up with alcoholic parents and explain how Alateen has helped them.

Children of Alcoholics

Type: VHS video
Length: 30 min.
Cost: Rental $75, purchase $395
Distributor: Coronet/MTI Film and Video
108 Wilmot Road
Deerfield, IL 60015
Date: 1989

Seventeen-year-old Lisa Blaine and her 12-year-old brother, Michael, dramatize the different ways kids try to cope with a parent's drinking problem. Health professionals from Harvard University Medical School talk about the scenes and discuss alcoholism as a family disease. The videotape also contains suggestions for coping.

Children of Denial

Type: VHS video
Length: 28 min.
Cost: Purchase $39.95
Distributor: M.A.C. Publishing
5505 East 39th Avenue
Denver, CO 80207
Date: 1990

Claudia Black speaks to adolescents and adults about the three basic rules they face in their dysfunctional families: do not trust, do not talk, and do not feel. She explores how an alcoholic affects his or her family in a sensitive manner.

Codependents

Type: VHS video
Length: 30 min.
Cost: Rental $75, purchase $395
Distributor: Coronet/MTI Film and Video
108 Wilmot Road
Deerfield, IL 60015
Date: 1989

A companion to *Children of Alcoholics,* this tape centers on Nancy Blaine, the mother of Lisa and Michael. Adolescent viewers can begin to understand the role their nonalcoholic parent plays in the family system.

Different Like Me

Type: VHS video
Length: 30 min.

Cost: Purchase $525
Distributor: Johnson Institute
                7151 Metro Boulevard
                Minneapolis, MN 55439-2122
Date: 1990

Jason, a teenager with an alcoholic father, seems like an average kid who does not have a problem in the world. But at home, he is upset and confused as he tries to hold his crumbling family together. A fight with his father drives him to a support group for children of alcoholics, where he discovers that he is not alone and that there are ways he can make his life better despite his dad's addiction to alcohol.

Drinking Parents
Type: 16mm film, VHS video
Length: 10 min.
Cost: Rental $75, purchase $250 (film); rental $75,
                purchase $225 (video)
Distributor: Coronet/MTI Film and Video
                108 Wilmot Road
                Deerfield, IL 60015
Date: 1980

A recovering alcoholic mother and her daughter discuss their individual frustrations. This video urges teenage children of substance abusers not to remain isolated but to seek help from community resources.

Everything's Fine
Type: VHS video
Length: 16 min.
Cost: Purchase $189
Distributor: Intermedia
                1300 Dexter North
                Seattle, WA 98109
Date: 1989

Ed Asner narrates this look at the effects chemical dependency has on family members. This program examines the roles people who grow up in dysfunctional families play—often throughout their lives. Sensitive and supportive, the film gives viewers the message that they do not need to pretend that everything is okay when it is not and that they can get help.

Families of Alcoholics
Type: 16mm film, VHS video
Length: 15 min.

Cost: Rental $75, purchase $290 (film); rental $75,
               purchase $250 (video)
Distributor: Coronet/MTI Film and Video
               108 Wilmot Road
               Deerfield, IL 60015
Date: 1980

Narrated by Geraldo Rivera, this film follows two families as members face the road to recovery together. It was produced by the ABC news program *20/20*.

Family Baggage

Type: VHS video
Length: 120 min.
Cost: Purchase $199
Distributor: Parkside Publishing Corporation
               205 West Touhy Avenue
               Park Ridge, IL 60068
Date: 1985

Family Baggage takes a humorous look at growing up in a dysfunctional family. Taped at a live performance at the Boulder Theater in Boulder, Colorado, this program is an excellent way to learn about dysfunctional family issues and to begin to deal with them. Most viewers will recognize at least some of their family's characteristics in this tape.

Francesca Baby

Type: 16mm film, VHS video
Length: 46 min.
Cost: Rental $75, purchase $735 (film); rental $75,
               purchase $555 (video)
Distributor: Coronet/MTI Film and Video
               108 Wilmot Road
               Deerfield, IL 60015
Date: 1977

A teenager and her younger sister try to survive living with an alcoholic mother. Although their mother's problem has a profound impact on their lives, they manage to find help through Alateen.

I Live in an Alcoholic Family

Type: VHS video
Length: 30 min.
Cost: Purchase $189

Distributor: Sunburst Communications
                  39 Washington Avenue
                  Box 40
                  Pleasantville, NY 10570-9971
Date: 1988

Three teenagers talk about what it means to live in an alcoholic home. The main emphasis is placed on the three C's: They did not *cause* the problem, they cannot *control* it, and they cannot *cure* the disease.

If Someone in Your Family Drinks
Type: Filmstrips on VHS video
Length: 26 min.
Cost: Purchase $145
Distributor: Sunburst Communications
                  39 Washington Avenue
                  Box 40
                  Pleasantville, NY 10570-9971
Date: 1987

This video explores the distinct roles each member of an alcoholic or chemically dependent family plays. Teenagers are given suggestions about how they can stop their denial and get help. A teacher's guide is included.

How To Stop the One You Love from Drinking and Using Drugs
Type: VHS video
Length: 56 min.
Cost: Purchase $24.95
Distributor: Network Publications
                  P.O. Box 1830
                  Santa Cruz, CA 95061-1830
Date: 1988

Through dramatic scenes and commentary, host Mariette Hartley explains the process of intervention. Based on Mary Ellen Pinkham's book by the same title, this program also helps family members learn to protect themselves from the emotional pain of living with an alcohol or drug abuser.

A Letter to Dad: A Story of Codependency
Type: 16mm film, VHS video
Length: 60 min.
Cost: Rental $100, purchase $600 (film); rental $100,
                  purchase $575 (video)

Distributor: Gerald T. Rogers Productions
5217 Old Orchard Road
Suite 990
Skokie, IL 60077
Date: 1989

Megan Riley, the divorced mother of two teenagers, confronts the damaging effects of growing up with a violently alcoholic father and a codependent mother.

Living with Trouble: Crisis in the Family
Type: Filmstrips on VHS video
Length: 38 min.
Cost: Purchase $175
Distributor: Sunburst Communications
39 Washington Avenue
Box 40
Pleasantville, NY 10570-9971
Date: 1984

Three teenagers coping with family crisis tell their stories. This tape explains techniques teens can use to help themselves cope.

Lots of Kids Like Us: How Young Children Learn To Understand a Parent's Alcoholism
Type: 16mm film, VHS video
Length: 28 min.
Cost: Rental $70, purchase $450 (film); rental $70, purchase $380 (video)
Distributor: Coronet/MTI Film and Video
108 Wilmot Road
Deerfield, IL 60015
Date: 1983

Ben and his sister, Laurie, attempt to cope with and understand their father's alcoholism in this film. Not only do they feel guilt and unhappiness, but they also suffer physical and emotional abuse. Although the protagonists of this sensitive video are young children, the program provides a thought-provoking look at life in an alcoholic family for kids of all ages.

"Mom, Louie's Looking at Me Again"
Type: VHS video
Length: 60 min.
Cost: Purchase $39.95

Distributor: Parkside Publishing Corporation
205 West Touhy Avenue
Park Ridge, IL 60068
Date: 1989

Comedian Louie Anderson has a gift for getting a message across and making viewers laugh at the same time. This tape, without ever mentioning the words *alcoholism* or *addiction,* explores the acting out, low self-esteem, and people-pleasing behaviors that are part of dysfunctional families. The tape comes with a viewing guide.

My Father's Son
Type: 16mm film, VHS video
Length: 33 min.
Cost: Rental $100, purchase $525 (film); rental $100, purchase $475 (video)
Distributor: Gerald T. Rogers Productions
5217 Old Orchard Road
Suite 990
Skokie, IL 60077
Date: 1984

Sixteen-year-old Michael tries to live a normal life despite having an alcoholic parent. This film explores the legacy of chemical addiction and the susceptibility of adult children to becoming addicted themselves.

"Numb" . . . Children of Alcoholics
Type: VHS video
Length: 60 min.
Cost: Purchase $49.95
Distributor: Health Communications, Inc.
Enterprise Center
3201 Southwest 15th Street
Deerfield Beach, FL 33442-8190
Date: 1990

Life in an alcoholic family is seen through the eyes of 15-year-old Eddy, a Family Hero who has become emotionally numb after years of being raised by an alcoholic father. This video offers commentary by and interviews with a number of people who grew up in alcoholic homes. It is the winner of two Emmy Awards.

Out of the Past: Adult Children of Alcoholics
Type: VHS video
Length: 52 min.

Cost: Rental $75, purchase $445
Distributor: American Filmmakers Library
                124 East 40th Street
                New York, NY 10016
Date: 1991

This video, which won an award at the National Adolescent Addictions Conference in 1990, features adult children of alcoholics remembering how it was to grow up in a family shattered by a parent's drinking. The focus is not only on how a parent's alcoholism affects children, but also on the steps adult children are taking to keep from repeating the cycle in their own lives.

Picking Up the Pieces
Type: VHS video
Length: 48 min.
Cost: Purchase $225
Distributor: Intermedia
                1300 Dexter North
                Seattle, WA 98109
Date: 1989

Sixteen-year-old Patty lives with an alcoholic mother, and nobody in her family talks about it. Instead they try to pretend the problem does not exist. Patty is miserable until a friend introduces her to Alateen, where she finds that she can begin to work on her own survival.

She Drinks a Little
Type: 16mm film, VHS video
Length: 31 min.
Cost: Rental $75, purchase $500 (film); rental $75,
                purchase $250 (video)
Distributor: Coronet/MTI Film and Video
                108 Wilmot Road
                Deerfield, IL 60015
Date: 1981

Cindy, a teenager, has an alcoholic mom whose drinking is destroying both of them. A male classmate with a similar problem leads Cindy to Alateen, where she learns to deal with her anger and guilt and how to live with her mother.

Together: Families in Recovery
Type: VHS video
Length: 30 min.
Cost: Purchase $500

Distributor: Parkside Publishing Corporation
                 205 West Touhy Avenue
                 Park Ridge, IL 60068
Date: 1989

This video shows the progress of three families in recovery and highlights the fact that everyone in the family needs help recovering. The focus is on how to heal emotional scars and how to recognize and avoid relapse.

Trust in Yourself: Adult Children of Alcoholics
Type: 16mm film, VHS video
Length: 25 min.
Cost: Rental $75, purchase $475 (film); rental $75,
                 purchase $400 (video)
Distributor: Coronet/MTI Film and Video
                 108 Wilmot Road
                 Deerfield, IL 60015
Date: 1988

What happens to children of alcoholics when they grow up? This video answers that question by looking at the lives of five adults who were raised by alcoholic parents. Addressing the confusion and denial in these adults, the film goes on to explain the healing that can come from group therapy and forgiveness. It is narrated by Robert Ackerman, cofounder of the National Association of Children of Alcoholics.

When Your Parent Drinks Too Much
Type: 16mm film, VHS video
Length: 17 min.
Cost: Rental $85, purchase $550 (film); rental $85,
                 purchase $495 (video)
Distributor: Coronet/MTI Film and Video
                 108 Wilmot Road
                 Deerfield, IL 60015
Date: 1987

This tape focuses around a support group and explains the issues children of alcoholics must face and how they can cope with those issues.

When Your Parents Drink
Type: VHS video
Length: 25 min.
Cost: Purchase $290

Distributor: Britannica Educational Corporation
310 South Michigan Avenue
Chicago, IL 60604
Date: 1988

Dramatized scenes and interviews in this video teach teenagers that a parent's drinking can have a big impact on their lives. The video also covers how to reach out for help.

Why Does Mom Drink So Much?
Type: VHS video
Length: 35 min.
Cost: Purchase $185
Distributor: Guidance Associates
P.O. Box 1000
Mount Kisco, NY 10549-0010
Date: 1989

Ways of coping with a drinking parent that do not work are compared to ways that do work in this video, which contains interviews with experts in the Adult Children of Alcoholics field. The focus is on feelings.

Organizations

Adult Children of Alcoholics
6381 Hollywood Boulevard, Suite 685
Hollywood, CA 90028
(213) 464-4423

This international group, which was founded in 1984, is based on the Twelve Steps of Alcoholics Anonymous. Its focus is on recovery for adults and teenagers who were raised in a dysfunctional family.

Al-Anon/Alateen Family Group Headquarters, Inc.
P.O. Box 862, Midtown Station
New York, NY 10018-0862
(212) 302-7240

Al-Anon was organized to help family members and friends of alcoholics. Group members share their concerns and, using the Twelve Steps of Alcoholics Anonymous, work on their own recovery from the chaotic life that comes from currently living with a substance abuser.

Children Are People, Inc. (CAP)
493 Selby Avenue
St. Paul, MN 55102
(612) 227-4031

CAP develops educational tools for working with children of alcoholics and those who have parents with other chemical dependencies. This organization also offers support groups for younger children in the state of Minnesota. In addition, it trains counselors and teachers to start support groups in their own areas.

Children of Alcoholics Foundation, Inc.
200 Park Avenue
31st Floor
New York, NY 10166
(212) 949-1404

This group works primarily to educate people about the issues surrounding growing up in an alcoholic home. It publishes educational materials that can be used in the middle school classroom and also provides reading lists and videotapes.

Codependents Anonymous (CoDA)
P.O. Box 33577
Phoenix, AZ 85067-3577

CoDA describes itself as a fellowship of men and women whose common problem is an inability to maintain functional relationships. Most members grew up in dysfunctional families. They share with each other using the Twelve Step model in the hope of solving their problems and helping others recover.

Families Anonymous (Families of Substance Abusers)
P.O. Box 528
Van Nuys, CA 91408
(818) 989-7841

This national organization with over 400 chapters helps relatives and friends of substance abusers grow in their own recovery. The program is based on the Twelve Steps of Alcoholics Anonymous.

National Association for Children of Alcoholics (NACA)
32582 Coast Highway, Suite B
South Laguna, CA 92677
(714) 499-3889

Founded out of deep concern for all those affected by alcoholism, NACA provides support and information for children of alcoholics of all ages. It puts out a quarterly newsletter, refers people to groups, and helps people start groups in their hometowns.

Hotline

Al-Anon Family Group Headquarters
(800) 356-9996
Monday through Friday 9:00–4:30 E.S.T.

By calling this toll-free number, you can request a packet of information about Al-Anon or find out how to contact local groups in your area.

Index

Smokeless Tobacco: The Sean Marsee Story, 145

Smokeless Tobacco! Yolanda and Mark Talk to Teens, 141

Smokers Anonymous, 148

Smoking. See Marijuana; Tobacco; specific drugs

Smoking: It's Your Choice, 145–146

Smoking: Personal Pollution, 146

Smoking: The Choice Is Yours, 145

Smoking Not Allowed, 138–139

Smoking, Tobacco & Health: A Fact Book, 141

Snow Ghost, 95

Snuff, 129, 133, 139–140, 141, 143, 144–145

Snyder, Anne, 43

Snyder, Solomon, 100

Snyder, Zilpha Keatley, 96

Solvents. See Inhalants

Speak Up, Speak Out: Learning To Say NO to Drugs, 121

Special Focus: Preventing Alcohol-Related Birth Defects, 47

Speed. See Amphetamines

Spence, Annette, 12

Spence, W. R., 104